THE AMERICAN CHARACTER

THE AMERICAN CHARACTER

Views of America from
The Wall Street Journal

Edited by
DONALD MOFFITT

George Braziller
NEW YORK

EDITOR'S NOTE

The articles that appear in this book have been published as they originally appeared in *The Wall Street Journal*. The reader should keep in mind that, because of the passage of time, certain facts, assertions and conclusions may no longer remain valid.

—D.M.

Published in the United States in 1983 by George Braziller, Inc.

Copyright © 1980, 1981, 1982, 1983 by Dow Jones & Company, Inc.

Grateful acknowledgement is made to Velvet Apple/Tree Publishing Co., Inc. for permission to reprint lyrics from "9 to 5" by Dolly Parton.

All rights reserved.

For information address the publisher:
George Braziller, Inc.
One Park Avenue
New York, NY 10016

Library of Congress Cataloging in Publication Data
Main entry under title:

The American character.

   1. United States—Social conditions—1945-   —Addresses, essays, lectures. I. Moffitt, Donald.
II. Wall Street journal.
HN57.A585 1983   306'.0973   83-6353
ISBN 0-8076-1076-3

Design by Jennie Nichols/Levavi & Levavi
Printed in the United States of America
First edition

THE AMERICAN CHARACTER

INTRODUCTION by William E. Blundell   10

THE NATION: The Land and Its People

"To Loggers, the Woods Are Dark and Deep—But Far From Lovely"
   WILLIAM E. BLUNDELL   14

"Job of Arctic Driller Is Dirty, Dangerous and Very Lucrative"
   KATHRYN CHRISTENSEN   21

"The Days of a Cowboy Are Marked by Danger, Drudgery and Low Pay"
   WILLIAM E. BLUNDELL   27

"Tenant Farming Gains, Troubling Proponents of Family Ownership"
   MEG COX   34

"Arizona Indians Win Victory Over U.S.: Refuse $33 Million"
   WILLIAM E. BLUNDELL   39

THE WORKPLACE: Americans at Work

"Extra! Joseph Gomez Tells How He Runs Sidewalk Newsstand!"
   DANIEL MACHALABA   44

"Steno Pool's Members, Buried by Paper Flood, Yearn for Other Things"
   KATHRYN CHRISTENSEN   49

"Women Coal Miners Fight for Their Rights to Lift, Shovel, Lug"
   CAROL HYMOWITZ   55

"Assembling Computers Means That Happiness Doesn't Come Till 4:30"
ROGER THUROW   61

"Many Managers Resist 'Paperless' Technology for Their Own Offices"
LAWRENCE ROUT   67

"End of CETA Program Portends Loss of Jobs For Unskilled Workers"
MARILYN CHASE   72

"Carolina Research Park Illustrates Innovations In Nation's Work Sites"
JANET GUYON   78

BUSINESS: Large & Small

"Wood-Stove Maker Has Hot Love Affair With Its Customers"
WILLIAM M. BULKELEY   86

"The Attractions of Starting a New Venture Prove Irresistible to Some Entrepreneurs"
WILLIAM M. BULKELEY   91

"A French-Fry Diary: From Idaho Furrow to Golden Arches"
MEG COX   97

"Trailing the Japanese, U.S. Steelmakers Seek To Use Their Methods"
DOUGLAS R. SEASE AND URBAN C. LEHNER   101

"At Procter & Gamble, Success Is Largely Due to Heeding Consumer"
JOHN A. PRESTBO   107

CITIES: Small Towns to Urban Centers

"Small-Town Revival, Like Most Trends, Bypasses Strandburg"
LAWRENCE ROUT   116

"Bisbee Learns What Happens When Boomtown Goes Bust"
WILLIAM E. BLUNDELL   121

"Elmira Will Never Be What It Used to Be, But Is Far From Dying"
JAMES M. PERRY   124

"Indianapolis Thrives on Partnership of City, Business, Philanthropy"
FREDERICK C. KLEIN   130

POLITICS: Grass Roots On Up

"Town of Pella, Iowa, Talks of Little Other Than Nuclear Attack"
JOHN J. FIALKA   138

"Mayor Schaefer Guides Baltimore Renaissance With a Personal Touch"
DEBORAH A. RANDOLPH   144

"Brash B. T. Collins Handles the People For the Brown Camp"
CARRIE DOLAN   149

"A Registered Agent Helps Saudis Fathom And Sway Washington"
KAREN ELLIOTT HOUSE   154

"Spiritual Descendants Of Old Sam Maverick Enliven the Congress"
DENNIS FARNEY   160

"Design of Proposed Memorial to Vietnam Dead Is Reopening War Wounds Meant to Be Healed"
ANDY PASZTOR   165

CRIME: On the Streets and In Corporations

"New York Fish Market Points Up a Pattern Of Extortion and Fear"
STANLEY PENN   172

"Dealing in Marijuana Can Mean Big Money—But Also a Life of Fear"
DAVID J. BLUM, LAUREL LEFF,
ROGER LOWENSTEIN AND STANLEY PENN   179

"How a Park Mugging Led to Impulse Killing Of a New York Lawyer"
STANLEY PENN   186

"Court Records Detail Celanese Man's Years As an Industrial Spy"
JIM MONTGOMERY   193

"More Riots Are Feared As Overcrowding Fuels Tensions Behind Bars"
ROBERT E. TAYLOR   199

SOCIAL TRENDS/LIFESTYLES

"Sharp Differences in Attitudes On Social Questions Divide U.S."
SAM ALLIS   206

"Integration Is Elusive Despite Recent Gains; Social Barriers Remain"
CHARLES W. STEVENS   208

"Era of Middle Class Has Arrived, But It's Hard to Say Who's in It"
SAM ALLIS   214

"Some Cried A Lot, But Youths Survived Week Without TV"
JANE MAYER   217

"For Middle-Aged Man, A Wife's New Career Upsets Old Balances"
MARY BRALOVE   221

"Welfare Mother Begets 3 Welfare Daughters, Perpetuating Life Style"
JULIE SALAMON   226

"Homeless Northerners Unable to Find Work Crowd Sun Belt Cities"
GEORGE GETSCHOW   233

LEISURE AND THE ARTS

" 'The Hook': Songs of Pain and Double-Dealing"
MICHAEL L. KING   242

"The Texas 'Fandangle' Replays a Proud History"
EDWIN WILSON — 246

"Sam Shepard: Bleeding in Red, White and Blue"
EDWIN WILSON — 249

"Walt's Wonderful World Turns Out to Be Flat"
MANUELA HOELTERHOFF — 252

"The High-Flying Price of a Deadly Artform"
DOUGLAS MARTIN — 258

SPORTS

"It's 10 Below Zero in Walker, Minn., But at Least the Eelpout Are Biting"
WILLIAM H. LOVING — 262

"For Football Scouts And College Seniors, Today Is the Future"
JOHN HUEY — 264

"Some Old Masters Vault Nine-Foot Bar—And 70 Years"
DORON P. LEVIN — 270

JOURNALISM

"Evans, Novak Still Rile Readers After 18 Years of Right-Wing Purity"
JAMES M. PERRY — 274

"In Farm Wife News, Rural Readers Write Of Mice and Women"
LAUREL SORENSON — 281

"A Last Remembrance of a Newspaper's Days Past"
JAMES M. PERRY — 285

INTRODUCTION

For more than two centuries a procession of politicians, poets, historians and critics have struggled to explain America. Success has eluded them, the American people having stubbornly refused to sit still long enough to have a full-color portrait done. They have been too busy.

We can only hope to discern the American character in snatches of action, for the relentless impulse toward action dominates American life. We are not a reflective, backward-looking people. Don't just sit there, we say. *Do* something. And the incessant doing of it has made America one of history's engines of change, indiscriminately pouring out upon the world polio vaccines and nuclear weaponry, computer technology and disposable diapers, an extraordinary political idea and the perfect hamburger. We are loved and hated, feared and trusted, but seldom ignored—and just as seldom understood, even by ourselves.

This book seeks to promote understanding by catching contemporary Americans in motion, offering brief but telling glimpses into their character through their conduct in daily life and work. Their stories are drawn from the pages of *The Wall Street Journal*, the nation's largest daily newspaper and one highly respected for the quality, range and depth of its features. *Journal* reporters take us from coal mines to the meanest urban streets to farms to assembly lines, letting us see and hear our compatriots building tomorrow.

The manufacture of the future is the life and business of America. But it is increasingly a fragmented, specialized and urbanized endeavor; we are becoming a nation of isolated individuals ever more dependent on each other, and at the same time ever more ignorant of how we are connected.

So this collection of stories also serves to reintroduce us to each other. Taken to the big-tree logging woods, we learn of men who face extreme risk of injury and death every day so we can have the wood we need to build our bookcases. It is a good thing that we know the blood of our fellow citizens is on those boards, that the lettuce at the supermarket was not immaculately conceived in its produce bins, even that the french fries at McDonald's are good because a lot of money and corporate toil were expended to make them good.

The characteristic of America that resists any attempt at a definitive, lasting analysis of the nation is the constant upwelling of self-induced change in our society. We remake that society every few years, scrapping whatever isn't working and trying something new. Many of the stories herein are about change and the conflict that inevitably rises out of it, stories about women fighting discrimination and superstition to become coal miners, about men struggling to adjust to wives who seek careers and are changed by them, about paperless offices and other workplaces of the future.

But beneath the turmoil some things never change. As so many of these stories attest, we are now, as we have always been, one of the most individualistic of peoples. We insist on being treated as individuals and not as impersonal, faceless numbers, and we reward those who remember this, like a little soap company that listened hard to housewives and thereby grew up to be Procter & Gamble. While our political consultants shape candidates into inoffensive clones, we retain a sneaking fondness for politicians and others who remain very much their own men. We admire the likes of B.T. Collins, the bar-hopping, cheerfully profane aide to former California Governor Jerry Brown, who insults everybody and cracks dirty jokes while his ascetic boss watches a slide show on solar energy near Tibet.

Americans would rather build something new than run it, start something than finish it. Almost a half-million enterprises are launched here every year by people who gamble with the future and who wouldn't enjoy the game without the risk. This freelance, entreprenurial spirit pervades not only business but all of American life. But the deep strain of individualism from which it springs has darker aspects.

Individuals don't function well in impersonal, antlike environments, and it is ironic that America should have advanced and promoted mass production techniques and modern industrial organization to the rest of the world when its own people are so ill-suited to them. We see, in a steno pool and a computer assembly line, the crushing boredom and facelessness of such work. Our industrial genius too often has created jobs that stifle us and deny our nature as a people.

And we do not know what to do about those who cannot adjust, who are left behind by rapid change. If one aspect of civilization is the enduring, constant willingness of the fortunate many to provide for the unfortunate few, then we are not yet a completely civilized country; our natural compassion is always at war with our cherished belief that every man has the opportunity to make something of his own life if he really wants to. So we vacillate, offering help with one hand and snatching it back later with the other. The results are sad. A street sweeper in San Francisco who is losing his CETA job says: "This job's the best thing ever happened to a poor man. It's feeding babies. When it's over, I'll be putting cardboard in my little girl's shoes, like my mama did me."

We do not know, either, what to do about alienation and the plague of violence. In New York's Lower East Side, we join detectives tracking a killer through a jungle inhabited by teenage murderers and muggers who carry 12-inch knives and refer to their victims as "geese." These horrors are America too.

We cannot overlook them and we do not. But neither will we accept them fatalistically as permanent parts of American life, evils that can never be remedied. Having conquered a vast and hostile physical frontier, we convinced ourselves that we could conquer anything. At bottom, we still think so—and in this book the reader can see some of the new problems, the new challenges, the new frontiers, already under assault by the energy, optimism and sheer stubbornness of his compatriots. There is something supremely egotistical about the effort, and something glorious too.

William E. Blundell

THE NATION

The Land and Its People

NATURAL ENEMIES
To Loggers, the Woods Are Dark and Deep—But Far From Lovely

Men Take 'Proud Fatalism' And a Macho Demeanor To Their High-Risk Jobs

The Mason Family's Big Toll

BY WILLIAM E. BLUNDELL

KALAMA, WASH.   12/8/81

Let us say that you work in an office building with 1,000 people and that every day at least two are hurt on the job. Some suffer such ghastly wounds—multiple compound fractures, deep cuts severing muscle, sinew and nerve, shattered pelvises—that they may never return to their old posts. And every six months or so, a body is taken to the morgue.

Almost anywhere, this would be called carnage, and a hue and cry would be raised. But in the big-tree logging woods of the Pacific Northwest, it is simply endured with what logger-writer Stan Hager has called "proud fatalism," and few outside the loggers' trade even know of it. Miners trapped behind a cave-in draw national media attention, but in the

14

dim rain forests men fall singly and suddenly. There aren't any TV cameras.

Increased stress on training and safety in recent years has helped. But death and injury rates still are extraordinarily high—in part because loggers are an almost suicidally prideful and tradition-bound group, hooked on danger and suspicious of new equipment and techniques.

Resistance to Change

"There's tremendous macho, and I can't imagine any group of men more resistant to change," says Joel Hembree, the safety coordinator for Local 3-536 of the International Woodworkers of America, which represents loggers and millworkers in southwest Washington. The union, he adds, is thus in the awkward position of pushing measures that many of its own members oppose. "We're a bunch of dirty S.O.B.'s for trying to jam safety down their throats," he says.

In the forest, a few loggers sit in a bus reeking of old socks, wet wool and tobacco smoke, grousing about safety. "They've already got us decked out like Christmas trees," growls Howard "Spider" Mason, a 36-year-old Weyerhaeuser Co. "timber faller," or cutter, displaying a pair of heavy water-soaked leg protectors the law now says he must wear. Another logger recites a poem about the idiocies of the safety people that concludes, "Who's going to protect us against our protection?"

Even if the loggers did festoon themselves with every safety gadget available, the forest has a hundred treacherous ways to get them anyway. "To you the forest is a pretty place," says a union staffer. "To our guys it's dark, it's scary and it's out to hurt them."

Men are crushed to death by trees that simply fall over without being touched, or speared through by broken branches that fall 250 feet on a windless day, or maimed by rocks bouncing down hillsides.

The forest also is unforgiving of error, and a moment's carelessness can wound or kill. About 15,000 men are usually working in the Washington woods; over the past three years they have suffered a total of almost 28,000 injuries and 75 deaths. "It's you against the trees," says a veteran woodsman.

This toll is viewed with stoicism. Spider Mason, tall, dark and talkative ("Spider wore out two pair of lips before he was 18," says a co-worker), keeps his buddies laughing at his banter. But he is serious about the hazards of the job. "You go to work every day knowing death is in the trees," he says. "Your family knows it; my wife doesn't want to hear anything about what I do. But a logger has to *enjoy* danger or he isn't a logger."

Generations of the Mason clan have gone into the forest and, as with so many other families, it has made them pay for their fascination with it. The forest has already killed Spider Mason's uncle, grandfather, father and brother. The forest has also taken a big price from the town of Hayesville, N.C., population about 300; Clarence Stamey, woods business agent for the IWA local here, comes from Hayesville and can think of 10 fellow townsmen who have come to the Northwest woods to die. He may have forgotten a name or two, he adds.

The trade-off for all this? Membership in a fraternity.

* * *

At 4 a.m. bedroom lights go on in Kalama, Longview and smaller lumber towns—"the three-house, two-bar places," one logger calls them—buried in the green spires of the Cascade Range. A little later, the sleepy men board their "crummies," the aptly named crew buses that take them to their camps. All wear a uniform that hasn't changed in decades: caulked boots, heavy trousers cut off near the tops of the boots, work shirt, suspenders (no logger wears a belt), and usually a full beard or a brushy mustache.

By dawn the chain saws are snarling in the woods. The loggers won't get back home until dark—or well after dark as the days grow shorter. In between, they do some of the hardest physical work in American industry. Toiling "in the pit," at the bottom of infernally steep slopes, "choker-setters" struggle to fit 100-pound collars around the logs to be dragged uphill on one-inch cables grinding overhead. Laden with 50 to 100 pounds of gear, the timber fallers crawl up and down hills clogged with man-high brush to find their trees. In summer there is heat exhaustion, in winter the sheer misery of constant rain or snow.

It is the ability, and the will to endure such work that bind Northwest loggers together. To them, the loggers of the Southeast, where the trees are smaller, the land flatter and the climate benign, are mere woodchoppers. "*This* is logging," brags one foreman, indicating a virgin forest where monster Douglas firs eight feet in diameter and 250 feet tall can still be found. Nine miles east, Mount St. Helens rises like a white wall, its shattered summit banked in mist.

This is a male society. Few women apply for work requiring such great upper-body strength, and those who do confront a relentlessly macho atmosphere. At one camp men chose lots to sit next to a woman choker-setter on the crummy so they could harass her on the way home; she quit. A logging supervisor says, "The idea that a woman possibly could do what they do—well, it just kills them."

Few blacks work in the Northwest woods, either. Many loggers are from Southern families, and deeply ingrained racial attitudes persist. An old logger, arms covered with chain-saw scars, says earnestly, "A while back they tried real hard to get some of those niggers up here to work, but they didn't stick. I don't know why."

Everyone who enters the woods is hazed crudely and unmercifully. Does he have big ears? He is Dumbo forever. Is he a newlywed. Slip some dirty pictures into his empty lunchbox so his bride will find them. Put rocks in his gear bag, give him grueling, unnecessary chores to do. Test him. "The tender young boys don't last," says Spider Mason. One called Dimples so displeased the veteran logger he worked with that the latter picked him up overhead and threw him uphill with instructions never to return. He didn't.

In work so dangerous, it is vital to cull the unfit and the incompatible. A streak of meanness in the hazing often is the first sign that a man is on the way out, says Jack Coady, the superintendent of Weyerhaeuser's District 6, comprising 142,000 acres of forest east of Kalama. The victim may have his lunch destroyed or his clothes set afire; then another man may invite him behind a tree for a faceful of knuckles. Finally the hook tender—the boss union logger—may simply say, "Go on down the road. We don't want to see you anymore."

If a man is a good worker but cannot get along with his fellows, Mr. Coady will bluntly tell him that he is fouling up and that if he can't adjust to his next crew, he will be run off. Bluntness is always the loggers' way. "It's good, clean communication, one on one," he says. "No dancing around, no politics. Logging is an open society, and that's one reason I like the industry so much."

The woods are full of men who have repeatedly quit the miseries and dangers but who keep coming back. The open, rough camaraderie, the knowledge that they can do work others quail from out of fear or weakness, forges a sense of community they cannot find outside.

Greg Kruger, a strapping, fair-haired logger, says, "The beauty of the woods is that if you can do a damn good job, you can be any man you want, you can wear a clown suit or a tuxedo to work if you want. You'll get razzed to death—but you're accepted. You belong."

In 1974 a basketball-sized rock glancing off a canyon wall crushed Greg Kruger's left side. (One of the men who carried him out quit on the spot when he saw the wounds.) Now Greg's arm is a mass of scar tissue, and a piece of shattered pelvis still floats around inside him. Partly disabled, he works in the office at South Camp, the headquarters of District 6.

Work is somehow found for many men hurt seriously on the job—even though this may involve violating contract rules that require filling slots by seniority. Union representatives and company supervisors just look the other way; it is more important that the fraternity to which both belong takes care of its own. As for Greg Kruger, he wishes he could set choker again. But it is enough just to be here, still a member in good standing.

* * *

Thirty of the 210 men at South Camp are in a little contest. Divided into three groups of 10, they have been promised that if any group goes six months without an injury, the men and their wives will get a free dinner. "Shoot, they'll never collect," mumbles the logger. Three men on two of the teams were hurt within days after the list had gone up, thus having to start the six-month cycle all over again.

The 30 are South Camp's rack crew of timber fallers, the loggers who have the greatest risk of death. This camp hasn't lost a cutter in many years, but every old-timer on the crew knows someone who has been killed at this exacting craft. Conversation with fallers is a litany of tales about crushed skulls, broken backs, legs half-severed by chain saws. They also suffer scarred eyeballs from wood particles flying out of saw cuts, permanent hearing loss from saw noise far in excess of maximum federal standards, and damage to the capillaries and nerves of the hand because of vibration, damp and cold.

Safety Record

This is called white hand, and Roy Palmer has it badly. At times his hand turns a corpse-like white, and he loses feeling in it, a dangerous thing that Roy and the others shrug off. "You just clamp your fingers on with the other hand, and once in a while you burn it on the muffler (of the chain saw) till your glove starts to smoke," he says cheerfully.

At 62 and near retirement, Roy is still one of the most productive cutters. He went 27 years without an injury, an incredible record. Men have died around him, and once a partner, immobilized in front of an oncoming log when his foot got stuck, screamed to Roy to cut his leg off (he cut him out of his boot instead). But Roy himself escaped until recently.

He tore his hand on a running saw last year. And this past July, he had another accident while he was cutting a fallen tree into log lengths. When a tree is lying on uneven ground, it is full of areas of tension and compression called binds. After these are cut through, the sections can writhe like snakes or swing uphill or down, pivoting on rocks or stumps and crushing anything in their way. Roy Palmer fell as a tree moved, and his saw cut through muscles near his ankle and halfway into the bone.

There are scores of ways that loggers can die from a single mistake, and they are acutely conscious of the need for total concentration. Gary Trople, who is going through a divorce, says his production drops when marital troubles are on his mind because he won't touch a tree without having his entire attention on it.

Like others, he has a love-hate relationship with his job. Even at six, he wanted to be a timber faller; "I'd take a hatchet and beat on some of those little-bitty pine poles till they fell down," he recalls. But four months after he started in the woods, a snapping cable threw him against a stump, crushing his ribs, fracturing his skull and breaking his back in three places. "I swore I'd never come back," he says. "Five months later I was back. I went in the Army for four years and swore I'd never come back. Here I am."

Value of Narrow Escapes

Not long ago he felled a tree that brushed another tree in its descent, bending it like a 220-foot catapult. The tree sprang back to fire a deadly hail of broken limbs at him, but he escaped with lacerations. "Most of the time that would kill you," says his supervisor, a ginger-bearded logger named Jack Davis. But he adds that without close calls a faller can be lured into a false sense of security that may prove fatal. Jerry Baldwin, a young cutter, listens dubiously. "When I have a close call," he says "I just go home and shake for a while."

For this extra ration of danger, fallers get some of the top pay in the woods—$30,000 in a good year for an hourly paid union man, more for a good "gyppo busheler," a cutter working for a nonunion contractor and paid by the amount of wood he can lay on the ground.

Their psychic income is the satisfaction that comes from conquest of the great forest giants, and fallers always remember their biggest trees. "Lay one of those big dudes down just where you want, save it all, and you've done something damn few men anywhere can do," says one. A bad job that splits or breaks a tree can destroy 90% of its lumber value.

"Uphill! Uphill!"

In a virgin grove, Elmer Osborne and Paul Cline are working on a tree that was growing before Columbus sailed. It is about seven feet thick and 240 feet tall. After making the undercut, a thick wedge of wood removed in the desired direction of fall, Elmer cuts through the other side until only a thin slab of "holding wood" supports hundreds of tons above. Its equilibrium altered, the tree creaks, the wood tears away, and Elmer yells, "Uphill!" (No one yells, "Timber!" anymore.) The fir falls slowly, striking with a mighty *whump* that shakes the earth. It is a perfect fall, saving intact about $6,000 in logs and much more in lumber value at retail. "I'll take that one. That's a good one." Elmer says with a broad smile. It doesn't matter now that an hour earlier a 160-foot dead tree falling the wrong way almost wiped him out.

Such scenes grow rarer. On the private lands of the big timber companies, the enormous trees of the virgin forest are quickly disappearing; in their place are strange, monotonous woods that seem almost dead by comparison—filled with trees of the same height, thickness and species, all planted by men. They will never be allowed to reach the size of the old giants because that is uneconomical. Harvesting them will be far safer than working in the virgin forest, with its treacherous rotting trees, snarls of interlocking top branches, and leaning trees. But much of the glamour of logging will fade with that natural forest, too.

"That's why I've got pictures of the biggest trees I've cut," says Jack Davis, the supervisor. "For the kids, so they can see what it was really like. The day is coming when men in the woods will laugh if you tell them there were really trees 10 feet thick here."

Job Of Arctic Driller Is Dirty, Dangerous And Very Lucrative

Bill Walter, 24, Makes $90,000 A Year Searching for Oil; Divorce & Dogeared Books

BY KATHRYN CHRISTENSEN

THE BEAUFORT SEA — 4/14/81

Midnight approaches, and fatigue lines are carved in Bill Walter's unshaven face. Since noon, he and his six-man crew have been trying to jar loose the obstruction clogging the 15,000-foot hole they're drilling through a sandbar off Alaska's northern coast.

His eyes on the gauges in front of him, Mr. Walter keeps one gloved hand on a control lever and another on a long brake handle; he is working a block of pulleys hanging in a derrick that towers 175 feet above the ground. The machinery screeches like a wounded elephant as it is raised, then slams down with a force that sends shudders through the rig floor. The monotonous process halts only long enough to thaw the machinery that freezes in the Arctic temperature of 40 degrees below zero.

Just before his 12-hour shift ends and another crew takes over, Mr. Walter is able to free the obstruction to some extent. Splattered with mud, he heads for camp knowing that the actual drilling of this wildcat, or exploration, well may not resume for days. But whether the task is drilling or "fishing"—oil-field jargon for recovering equipment lost in the well—it is 24-year-old Mr. Walter who is directly in charge of Rig 84 while his crew is on duty.

A Blindfolded Surgeon

Some have compared Mr. Walter's job as an Arctic driller to that of a blindfolded surgeon performing an operation while standing across an auditorium from the patient. Using a collection of levers and knobs, Mr. Walter manipulates 1,500 horsepower and tons of iron through a hole that is already miles below and beyond him. His work is cold, dirty and dangerous. It is also lucrative: He is paid more than $90,000 a year.

As a high-school graduate, Mr. Walter is aware that he's earning more money than many men who have extensive educations and who are twice his age. Nevertheless, he says, "We're earning it up here."

"Up here" is the site of the West Mikkelsen No. 3 well in the Beaufort Sea. Just east of Alaska's Prudhoe Bay field, the Beaufort was opened for drilling in late 1979 and is one of the state's newest exploratory fields. Drilling here this year is limited to the period between Nov. 1 and April 14, the time when ice is the strongest and thus most capable of preventing damage to wildlife and the landscape in the event of oil spills.

Shell Oil Co. and its partners are spending more than $70,000 daily to drill at West Mikkelsen No. 3 well. High as those costs are, the potential rewards make drilling in the Beaufort Sea a gamble that Shell and other big oil companies are eager to take. Although no production has begun yet in the Beaufort, U.S. Geological Survey estimates say the area "most likely" holds 7.8 million barrels of still undiscovered but recoverable oil and 27 trillion cubic feet of undiscovered but recoverable gas.

But if the oil companies are counting on the promise of what may lie beneath the Beaufort, most of the 55 men working on this well are already banking on it. Some are former teachers or lawyers, others once were carpenters or bartenders. Ask what brings them to this isolated and frigid place—where most work 14 consecutive 12-hour days before taking seven days off—and they reply frankly that you can measure a man's greed by how far north he has come. Mr. Walter answers: "Money, mainly. I sure can't say I came because it's 90 (degrees) below."

Mr. Walter is an employe of Brinkerhoff Signal Inc., the drilling contractor on West Mikkelsen No. 3. He has worked in oil fields from Wyoming to Canada since the age of 17, when he became discouraged by the prospect of laboring on his family's Montana farm for $500 a month. And he is adamant about staying in Alaska. Though he has a home in Wyoming, he has rented one in Anchorage, 800 miles south of here, and plans to build a house there. "They'd have to drag me back," he declares. "You learn a lot on this kind of well; up here, there are challenges you can't find anywhere else."

One of the biggest challenges on this well involves the direction at which the hole is being drilled. While Rig 84 sits less than a mile offshore on a sandbar indistinguishable from the snow-covered frozen sea, the hole it is drilling angles off diagonally more than a mile under the sea. "With such a deviated hole," Mr. Walter says, "you're asking for trouble."

And trouble has been obliging. To protect the pipe as it angles through the hole's iron casing, the drilling crews headed by Mr. Walter and Bruce Snodgrass have put 150 thick rubber protectors resembling collars on the top 4,500 feet of pipe. The "fishing" procedure that followed was necessary because, Mr. Walter says, "when we came up out of the hole, none of those rubbers were on the joints. Something down there was tearing them out."

The problem of breaking up and retrieving the rubbers requires special equipment and delays drilling by more than a week. But such complications aren't unexpected on an oil rig. Earlier this year, Mr. Walter says, "I dropped two joints (30-foot lengths of pipe) down the hole." He is still incredulous that such a thing could have happened while he was at the controls. "I was positive I'd be run off (fired)," he says.

His first reaction was to peer down the miles-deep hole, an absurdly futile act that would have sent the roughnecks on his crew into howls if the situation hadn't been so serious. In the oil business, dropping so much as a wrench down the hole is grounds for dismissal. As it turned out, however, Mr. Walter was back on the rig shortly. "Bill's young, and he's a very good driller with lots of potential," says Robert Grote, a Shell foreman. Because of that and the fact we were considering altering direction (of the hole) a little anyway, we kept him. One thing we know is that he'll never make that mistake again."

Although Shell is the operator of this well, fewer than six of the 55 men here are Shell employes. Most work for the drilling contractor; the rest are employed by data-logging, food-preparation and special consulting companies. From the more than $90,000 paid to each of the two drillers and tool pusher Terry Coleman, their supervisor, wages drop to about $40,000 for the man who helps the cook and makes the beds. Even that lesser figure can be a fortune, however, considering that these workers have no living expenses during their hitches on the rig. "You can come up here with five cents and go back loaded," says Mr. Walter.

The camp itself, a string of connected trailers resembling a barracks, stands about 50 yards from the rig but is barely visible because of the snow banked around it. In the surrounding terrain, subzero temperatures and ferocious winds create chill factors that, at 100 degrees below zero, are capable of freezing exposed flesh within seconds. Whiteouts strike frequently, making it impossible to distinguish the landscape from the sky beyond 25 feet.

Lack of snow, however, was a problem at one point during the drilling of this well. Shell had to complete by Nov. 1 a 17-mile ice road connecting the campsite with an airstrip; but at the time the road was being built, too little snow had fallen on the tundra to provide the base for a solid road.

Consequently, says M. L. Woodson, head of Shell's Alaska production operations, he ordered industrial snow-making machines costing a total of $180,000. "When that purchase order . . . hit Houston, they must've thought I was crazy," Mr. Woodson says.

Good Food

Life inside the camp is as comfortable as possible, and the food is both good and plentiful by any standards. Shell figures the men need about 6,000 calories a day. Four meals are served daily; one recent lunch included ham and turkey, several salads and vegetables and a half-dozen desserts prepared that morning by the camp baker. Steak is on the menu at least twice a week; prime rib, at least once.

The rules here are few but simple: no alcohol, no fighting, no drugs and no loud noise in camp. Infractions can send a man packing though a bit of discreet drinking in quarters is occasionally tolerated. Most gambling is also forbidden, but men here have permission to play quarter-ante poker.

Boredom is a big threat. Books and magazines in the camp quickly become dogeared, and the projector in the movie room runs almost continuously. "I like the isolation, but there are times when I wake up and don't know if it's noon or midnight, especially when it's dark all the time" (as it was from November until mid-January), says Mr. Walter, who spent Thanksgiving, Christmas and New Year's on the rig.

Time to Worry

Some men spend their time worrying that their families will have problems while they're away for so long; others fret that their families will get along too well without them. Several, including Mr.

Walter, are divorced; he says he is convinced that oil fields and marriages mix about as well as oil and water.

"Men who spend any time in the oil field usually end up with three things: a gold watch, a diamond ring and divorce papers," says Donald Wester, an independent drilling consultant who is one of Shell's foremen on this well.

Still Mr. Walter seems pleased with his life. Although he wants to be an engineer someday, he will go on to another drilling job for Brinkerhoff once this job is finished. "People think we're nuts to do this, but I wouldn't trade it for anything," he says. "Until I became a driller, I never really knew what it meant to be mentally tired and challenged. The oil field has been good to me in more ways than paying my taxes."

His biggest responsibility is for the safety of his crew, no small task considering the amount of machinery he controls. "Every driller knows he's going to hit a wrong lever sometime and hurt somebody," he says, "but if anyone was ever killed, I'd have to give up the job if it was my fault." (So far, the most serious injury in camp has been the frostbite suffered by one worker.)

Goofing Off

As their two-week hitches wind down, every man in this camp is anxious to leave for a week "in town." Shell flies the men to Anchorage, where some spend the week hunting and fishing. Others fly, at their own expense, to warm vacation spots or to families as far away as Arizona. None makes a gradual transition back to normal civilization.

"The best way I know to unwind is to party; sometimes I don't get to sleep for two days after I get out of here," says Mr. Walter. "I've goofed off as much money in seven days as I've made in 14. . . . Usually, though, after a week off, I'm ready to get back to the rig."

At the end of one recent two-week shift, Mr. Walter and a dozen other men fidget as they wait to board the cold Convair that Shell charters to transport them back to Anchorage. Cowboy boots and tight jeans have replaced heavy boots, stained work clothes and hard hats. Once they are on board and strapped in the worn seats scattered around the plane's cargo, their worst fear is realized. There will be no drinking during this flight, thanks to the drilling crew's rowdy celebration of Mr. Walter's birthday on the group's last trip from the rig to Anchorage.

Once in the city, they quickly make up for that setback. The pressure of spending two weeks on the rig comes off like a barely controlled blowout: and by the time Mr. Walter settles down for dinner later in the evening, two of his well-lubricated friends have devised a new example of oil-field humor to make this week off a memorable one.

He is still on his first glass of wine and only two bites into his salad when a stranger dashes through the dimly lit restaurant and smashes a gooey pumpkin pie into Mr. Walter's face. As he wipes it off, he growls that the least the pranksters could have done was choose a cherry pie. He asks: "Did I really say I like this kind of work?"

The Days of a Cowboy Are Marked by Danger, Drudgery and Low Pay

But Jim Miller Likes Work As an Arizona Cowboss; Social Security Next Year

'People and Cattle Don't Mix'

BY WILLIAM E. BLUNDELL

RAFTER ELEVEN RANCH, ARIZ.   6/10/81

The lariat whirls as the man on horseback separates a calf from the herd. Suddenly, the loop snakes around the calf's rear legs and tightens. Wrapping a turn of rope around the saddle horn, the rider drags the hapless animal to his crew.

The flanker whips the calf onto its back, and the medicine man inoculates the animal. Amid blood, dust and bawling, the calf is dehorned with a coring tool, branded in an acrid cloud of smoke from burning hair and flesh, earmarked with a penknife in the ranch's unique pattern (cowboys pay more attention to earmarks in identifying cattle than to brands) and castrated. It is all over in one minute.

Jim Miller, the man in the saddle smiles broadly as the released calf scampers back to his mother. Mr. Miller is 64 years old. Born and raised nearby, he has been working cows in Yavapai County since he was five. He will keep on until he can't throw a leg over a horse anymore. "It's all I know and I like it," he says.

The marks of his trade are stamped into his body: broken legs, a broken ankle, dislocated shoulder and elbow, a thigh torn open by a broken saddle horn. The fingers of the right hand are grotesquely broken, and he can't flex them fully. It is the roper's trademark, the digits that have been caught in the rope and crushed against the saddle horn, but Mr. Miller still wins roping competitions with that hand.

Jim Miller is a cowboy. There are still many cowboys in the West. Some wear black hats with fancy feather bands; they tear around in oversize pickups with a six-pack of Coors on the seat. These are smalltown cowboys. They don't know anything about cows, and the only horses they know are under the hood.

Others become cowboys at sunset, shucking briefcases and three-piece suits for designer jeans, lizard-skin boots and silver buckles as big as headlights. Then they go to Western nightclubs to see what everyone else is wearing. They are urban cowboys, and the only bulls they know are mechanical ones.

Finally, there is a little band of men like Jim Miller. Their boots are old and cracked. They still know as second nature the ways of horse and cow, the look of sunrise over empty land—and the hazards, sheer drudgery and rock-bottom pay that go with perhaps the most overromanticized of American jobs. There are very few of these men left. "Most of the real cowboys I know," says Mr. Miller, "have been dead for a while."

Hype and Illusion

A big man with a ready laugh, he is both amused and exasperated by all the cowboy hype. "It almost makes you ashamed to be one," he says. "You've got doctors and lawyers and storekeepers runnin' around in big hats and boots." None, he intimates, would want to step into a real cowboy's place today; their image of the life is an illusion.

The typical ranch hand in this traditional cattle country, he says, is in his late teens or early 20s—so green he often doesn't know how to shoe his own horse—and must do all sorts of menial chores. Nobody can now afford the "horseback men," aristocrats of the saddle who spurned all ranch work that they couldn't do from the top of a horse except branding. Most hands are local boys who commute to work from nearby towns, as does Mr. Miller himself. With few exceptions, the bunkhouses full of "bedroll cowboys," wanderers from ranch to ranch over the West, are no more.

Some things haven't changed, though. Punching cows, says Mr. Miller, "is still the lowest-paid job for what you have to know and do." In the '30s in Yavapai County, cowboys made $45 a month plus bed and board. The standard wage now is around $500 a month without bed and board. There is Social Security and the usual state coverage for job-related injuries, but there are no pension plans, cost-of-living adjustments, medical and life-insurance packages, or anything else.

Mr. Miller is one of the elite. His salary from Fain Land & Cattle Co., the family concern that operates the ranch, is $1,150 a month, but that is because he is the cowboss. The cowboss is the master sergeant of the ranch; he leads by example, works along with his men, and is in charge of day-to-day cattle operations. At various times the cowboss, or any other top hand, has to be a geneticist, accountant, blacksmith, cook, botanist, carpenter, tinsmith, surgeon, psychologist, mechanic, nurse and a few other things beside rider and roper. "There just isn't any point in a young fellow learnin' to be a top hand when he can make so much more today doin' practically anything else," the cowboss says sadly.

Then why do some still follow the life?

* * *

It is early morning on Mr. Miller's domain, more than 50,000 acres of rolling semiarid dun hills and mountain slopes. The cowboss and two full-time hands work this country by themselves. They are going today to 7,800-foot Mingus Mountain to collect strays missed in the recent spring roundup. Mr. Miller surveys the land critically. Here and there the grama grass is greening up, but good summer rains will be needed to get the range in condition.

There is absolutely nothing that the cowboss can do about it except pray. The land is just too big. In almost every other occupation, man seals himself off from nature in factory or office tower, struggles to bend a little patch of it to his will, or tries to wrest away its riches by force. But the cowboy knows he is only a speck on the vast plain, his works insignificant, his power to really control the land almost nil; nature herself is the only manager of the Rafter Eleven or any other ranch. So the cowboy learns to bow humbly before the perils and setbacks she brings, and to truly appreciate her gifts.

A big buck antelope squirms under a fence and sprints over the plain, hoofs drumming powerfully. "Now that's one fine sight," murmurs a cowboy.

The party is not sauntering colorfully over the hills on horseback. It is bouncing over them in a pickup. The cow ponies are riding comfortably behind in a special trailer; they, too, commute to work now. Though he grew up in the days of chuck wagons, line camps, bunkhouses and the great unfenced ranges, Mr. Miller is a strong believer in modern methods. He uses an electric branding iron because it is faster, and he will even use a trailer to take small groups of cattle from place to place on the ranch rather than drive them on foot. One pound sweated off a steer costs the ranch about 67 cents.

But he and every other experienced cowman draw the line at replacing the horse. There is a strange chemistry between horse and cow, a gentling effect, that he declares irreplaceable. "Some dummies around here tried motorcycles once. Didn't work worth a damn," snorts the cowboss. No machine, he adds, can ever duplicate the instincts and balletic ability of a fine cutting horse dancing into a herd to separate steer from heifer.

At Mingus Mountain the horses go to work. There is no glamorous dashing about on the plain, only a laborious, slow plod up a mountain canyon that is rocky, steep-sided, clogged with brush. Jagged tree branches jab at the riders. It is grueling, hazardous work, but a nice piece of high country is a valuable asset to any ranch here. In winter it is actually warmer for the cattle because the cold air settles in the valley below, and the nutritious scrub oak and other bushes are available year around and grow above snow.

In a high clearing fringed by oak, juniper and pine, 18-year-old Troy Tomerlin pauses awhile, chewing on a twig, to consider his future. He can operate a backhoe and could make almost twice as much doing that as the $500 a month he gets now. "But I don't know how I'd like diggin' septic tanks day after day," he says. "Here I can see animals, work with animals, move around a lot of country. In an office you can't see nothin' but a desk, and I don't like people lookin' over my shoulder. Jim tells us what to do, and how you do it is up to you. I like that."

Suddenly, dark clouds begin to boil up over the mountain. Last week the cowboys were pelted by hail the size of golf balls, but that is just part of the job. Lightning, however, is much feared by any mounted man caught on the open plain, and many cowboys have been killed by it. Last summer a bolt barely missed Troy and knocked him unconscious. Other cowboys have been killed or crippled when their horses fell on them and leaped back up to gallop in panic with the rider entangled in rope or stirrup. "I've had three real good friends dragged to death that way," Mr. Miller says softly.

Lariats Used Sparingly

The clouds pass over harmlessly and 18 head coaxed out of the rocks and brush are driven toward the plain. Tommy Stuart, a fine rider with rodeo experience, crashes through brush again and again to divert straying animals. The men cry out to the cattle in a strangely musical series of yips, calls and growls. Tommy has to rope a balky calf, the only time anyone uses his lariat; the cowboy who does so frequently doesn't know how to drive cattle, Mr. Miller says.

The trick, he says, is to watch the way their ears are pointing and so anticipate their direction. Mr. Miller also rests cattle frequently on drives to let cows and calves "mother up" so they're more easily driven, or to calm trotty (nervous) animals. "If you don't rest them," he says, "they'll start to run, they'll get hot, then they'll get mad. Then there's no turning them. You've got to keep your cattle cool."

The fall weaning is a particularly sensitive time. Separated from their mothers until the maternal bond is broken, the calves, now sizable, are under stress that can cause pneumonia. When the animals finish days of bawling and finally lie down, the sound of a car, a dog's bark, even the cry of a night bird, may set them back on their feet and running in stampede, mowing down fences, crushing each other in the pileup of bodies. This happened to Mr. Miller twice when he was cowboss on the big Yolo ranch.

Nothing untoward happens on this drive, and the riders finally reach the plain. No chuck wagon rolls up with a bewhiskered Gabby Hayes type ready to ladle out son-of-a-bitch stew—classically, a concoction of cow brains, tongues, hearts, livers and marrow, with a handful of onions thrown in to conceal the taste. Instead everyone rumbles back to the ranch house and the cowboss himself fixes lunch for his men: steaks, beans, bread smothered in gravy, and mayonnaise jars full of iced tea.

How to Get Fired

By tradition, the cowboss looks out for his cowboys and hires and fires them himself. Besides incompetence, two things will get you fired by Jim Miller: abuse of horses and bellyaching. The latter is a breach of a cowboy code still in force. For $500 a month, the ranch expects and almost always gets total and uncomplaining loyalty to the outfit. Unionism is an utterly alien concept to cowboys; if a man doesn't like his boss, his job or anything else, he quits on the spot.

Firing is as simple. There are no hagglings over severance pay, no worries about employe lawsuits. "I just tell them, 'This is it,' and they go," says Mr. Miller.

Once, when a cowboss needed good hands, he would just drop in at the Palace Bar on Whisky Row in Prescott. This was the hiring hall and water hole, full of men who had been on the range for months and were "getting drunker'n seven hundred dollars," as Mr. Miller puts it. He doesn't go there anymore. "Now it's full of hippies and such as that, people who don't know a horse from a cow," he says. Instead, cowboys call him at home when they need work.

Lunch is over, and the men get off their rumpsprung old chairs and go out to nurse a young heifer internally damaged when calving. If they don't get her up to walk, she will die.

* * *

At the offices of Rafter Eleven, Bill Fain has been told by his computer that the cattle he soon will sell will have cost about 68 cents a pound to raise and fatten. He expects to get 67 cents for them. That's the cattle business today, says Mr. Fain, vice president of Fain Land & Cattle and the third generation of his family on this ranch. And such thin margins make men like Jim Miller particularly important.

The cowboss is considered one of the canniest judges of livestock in the area, and buys the registered bulls and replacement heifers for the ranch. It is he, more than anyone else, who maintains the quality of the herd. He coaxes an 80% calf crop out of the 700 mother cows here, a good ratio. He does not overburden the land, letting it rest and renew.

"Our product isn't cattle. It's grass," says Mr. Fain, "and Jimmy knows that. A lot of people can rope and ride and love the life, but there are damned few left who can do all the things he does."

Outside, cars whiz by on the road that crosses what used to be called Lonesome Valley. Some 6,000 people live there now because the Fains, trying to diversify out of an increasingly risky reliance on cattle, sold a piece of the ranch to a developer who built a town on it. The Fains developed another piece themselves.

This has made the cowboy's job harder. Cattle have been shot and cut up on the spot with chain saws by shade-tree butchers who throw the pieces in the back of a pickup and drive off, leaving head and entrails. People tear down cattle feeders for firewood, shoot holes in water tanks, breach fences to maliciously run down calves. "People and cattle don't mix," concedes Mr. Fain. "It's a sick thing," says Jim Miller, and there is an icy anger in his blue eyes.

Meanwhile, the old family ranches are being sold, most of them to investors who don't know one end of a Hereford from the other and are more interested in tax shelter than running a good spread. This has driven ranchland prices so high that a young man who really wants to raise beef either can't afford to buy or has no hope of getting a return on his investment. "I really can't see much future in the cattle business," Mr. Miller says.

Cougars and Grasshoppers

Perhaps not. But around Yavapai County the cycle of ranch life continues unchanged on the surviving family spreads. In Peeples Valley, cougars have taken 15 calves this year and lion hunter George Goswick is tracking them through the Weaver Mountains. In the pastures, mares are heavy with foals; in time some will find their way into the gentling hands of Twister Heller, the horse breaker. On the Hays ranch, owner John Hays is stabbing a wild-eyed Hereford bull in the rump with a needle full of antibiotics and fretting about the grasshoppers that are all over his property. There is too much ranch and too many hoppers, so he must simply accept them.

At evening, Jim Miller comes home to a house and five rural acres with horse corral outside Prescott. He and his wife, Joan, have lived here 10 years; for the first 27 years of their marriage they lived on the local ranches he worked, raising four sons and two daughters, teaching all to rope and ride. None have followed in his footsteps because there isn't any money in it.

Next year, when he's 65, Mr. Miller plans to quit as cowboss at the Rafter Eleven and start collecting Social Security. But he says he will never stop working. Few men around here who have spent their lives on a horse seem able to get off. Jim's friend Tom Rigden still rides roundup and castrates calves on his ranch, though he has been blind for almost eight years.

Mr. Miller doesn't expect any trouble finding day jobs on ranches. At a time when there are so few real cowboys left, he says, there is always work for a top hand.

SPROUTING LEASES

Tenant Farming Gains, Troubling Proponents Of Family Ownership

Poor Management Is Feared: Will Speculation in Land Cause a Food-Price Rise?

A Lawyer's Best Investment

BY MEG COX

Clyde Hagemann

HAMPSHIRE, ILL.   10/6/81

Clyde Hagemann farms as far as he can see in every direction, a total of 3,500 acres. He owns eight tractors, two combines, several semitrailer trucks and grain storage bins that dwarf the local grain elevator. He employs three hired hands.

But Hr. Hagemann doesn't own a square inch of land. Even his house is rented. This sophisticated farmer is a tenant, a sharecropper. He is also, perhaps, the farmer of the future.

"If everybody owned land but me, I might be bothered," says the 37-year-old Mr. Hagemann, a soft-spoken man with sandy hair and freckles. "But the trend is toward doing what I'm doing."

The General Accounting Office says that less than half of U.S. farmland is owned by the people who farm it. A detailed 1980 study by a Sioux City, Iowa, Roman Catholic group dedicated "to preserving family farms" found that in some of Iowa's richest farming counties, as much as 77% of the farmland is rented. Given the older average age (over 50) of farmers, recent tax-law changes and current farm-income problems, many experts say the gulf between farming and land ownership will widen.

The implications are profound. A 1980 farm-ownership report by the Senate Select Committee on Small Business predicts that "the land will be less carefully stewarded, farmland will become the subject of price speculation and unwise farm development, and the family farm system as this country knows it will be undermined."

"I think the situation is alarming, and I don't think the public is aware of it," says former Agriculture Secretary Bob Bergland, who in 1979 directed an extensive study on the outlook for the family farm. "We have fewer landowners today than we've had in all history." The more land that outside investors buy, the higher land prices go and the higher rents are raised, until "land values are driven by factors that have nothing to do with crop prices or farming," argues Mr. Bergland. "Eventually, those higher land prices translate into higher food costs."

Despite U.S. decrees and homesteading acts designed to create the maximum number of independent farmers, there has always been a significant amount of tenancy. Even in 1880, when there was more than enough land to go around, one-fourth of U.S. farmers were tenants, the Agriculture Department says.

Drastic Changes

Tenancy isn't necessarily bad; the U.S. would be in grave trouble without it, says Prof. Neil Harl, an agricultural economist at Iowa State University. "A healthy agriculture ought to have a mixture of owned and rented land," says Mr. Harl, "in order for new entrants to farming to get a toehold."

Renting has long served this vital function for newcomers, and even larger, settled farmers often rent some land. More than half of U.S. farmers both own and rent, Agriculture Department figures show. But the agency has never analyzed landlords and rental arrangements, and they are undergoing drastic changes.

"There has historically been a high proportion of landlords who are retired farmers or sons of farmers," says Gene Wunderlich, an Agriculture Department economist, but "we suspect there is a greater tendency now for these landlords to be people with no farming experience."

It isn't that corporations are taking over farming or that foreign investors are invading. The Agriculture Department estimates large corporations own 1.6% of U.S. farmland, much of it on the West Coast, and foreigners own 0.5%.

35

Inflation and Security

What has happened is this: Fewer Americans wanted to stay on the farm, while more and more wanted to own farmland, attracted by the sharp price rise over the past decade. As increasing numbers of farmers retire, they and their offspring are keeping the land regardless of whether they plan to farm.

"A lot of heirs who don't want to farm have hung on to the land as an investment, while in a previous generation they probably would have sold out," says Philip Raup, a University of Minnesota land economist. "What's made the difference? Inflation and a search for security."

One of Mr. Hagemann's landlords here in Hampshire who is both an heir and an investor is Chicago lawyer John Damisch. (Of Mr. Hagemann's 12 landlords, six are land speculators or developers, six are widows or retired farmers and only one lives on the farm property.) Mr. Damisch inherited one-fifth of a 1,000-acre farm homesteaded by his ancestors in 1835. He didn't have any intention of farming, but once he owned part of a farm, Mr. Damisch got the urge to buy a whole one for himself. And because that turned out to be the best investment he ever made, he bought four more farms.

"I bought the first farm in 1958, for $325 an acre, and it would easily bring $3,500 an acre now," says Mr. Damisch. Farmland prices overall rose 300% between 1968 and 1979, says the Agriculture Department, and, in Iowa, the rise has been 456% since 1967.

Such price leaps can be a bonanza to established farmers, but younger farmers trying to get started or build on to a budding operation are simply priced out of the market.

"Today you have to choose between land and equipment," asserts Warren Nesler, who farms 2,200 acres near Mr. Hagemann and only owns 80 acres. Mr. Hagemann says he himself couldn't afford the $1 million investment he has in equipment if he had land payments, too. Mr. Hagemann says he spends $70,000 a year on fertilizer alone.

Using Iowa State University estimates for production costs, yields, land prices and interest rates (12% at the Federal Land Bank), it becomes clear that the difference between buying and renting farmland these days is the difference between brutal losses and survival.

If a farmer bought land for $2,100 an acre, the current average for Iowa, he would have annual interest costs of $252 an acre, twice the average Iowa rent of $125 an acre. Adding the costs of such necessities as seed and fertilizer, a farmer who bought 100 acres would lose

$13,265 if he planted soybeans and $8,875 if he planted corn. But if he rented 100 acres, he would lose only $565 on beans and would earn $3,825 on corn.

Farmers report a variety of changes in rent arrangements with absentee owners that put more pressure on the farmers and on the land. Mr. Hagemann says 10-year leases were common in his father's day, but most leases currently are for two or three years at most. And many farmers say that although they prefer renting "on shares, 50-50," so that landlord and renter share equally in bad crops and good, non-farmer landlords are more likely to demand an unvariable cash rent.

Some areas report a breakdown in the traditional practice of renting land to the same tenant nearly indefinitely. "Some absentee landlords are putting the lease up for auction," says Donald Wieland, vice president of Farmers National Bank of Cherokee, Iowa. "Last year, 40 farmers bid for one 120-acre farm, which drives up all the rents."

Issue of Erosion

Without land, a farmer's existence is shakier all the way around, says James Kramer, a Hugoton, Kan., farmer. "Tenant farmers are the ones who'll go by the wayside whether they're efficient or not, because they're the ones who'll get shaken out in bad times," says Mr. Kramer.

Mr. Bergland, who himself started out as a renter and who now leases his Roseau, Minn., farm to his daughter and son-in-law, agrees. "There is no equity in equipment, which depreciates 10% a year," he notes, while U.S. farmland prices as a whole haven't fallen since 1941.

Also farmers generally have a much greater stake in keeping farmland producing food, Mr. Bergland notes. Especially near growing towns and cities, non-farm landlords may eagerly seek developers, which could increase the rate at which farmland is being lost. (The Agriculture Department estimates a yearly loss of three million acres, out of a total farm acreage of around one billion.)

Finally, there is the hotly contested issue of soil erosion and long-term husbandry of the land. "Most investors take tremendous pride in ownership," says Joel McNeill, an executive with Doane-Western Inc., a big farm-management concern. "They know the land will depreciate in value if they allow erosion."

But many farmers admit they just don't treat land as well if it isn't theirs. "I tried to do a good job when I was a renter," says Kenneth Ver Steeg, a Rock Rapids, Iowa, farmer. "But it's different when you own it. I plan further into the future in terms of things like fertilizer and tillage; you give it the best care possible even if it costs extra now. But when you're renting, you just put in what you can get out this year."

Several factors suggest the trend toward tenant farming and absentee ownership will accelerate. To begin with, investors are dominating farmland purchases, says Mr. McNeill of Doane. Investors have dominated the market for several years, he adds, while slumping farm income has limited buying by farmers. Inflation-adjusted farm income hit a 10-year low in 1980, remains depressed this year and isn't expected to recover much in 1982.

An enormous share of U.S. farmland will be changing hands over the next 20 years, and recent estate-tax reforms could translate that into increased tenancy, some economists say. Nearly 70% of farmland is owned by people over 50, and the new tax laws will give those owners who are farmers more incentive than ever to keep land in the family when they retire, regardless of whether heirs want to farm.

"Perfect Shelter"

Provisions that make transfer to a spouse tax-free and reduce the tax bite in other ways will also make farmland more attractive to investors and "will probably result in increased tenancy," says Prof. Harl. There were already tax advantages (such as preferential treatment for capital gains) in owning farmland that, the Senate committee's farmland report notes, "are of greatest benefit to those in the highest tax brackets." And investors may like the fact that while landowners used to have to keep farming 15 years to get a lower "current use" tax rate, the new tax laws say they only have to farm the land 10 years for the lower rate.

"I think farmland will become a perfect shelter for people under the estate-tax changes," says Mr. Bergland. "We're going to see trust funds, pension funds and industrial buyers snap up farmland."

Short of forbidding non-farmers to buy land, as some Scandinavian countries do, how can an acceleration in tenancy and absentee ownership be prevented? Most critics of absentee ownership urge the government to increase support for moderate-sized farmers who own and run their operations, while discouraging non-farm investors.

Mr. Bergland suggests that the capital-gains tax rate only apply to that amount of capital investment required for "the most efficient-sized farm," which he says is about 1,000 acres in the Midwest. By taxing any gains beyond that at the higher ordinary-income rates, Mr. Bergland says, "speculation would be discouraged."

Arizona Indians Win Victory Over U.S.: Refuse $33 Million

Opposition by Yavapai Kills Plan to Flood Reservation; Trail of Broken Promises

BY WILLIAM E. BLUNDELL

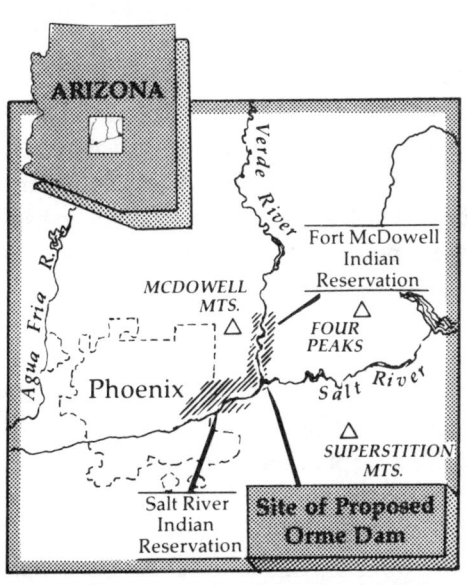

FORT MCDOWELL, ARIZ.
12/17/81

The 360 Yavapai Indians on this small reservation, the shrunken remnant of thousands who once lived on 10 million Arizona acres, have won their first great victory over the white man. He wanted to stuff some $33 million into their pockets. They told him to get lost.

The money would have been paid for a patch of Yavapai desert flooded by the proposed Orme Dam, the keystone of a $1 billion federal water project that practically every element of Arizona's political and economic power structure has lusted after for 13 years. But the huge dam at the confluence of the Salt and Verde rivers would have inundated up to 17,000 of the 25,000 acres the tribe has left, and forced its relocation.

So the Yavapai (pronounced yah-vuh-PIE), who were never even consulted about the dam when it was first authorized in 1968, dug in for a last stand. They lobbied in Congress, marched on a "trail of tears" to the state capitol, and picketed Sen. Barry Goldwater at a public appearance. "This was our last piece of homeland," says tribal chairman Norman Austin. "There was no other place for a people who had been sent wandering over the desert for so many years."

Government Caves In

The government, of course, could have just condemned the property, kicked out the Yavapai, and paid them off anyway. But confronted by their refusal to sell voluntarily at any price, by rising public sympathy for them, and by the certainty of a lawsuit by the Indians and their environmentalist allies (the dam would have drowned the south Verde's riparian habitat, bald-eagle nesting sites and archaeological ruins), the dam's proponents are caving in.

Now most of them have reversed course, to support an alternative plan that won't affect the Yavapai. The final decision will be made by Interior Secretary James Watt, who has already informally backed the alternative; official approval won't be announced until environmental-impact statements are completed, but it is generally agreed that the Orme Dam is dead.

"It's pretty amazing," says Lawrence Aschenbrenner, an attorney for the Native American Rights Fund who aided the Yavapai in their struggle. "All sorts of well-intentioned people told the Yavapai they were sticking their heads in the sand, that if they'd just negotiate, they could make a heck of a deal. The $33 million was a tentative bargaining offer, really. What these people have done is an example to other tribes who can now say, 'By God, if we get together and don't give up, we can win too.'"

Meanwhile, on their mountain-ringed piece of Sonoran desert, the Indians celebrate because they don't have to take Uncle Sam's money. When news of Secretary Watt's preliminary opinion was announced a month ago, some elders wept or cried out with joy. "I ran down here hollerin' and my daughter said, 'Are you sick? Are you crazy?'" recalls Bessie Mike, a 73-year-old basket weaver.

A great billowing woman in a print dress, she sits under a tree outside a tiny cinderblock home painted lilac: a rusting Plymouth Fury is sinking into the desert nearby. She has just received $1,100 for basketry it took her four months to make. Couldn't she use $100,000 or so? Why not sell the land? "This is our place," she says simply.

Not all the Yavapai opposed the dam. One living off the reservation, Michele Guerrero of Mesa, has publicly criticized the tribe's decision, saying that the money could have been of immeasurable help in raising the tribe's standard of living and educational level. Many whites also find the decision incomprehensible for the same reason. "I still think they made a mistake," says one state official. "Just think of what they could have done for themselves with all that money."

But some Yavapai cheerfully admit they would probably just blow much of it on a spending binge. One tells of a cousin who got $1,500, part of an overall $5.1 million land-claim settlement distributed among the tribe in the mid-1970s. He splurged on an expensive Western outfit, including red boots, started nipping on a jug, and extended grants and loans to hangers-on. He awoke the next morning sans money and everything else. Even the boots were gone.

So to the Yavapai, the white man's money is ice, but the land is diamonds. A profound and mystical connection to that land, something many whites don't comprehend, is at the root of the Yavapai resistance. In a tribal vote five years ago, 144 of them voted to hold the land and 57 voted to sell it, with most of the latter votes apparently coming from tribal members living off the reservation. Today, it is difficult to locate anyone living at Fort McDowell who admits he voted to sell.

Like other tribes, the Yavapai hold their land in common, not as individual plots, and they view it as an integral part of their religion and culture. "Land should not belong to people—people belong to the land," says Virginia Mott, an outspoken opponent of the dam.

Tribal religion and culture have been in decline, slowly eroded by neglect and by white influences. The Yavapai tongue is dying out, the last medicine man is gone, and knowledge of the old faith and customs resides mostly among the elders. But enough of the Yavapai way remains in the tribal consciousness to make even the thought of drowning the land a desecration.

Honored Dead

There are prayer grounds here consecrated by medicine men of old. There is the neatly tended cemetery, all graves aligned to face the sacred mountain called Four Peaks. To the Yavapai, the dead remain a part of the community, and to disturb them would be deeply troubling. (One grave holds the honored bones of Carlos Montezuma, a Yavapai physician and a powerful spokesman for all Indian interests until his death in 1923. He had predicted that the whites one day would try to build a dam that would flood the reservation. "White people's heads are long," he wrote. "They can see many years ahead" about the future need for a dam.)

Finally, there are the Kakakas, the secretive Old Ones who are the guardians and protectors of the Yavapai. In tribal lore, they are tiny people, three or four feet tall, immortal, and live on Four Peaks, Superstition Mountain, and Red Mountain, as well as in ruins at Fort McDowell that the Yavapai avoid. Flood out the Kakakas? Unthinkable.

Beyond their reverence for the land itself, the Yavapai also harbor a historically justified skepticism about white promises. In the 1860s the U.S. cavalry promised them food, clothing and land if they would settle near Army forts; they got starvation and smallpox instead. Lumped in with the far more warlike Apache (they still are called Mohave-Apache, though their language is entirely different), they were mowed down by Army rifles at Skeleton Cave, Bloody Basin, Skull Valley.

Landing on Reservation

Rounded up again on land they were told would be theirs, they were again displaced and sent on a forced march of 180 miles to the Apache reservation at San Carlos. Many died. They finally got their own reservation here in 1903 and have clung to it since, despite repeated threats to move them into the nearby Salt River reservation with their ancestral foes, the Pimas.

Thus, they were wary of white promises about the benefits they would enjoy from the dam. One was exclusive concessions for boating and fishing on the lake it would form. Beyond the fact that Yavapai hate fish and don't like still water, it wasn't made clear until recently that the lake level would fluctuate so drastically that the place would be a mud flat much of the time, which would have left the Indians operating the only landlocked marina in the U.S.

Though they apparently have won the fight against the Orme Dam, the Yavapai and their allies have little confidence that they will be left alone from now on. Carolina Butler, a feisty white housewife from Scottsdale who has aided the Yavapai from the beginning, wants an endangered-Indian law to protect small tribes everywhere from destruction by such projects. Tribal member Phil Dorchester, noting that water wells in Phoenix and Scottsdale have been poisoned by chemicals, says fatalistically: "They'll come up here sooner or later to try to get more water from the Verde. They'll have to."

The young will have to be vigilant, says John Williams, 77 and wheelchair-bound. "I am a man of rubber now," he says, indicating his useless legs, "but I would tell the young people this: The God behind blue heaven made this land for his people. Hold it. Put writing on papers. Do not sell it. Do not lease it. Pass it down. All this my own father told me too."

THE WORKPLACE

Americans at Work

Extra! Joseph Gomez Tells How He Runs Sidewalk Newsstand!

New Yorker Braves Robbers, Cold, Competitors' Barbs; All the News, Plus Candy

BY DANIEL MACHALABA

NEW YORK 2/19/82

Signs state clearly that the corner is that of East 77th Street and Lexington Avenue, but they don't forestall the passerby's question: "Where's 77th and Lexington?"

"You're there," answers Joseph Gomez, by now accustomed to the query that he hears from morning to night, day in, day out. Still, he mutters to himself: "This business is crazy, crazy."

The business is the A&J Newsstand operated by Mr. Gomez and his wife, Aurora, on the corner of—where's that again?—yes, 77th Street and Lexington in Manhattan. Among other bits of craziness attendant to his job, Mr. Gomez says, is the fact that the installation of a clock in front of the stand hasn't cut down on requests for the time of day and the fact that a hot seller in this Upper East Side neighborhood is San Francisco magazine.

All this takes place in and around a 48-square-foot aluminum shed that abuts the stairwell leading down to the Lexington Avenue subway line and is a few feet away from the entrance of Lenox Hill Hospital. The Gomezes have been operating A&J for eight years, serving a clientele that averages 1,500 people a day and that ranges from the famous (Richard Nixon and New York City's Mayor Edward Koch have bought newspapers from A&J) to the unknown likes of common street thieves.

Unenviable Job

All told, close observers say, it isn't an enviable job. Stephen Stollman, a carpenter who has built and repaired newsstands throughout the city, says, "Newsstand operators work long hours for not enough money, and they face the weather and people who can be obnoxious—if not dangerous."

Mr. Gomez has been robbed at gunpoint or knifepoint three times in the past two years. But of even greater concern is that he's in a declining business. Here in New York, the city's Consumer Affairs Department, which licenses most of the outdoor newsstands, says the number of such stands has declined from about 1,325 in 1950 to 408 today. Similar declines have occurred in Chicago, Philadelphia and the dwindling number of other cities that still have sidewalk stands.

A key reason that newsstands are folding is that there are fewer newspapers for them to sell. New York City, which boasted seven daily papers in 1950, now has three. One of the three, the Daily News, is in danger of dying if a buyer for it isn't found soon. "That would be one more reason why newsstands are closing," says Mr. Gomez, who today serves about half as many customers as he did when he first got in the business.

Small wonder that many in the city look upon A&J as a museum piece. "Parents bring their children and say, 'This is what a newsstand used to look like when we were kids,' " Mr. Gomez says. And such comments, he adds, make him "feel great."

The 49-year-old Mr. Gomez came late to the newsstand business. Until 1973, he was a bookbinder; but in that year his eyesight became impaired by glaucoma, forcing him to give up his trade. He was hired as a checkout clerk at a cigar store; but on his first day, he made a cash-register error and was dismissed. Then, because of his eye condition and because Mrs. Gomez had been blind from birth, the couple were offered free use of one of the more than 100 New York City sidewalk newsstands owned by the New York State Commission for the Blind and Visually Handicapped.

For the Gomezes, the offer was a welcome alternative to working in a sheltered shop for the blind or "being in the house and feeling like a vegetable," Mr. Gomez says. He adds: "It means a lot to blind newsstand dealers that we don't have to be a leech on society." (Mr. Gomez has enough sight in his left eye to count change and to make out the forms of people.)

Cigarets and Candy

The Gomezes were assigned the commission's first vacant stand—the 77th and Lexington location—which they christened A&J after the initials of their first names. Mrs. Gomez bought the stock, which at first consisted solely of magazines and newspapers. However, in 1979 Mayor Koch signed regulations permitting newsstands to increase their selling area by 50% and to diversify into such non-news products as cigarets, candy, razor blades and packaged foods. In response, the Gomezes reduced A&J's magazine selection by one-third, to about 130 titles, to make room for candy and cigarets. They also installed a stamp machine as a service to customers; and Mr. Gomez has become an agent for Lotto, a New York State gambling game.

(The mayor's regulations, according to the mayor himself, were aimed at increasing the profitability and number of newsstands, which, he said, "can add to the street life and safety of a neighborhood." But they weren't greeted with enthusiasm by news officials. William McDonald, the circulation director of the Daily News, complains that many newsstands now have relegated newspapers to the background. "They push candy and cigarets, and they don't care if the President is shot or if an atom bomb goes off in New York City," Mr. McDonald says.)

At any one time, the Gomezes' stock is valued at about $2,000. A&J makes about five cents a copy on a newspaper that sells for a quarter and 20% of the cover price of most magazines. On Lotto sales, the Gomezes make a commission of 6.38%, which amounted to a total of $1,038 in 1981.

All told, A&J generates profits of about $5,500 a year on sales of more than $40,000. (The newsstand's location is considered "medium good" by those in the business; "great" locations, such as those outside the city's railroad stations, produce annual revenues of $200,000 or more.) A&J's profits supplement Mr. Gomez's $470-a-month Social Security payments from his years as a bookbinder.

A&J is open for business Monday through Saturday. Mr. Gomez usually leaves his house in the New York City borough of Queens at about 4:45 a.m., arrives at the stand at 5:10 a.m. and is open for business at 6 a.m. Mrs. Gomez usually joins him at the stand at 10:30 a.m. and stays until late afternoon. The stand is usually shut down at 6 p.m., although closing time on Saturday is somewhat earlier.

The morning rush starts about 7:15 and continues for approximately two hours. That's followed by a slack period, during which time Mr. Gomez rolls up coins and listens to the radio. Another, smaller rush occurs around lunchtime, followed by more slack time and then the evening surge, which begins sometime after 4 p.m. A&J's best seller is the tabloid New York Post (400 copies a day), followed by the New York Times (300 copies) and the Daily News (200 copies). The stand's best-selling magazine is Cosmopolitan (50 copies a month).

Newsstands like A&J get their publications from large distributors, most of whom don't consult the newsstand operators about what titles—or quantities—are preferred. For example, Mr. Gomez says he could probably sell 20 copies of Seventeen magazine each month but received only nine in a recent shipment.

The stands are also frequently used as testing grounds for new publications. "A new magazine may not be authorized to go into a chain store, so the street dealers end up getting all the junk," acknowledges Michael Cohen, a principal of Hudson County News Co., a magazine distributor.

Mr. Gomez says he has his problems selling some of the new titles; for example, he says he hasn't moved many copies of Twilight Zone, a new science-fiction magazine. When it comes to magazines, he says, sex-oriented covers sell best of all—but he keeps most of the stand's racier publications off his display racks. "I have my wife here," he says, explaining that Mrs. Gomez "doesn't care much" for selling sexy publications.

Mrs. Gomez usually remains inside the stand, whose seating accommodations comprise a stool and two boxes. For warmth in the winter, the couple keep two electric heaters blasting. (Their electric bill last month came to $123—which was $30 higher than the January electric bill for their house in Queens.)

The Gomezes keep a coffee pot simmering on a hot plate but fetch their lunch (most often a sandwich) from a nearby coffee shop. They have an arrangement with Lenox Hill Hospital to use the institution's first-floor bathrooms.

Lenox Hill also allows Mr. Gomez to sell newspapers room to room. For that task, Mr. Gomez says, he usually depends on friends. He considers the hospital rounds a special service, conducive of good will rather than a big moneymaker.

Mr. Gomez's special services also run to extending small amounts of credit to steady customers and remembering those customers' habits and preferences. "When Joe knows I'm here, he has a (subway)

47

token and a Washington Post out for me—I don't have to ask," says Edward Hagan, a bank official who buys his papers at A&J. The Gomezes' newsstand, Mr. Hagan maintains, is "one of the better stands in the city."

But along with his fans, Mr. Gomez has his detractors. One is Max Morgen, the owner of a nearby candy and cigar shop who wasn't at all pleased when A&J began to stock chocolate bars. "In the summer (the chocolate) will melt, and it can't be very healthy," Mr. Morgen says. (Mr. Gomez replies that A&J won't stock chocolate during the hot months.)

Harvey Rotenberg, the manager of another cigar store in the vicinity, grouses that Mr. Gomez "pays no rent, no nothing, and he's allowed to carry what I carry." He adds: "I'd like to get a match and burn (A&J) down, to be frank."

Mr. Gomez, although not so vehement, has his own complaints about competition. He bemoans the fact that several years ago a local grocery began stocking newspapers. And more recently, he says, a newsstand in the subway station broadened its stock to include magazines; that competition, Mr. Gomez says, has "cut my magazine business in half."

Still, A&J's operator has been known to turn the other cheek. Not long ago, when deliverymen staged a walkout, Mr. Gomez went to a distribution point across town, got 1,000 copies of the New York Times and took them back to his stand in a taxi. Although the action was mostly to keep his own customers happy, Mr. Gomez also spread some 300 of the 1,000 papers among his competitors at the cigar stores and the subway-platform newsstand. What's more, he says, "I didn't even charge them cab fare."

Steno Pool's Members, Buried by Paper Flood, Yearn for Other Things

*But the Pool Has Its Points:
It Is Relatively Well-Paid
And Both Clean and Safe*

Ink Spots for a Mystery Lady

BY KATHRYN CHRISTENSEN

*Working 9 to 5; what a way to make a living,
Barely getting by; it's all taking and no giving.
They just use your mind, and they never give you credit.
It's enough to drive you crazy if you let it.*
—*"9 to 5" by Dolly Parton*

SAN FRANCISCO   5/6/81

It's only midmorning, but the fancy electric typewriters and other machines are already pounding with the sound and rhythm of muffled jackhammers. Another boss in a vest enters the room, clips a blue work order to the six-page penciled memo he is carrying and—without a word or an expression—piles it on to the stack of paper on a supervisor's desk.

The man in the vest doesn't mean much to Teresita Clamucha, Jean Hill or Mimi Tong, one of whom will soon be typing his memo. He is just another contributor to the paper flood that constitutes daily life in the government-affairs stenography pool of Chevron USA Inc.'s public-affairs department.

Life in the pool—seven hours of typing and filing, broken up by occasional dictation duties—is clean, safe and fairly well paid. It is also dull, according to stenographer Jean Hill. "If I could possibly earn my living any other way, I'd do it," she says. "Sheer necessity and lack of education, that's why I'm here."

The pool is crowded and stuffy; rows of file cabinets eat up one-third of the space, and two fans with aqua blades push the stale air around. There aren't any windows; a mural with a forest scene provides the only "view."

Each member of this Chevron pool harbors some fantasy about working elsewhere. On most corporate ladders, the steno pool remains only a rung or two above the bottom. Few aspire to it, and it still is almost exclusively the province of women. They are as likely to be former teachers as they are to have barely finished high school. Some hope the pool will be the first step toward becoming an executive's personal secretary—as in the movies—but many more regard it simply as a steady paycheck. The most common gripe is that management doesn't appreciate the work and rarely says thank you.

Members of the Chevron government-affairs stenography pool (clockwise from upper left): Mimi Tong, Sergio Alexandre, Jean Hill and Teresita Clamucha.

More Impersonal Now?

Although much of this complaint is as old as the typewriter itself, the recent advent of sophisticated word-processing technology has wrought considerable change—and some new dissatisfaction— among the five million people in this country who, according to the Labor Department, earn their livings as typists, stenographers and secretaries.

Steno work isn't restricted any longer to taking letters in shorthand and typing them. Word processors capable of almost instantly turning out hundreds of error-free "original" letters have transformed some stenographers, at the pool here and at other offices, into computer operators, too. And the processors have almost precluded the luxurious old concept of providing every manager with his own secretary.

Many managers hail the increased productivity made possible by this new technology. But some workers think their jobs have been made even more impersonal than they were before. They feel they are beginning to take on the traits of the machines they operate.

"We can't really spend any creative energy at our work; I guess you'd say we're kind of like cogs in a machine," says Miss Tong, a senior clerk-typist. "The best we can do is work quickly and not make mistakes." Miss Clamucha, who is classified as a management stenographer, adds: "They (the managers) do all the thinking around here, we just do the punching."

That, of course, is as management intended. "Everything we do is to serve management better," says Edward Coy, the Chevron executive in charge of the office-services group that includes 17 mail clerks, typists and stenographers who work for the public-affairs department here. These support people form three pools that work for some 70 staff members.

Despite the clear demarcation line between "staff" and "support" troops, Mr. Coy makes it clear that Chevron tries to make pool life in the 1980s less demeaning than it used to be. Chevron policy, he says, forbids "subservient jobs at any level." He winces upon hearing indirectly that managers occasionally ask stenographers to run their personal banking errands.

Such managers have to be reminded, Mr. Coy says, "that there are no 'go-fers' or servants around here."

Though they are protected from servitude, the members of the government-affairs pool regard terms like "job satisfaction" as empty phrases for them. Still, they are grateful for their jobs, and they say they are lucky to be working for Chevron, particularly in its public-affairs department.

"I hate to say it because it's such a cliche," says Mrs. Hill, a 58-year-old widow who has worked in many other offices, "but as far as this kind of work goes, this company is the cream of the crop. I get no sense of identity from my work, but for someone like me with minimum skills, this pays the best."

Salaries for employes in the pool members' classifications range from $12,000 to $20,000 (compared with an average range of $11,000 to $16,000 for all such jobs in the San Francisco Bay area), and the atmosphere is relaxed enough that they aren't required to account for every break or trip to the coffee maker. Moreover, a slot at the public-affairs department means frequent free tickets to baseball games, plays and museum exhibits, and to charity luncheons that Chevron supports by buying tables. Some pool members even get roles in films produced by the department.

Personal Problems

Some others in the three public-affairs pools agree with Mrs. Hill's assessment of the job, adding that the mix of personalities and backgrounds here helps to keep the routine from becoming oppressive. The 17 members of the pools range from 20 to 58 years old and from Vietnam veteran to aspiring gospel singer. Though they rarely socialize outside the office, they like one another well enough to arrange an occasional potluck "gourmet extravaganza," and they confide in one another about personal problems.

One woman is a victim of her husband's physical abuse. Another is having trouble kicking a drinking habit. One lies awake nights worrying because a creditor is about to garnishee her wages. One way or another, all are concocting ways to defeat the monotony of their jobs, and about half are trying to figure a way out of their steno pool.

Even at 58, Mrs. Hill would do practically anything to escape office work. Given to a theatrical style of makeup and described by one co-worker as "our mystery lady," she longs for work—however menial—in a more artistic field. Not long ago, she says, "I took one of those aptitude tests with the ink spots and everything. I was sure it would show some marvelously creative field I should study, but my only talents seems to lie in bookkeeping and accounting."

"Creatures on a Treadmill"

The thought appalls her. Early widowhood and five children to support drove her to the business world, she explains, and she can't shake her conviction that it is inhabited by "creatures on a treadmill. It's as though they're alien beings, and I'm working on their planet. I know they're human and they do valuable work, but I just can't put myself into it."

Since learning the discouraging results of her aptitude test, however, Mrs. Hill is more resigned to her working life. "I'll just have to work with what I've got," she says. Now she spends nearly every lunch hour practicing her shorthand at Chevron's training center because "it tightens my mind." By quitting time, she says, she is eager to catch the bus to the residence hotel where she lives and has the time to "think about adventuring."

While not quite as restless as Mrs. Hill about office work, her colleagues also were looking for something more challenging or prestigious.

To Miss Clamucha, a career in accounting looks like the answer. "I don't really want to be a secretary; I want to be on my own," says the 28-year-old Filipino. "That's why I go to school two nights a week; to better myself." A divorced mother of a seven-year-old boy, she says her other obligations mean that her education can't proceed as quickly as she would like.

For some, recognition of the impossible dream comes slowly. Miss Tong studied criminology for two years before she realized that with little stamina, and weighing less than 100 pounds, she wasn't going to become the star of the San Francisco Police Department. Now her dreams turn to religion. Born a Buddhist but a convert to Christianity, the 28-year-old Chinese-American woman says that her idea of a dream job would be joining the staff of a Christian organization. But she is also hoping to move up a notch or two at Chevron, and, toward that end, she too is going to night school.

A Smile for a Mask

A fourth member of the government-affairs pool, 37-year-old Sergio Alexandre, who handles the filing, photocopying and envelope-stuffing, also has his aspirations. A tall, husky man whose former jobs have included lifting boxes for supermarkets, Mr. Alexandre says he chose to work in an office because "at least you're around people with brains." But, he says, the smile he wears as he assembles and staples 30 copies of a report is just a mask for a wandering mind: He fantasizes about being a professional comedian or an actor. He is realistic enough, however, to be studying how to operate a word-processing machine.

The possibility of breaking out of the steno pool isn't just an illusion, according to Carol Summers, the supervisor for the public-affairs department's office-services group. Nor, judging from Mrs. Summer's experience, must it take forever to accomplish. Now 25 years old, she began working in a steno pool two years ago. Her starting salary was about $11,800. Within a few months, she began receiving promotions and now earns more than $25,000. Though she does have a college degree, she points to other women in the company who have moved from a steno pool to jobs higher than hers with no college experience.

For a time Mrs. Summers moved her desk into the steno pool

where Mrs. Hill, Miss Clamucha, Miss Tong and Mr. Alexandre work. The group, she says, had been making too many errors, and there had been complaints from management. She felt that on-the-spot supervision would help, and she says it did. "Jobs like mine are often mothers' jobs," she says. "It's kind of like I have 17 kids to watch."

Mrs. Hill uses a different analogy to describe the role of stenographers in the office. "It reminds me of a dinner party," she says. "The executives are giving it, and we're the kitchen help."

IN THE PITS
Women Coal Miners Fight for Their Rights To Lift, Shovel, Lug

The Pay May Be Attractive, But Hazing and Abuse Are Among Drawbacks

Eyes at the Bathhouse Wall

BY CAROL HYMOWITZ

9/10/81

Diane Kuhn is a coal miner. She knows how to work on her hands and knees in a dark tunnel 230 feet underground. She can shovel tons of coal, lift a 50-pound bag of rock dust and lug a massive beam.

Mrs. Kuhn has learned that, in addition to physical stamina, her job at Consolidation Coal Co.'s Shoemaker mine in Benwood, W. Va., requires emotional grit. Most of her co-workers and all of her bosses are men, and many of them resent her presence.

Some of the men have scrawled coarse graffiti about women miners on mine-shaft walls. A foreman once cornered Mrs. Kuhn underground, she says, and threatened to make her job more difficult if she weren't "nice" to him. And her female co-workers recently discovered a hole in the wall of their bathhouse through which, they believe, mine supervisors have been spying on them.

Of all the traditionally male, blue-collar jobs in which women have sought to establish themselves, coal mining has proved to be the most resistant. Most coal companies have hired women only because of government importunings. And although some coal operators report lower absenteeism and higher productivity in mines where women are working, others continue to insist that women don't belong in the pits. "They don't have the nerve to do the work," says Melvin Triolo, the president of the Logan County, W. Va., Coal Operators Association.

Doing the Dirty Work

For their part, female miners say they aren't given a fair chance. They complain that they have been relegated to the toughest and dirtiest jobs, that they have been intimidated and that they have had to fend off sexual advances.

As recently as 1972, there were no women miners employed in the U.S. But as the number of female miners increases—to about 2,600, or 1% of the nation's mining work force, last year—more women are fighting what they see as sex discrimination. At the same time, certain coal companies are making an effort to address women's grievances by issuing formal guidelines denouncing sexual harassment, for example, and by instituting special training programs geared to help women advance.

Women also are beginning to win the respect of male miners and officials of the United Mine Workers union. "Women can do any job there is to do underground, although some guys still don't want to admit that," says Eddie Sturgill, a member of the UMW's all-male international executive board.

One reason that acceptance of women as miners has been so grudging has to do with the nature of the work. "It's an extreme occupation—the most dangerous of all jobs—done in the dark below ground where your life can depend on whether your co-workers can handle the work," says Brigid O'Farrell, a researcher at the Center for Research on Women at Wellesley College. "Those extremes," she continues, "have made it harder for women, who have to prove they can be counted on."

Last Hired, First Fired

Women miners also must contend with simple prejudice. Some of the men still believe in an old superstition that a woman underground is bad luck. The belief that men and women belong in different realms runs deep in Appalachia. And there is economic resentment. With more than 20,000 miners out of work because of slack demand for coal in some regions, women are accused of stealing men's jobs, even though many women recently hired have been among the first to be let go.

Women currently employed as miners say they need the jobs as much as men do. More than half of the women who work underground are divorced or widowed and are the sole support of their families. Mining pays higher wages (about $85 a day, to start) and offers better benefits and job security than practically any other job in the coal fields. Mrs. Kuhn, a 33-year-old divorcee with two children who once worked as a nurse, more than doubled her income when she became a miner. "Mining is the only way I can make it," she says.

The Strong Survive

But although the pay is relatively high, the work can be backbreaking. As beginners, women are employed as general inside laborers, and in these positions they do the most arduous of all jobs underground. GIs, as these workers are called, spend a lot of time shoveling coal onto conveyor belts. In low-seam mines, the shoveling is done in tunnels that may be no more than three feet high. GIs also lay shuttle-car tracks, drag heavy power cables for mine machinery and spray walls with limestone to hold down dust.

This is work that many men can't handle, and the sight of women doing it elicits strong but varied reactions. Some male miners who pride themselves on their strength feel resentful, while others "become very protective and try to do the job a woman has been assigned, as well as their own work," says R. Page Henley, a coal operations executive at the Armco Coal Co. office in Charleston, W. Va. Some women, he says, try to take advantage of this male protectiveness, for example, by offering to trade home-cooked lunches for help with their work. But, ultimately, only those who develop their own muscles are likely to last, and most women who take jobs underground "come from coal mining families and know what they're getting into," says Mr. Henley.

The dirt and lack of such amenities as toilets underground bother some women more than the hard work does. Joyce Harman, one of the first women hired as a miner in West Virginia, has worked her way up from general inside laborer to mine foreman over the past eight years, but she has never become accustomed to the lack of toilets. She says she has developed a chronic kidney ailment because she won't urinate in the mines.

Other women report having to put up with physically threatening sexual harassment. Some say they have been subjected to initiation rites that include being stripped of their clothes and greased. Others say that they routinely are grabbed and propositioned, and some claim to have been assigned especially difficult and dangerous tasks when they spurned sexual advances.

In their hard hats, overalls and boots, male and female miners look remarkably alike, and "not very sexy," says Joyce Dukes, the assistant director of the Coal Employment Project Women Miners' Training and Legal Counseling Group. But, she says, "some guys seem to think that any woman who dares to go underground is asking for it." The darkness and the isolation of mines also may invite more overt kinds of harassment than female office workers generally face, Miss Duke adds. "There's this mystique about things happening in the dark."

According to an informal survey conducted by the Coal Employment Project last year, harassment is a common problem for women miners. Although some of the 59 randomly chosen women who responded to the survey said that they had never been bothered, 17% said that they had been physically attacked in the mines; 53% said they had been propositioned by their bosses; and 76% said they had been propositioned by co-workers. More than one third said that they had been "snubbed" or "verbally attacked" by jealous miners' wives.

But the main complaint of women miners is discrimination in job assignments. Although some women, such as Mrs. Harman, have been promoted, more than 90% are concentrated in entry-level GI jobs.

At unionized coal companies, miners bid for jobs on the basis of seniority. But before a miner can "bid up" for the best-paid, skilled jobs, such as machine operators, he or she needs machine training and experience.

Coal operators say that most women either don't have the requisite seniority or shy away from heavy-machine jobs. But women say that the traditional "buddy system" militates against them. As Connie Goff, a miner at Island Creek Coal Co.'s Pocahontas mine in Keen Mountain, Va., explains it, "most machine operators will ask another guy, not a woman, to work with them if they need a fill-in helper." Some foremen reinforce this practice, Mrs. Goff says, by "making it clear they don't want women on the machines. Every time a woman here has a chance to work on a machine, the foreman says he needs her shoveling."

Like many of her female colleagues who had to show a certain feistiness to become miners at all, Mrs. Goff isn't afraid to stand up for herself. After watching several men with less seniority than she leapfrog her, she rallied with other women at her mine who are fellow belt shovelers. (There are 12 women there altogether in a work force of about 400.) Mrs. Goff also enlisted legal advice from the Coal

Employment Project and the support of a sympathetic local union officer.

At a grievance procedure meeting with mine managers, Mrs. Goff says, she warned her mine superintendent that the women might file a discrimination suit. She says the superintendent, in turn, agreed to begin a machine-training program and to give women more of a chance to win promotions.

Other female miners are indeed filing sex-discrimination complaints. The Coal Employment Project estimates that in the past two years it has filed at least 150 complaints about job bias and sexual harassment with the Equal Opportunity Commission and with other federal and state agencies.

Mrs. Kuhn and seven other women filed a $5.5 million suit against Consolidation Coal Co. in June, charging the company with "malicious trespass" and "invasion of privacy." The suit, filed in the Wheeling, W. Va., federal district court, alleges that employes and officers of Consolidation Coal's Shoemaker mine cut a hole in the wall of the women's bathhouse and "on numerous occasions" over the course of more than a year secretly watched the women as they were showering and dressing. The suit also alleges that a foreman learned of the peeping several months before the women themselves found the hole but that he "failed to correct" the abuse despite the company's "duty to ensure" that the bathhouse is "safe and secure."

Officials of Consolidation Coal won't discuss the alleged incidents because, they say, they have been advised not to comment during the litigation. Officials also decline to discuss company policies generally pertaining to women. However, in a prepared statement, Roger M. Haynes, the vice president for employe relations, said "it is the policy of the company not to condone sexual harassment by an employe. We would take prompt and appropriate action to correct any abuse of the policy."

Other coal companies are making special efforts to deal with problems that affect women, if only to avoid the sort of potentially costly lawsuit Consolidation Coal now faces. Philadelphia-based Westmoreland Coal Co. has a training program for mine managers on the special problems of women miners. It also gives female employes instruction in filing grievances.

Amax Coal Co., which is based in Indianapolis has a foreman-training program for women. "They've made women feel welcome," says Charlotte Johnston, a miner with five year's experience who completed the training this year and is one of two female foremen at Amax's big underground mine in Wabash County, Ill.

Mrs. Johnston worried at first that male miners wouldn't want to work for a woman, but she says she has gained the respect and support of the men who work for her. Although she says she became a miner "just for the money" and "figures I wouldn't stay long," now she says "I can't imagine doing anything else."

Despite the hazing women are subjected to as novice miners, those who prove their competence may find, Mrs. Johnston says, "a lot more closeness between people underground than I've seen in other workplaces." And with women currently making up one-sixth of the work force at Amax's Wabash mine, "being a woman miner is no big special thing here," she adds.

Assembling Computers Means That Happiness Doesn't Come Till 4:30

That's When Tedium Halts; But the Wages Are Steady And the Bars Aren't Far

There's a Tendency to Dream

BY ROGER THUROW

SAN ANTONIO   6/1/81

At 9 a.m. the assembly line has been moving for only one hour, but already the day is dragging.

In position five on line four, Annette Fullbright catches the next circuit board crawling down the line. At the current pace, one board passes her work station every minute and a half. Forty down, 280 left to go today.

Over in quality control, Ismael Hernandez puts his soldering gun back in its holster, fidgets with his left shirt sleeve and steals a quick glance at his watch. Thirty more minutes before coffee break. Two and a half hours to lunch. Seven and a half hours more until quitting time.

Two aisles over to the right, Delta Pena checks the dates on a calendar hanging near her work station. A smile flashes across her face. Tomorrow is payday.

On the Datapoint Corp. assembly line here, where desk-top office computers take shape, everybody, it seems, has a special way of marking time. Prisoners of a relentless, mechanized dictator, these workers toil over long workbenches like bees, repeating the same tedious task hundreds of times a day. From the moment they enter the hive at 8 a.m. until 4:30 p.m. when the assembly line creeps to a halt, their lives are as programmed as the computers they're assembling.

"Sometimes I could just scream and rip the line apart," grumbles Mary Martin, unwinding after work at a bar called the Pressure Cooker. "Boring? You don't know boring until you've done this."

Generations of blue-collar workers have yawned over the monotony of assembly-line work since the days of Henry Ford. Over the years, as the American workplace has become more and more modernized, robot-like machines have freed many workers from the drudgery of the assembly line. But from the Detroit auto plants to Arkansas appliance factories, there remain millions of mind-numbing assembly-line jobs that require the human touch.

Such is the case in the booming electronic industry. For all their wizardry, one of the few things computers can't do is reproduce. They are born on moving conveyor belts, which carry electronic parts past rows of workers attaching diodes, applying solder and tightening screws.

A Certain Peace

It is a rare person who finds life on the Datapoint assembly line exciting, rewarding or challenging. Yet, the assembly line does offer a certain peace of mind that comes from knowing you'll be doing the same thing tomorrow that you did today. No gut-wrenching decisions have to be made, no tough responsibilities faced up to. More important, the assembly line also offers a steady paycheck.

"Why do I work on the line? The bottom line is money," says Mrs. Fullbright, who gets $3.77 an hour.

The Datapoint assembly line looks like a ladies' auxiliary quilting bee, a powderpuff version of the sweaty auto-assembly lines. Hundreds of women and a handful of men are hunched over their work stations, maneuvering a soldering gun or stripping and twisting wires or squeezing a needle-nosed tweezer to better handle the tiny integrated circuits.

"From Sex to School"

Early in the day, the air has the heavy scent of a drugstore perfume counter. The factory is well-lighted by fluorescent bulbs hanging from the ceiling. Sweating is frowned upon because the salt from perspiration corrodes the electronic components. The workers' private toolboxes are decorated like executives' desks, with family photos and favorite mementos lining the insides of the top covers. The subject of the muffled gossip ranges "anywhere from sex to school," says one worker, although most of the talk seems to center on husbands, boyfriends or grandchildren.

Mrs. Fullbright never dreamed she would be working in a place like this. Just two years ago she was living in Germany on a military base with her husband and young son, hoping that someday she might return to college and complete her physical-education degree. But in late 1979 she divorced her husband, moved in with her mother here and waded into the job market with few skills to offer. "Every job around that I would like involved typing, and I can't type," she says. "So I thought I'd start out at the bottom and move up."

For the past 15 months, the 31-year-old Mrs. Fullbright has spent her weekdays hunkered down over a metal conveyor belt, "stuffing" thousands of transistors, resistors, capacitors and diodes—none bigger than a fingernail—into tiny holes on electronic-circuit boards. After a couple of hours each day, the neck gets tight, the eyes become bleary, the fingers stiff. Just when she thinks she has handled all the boards she can stand for one day, here comes another one, bumping into the one she has just completed. The assembly line stops for no one.

The "stuff lines" operate like an endless relay team. On line four, where Mrs. Fullbright usually works, the boards are handed off from Rose to Norma to Angie to Connie to Annette. Each one is required to plug so many of the integrated circuits into certain holes, as designated by a color-coded pattern hanging in front of them. After Mrs. Fullbright finishes her work on a board, it crawls on down the line, past Gloria, Anita, Kathy, Robin.

The names and the faces of the women on the line don't matter much; it's the job that counts. Almost anybody can do it, but if just one little diode is inserted backward, the finished computer doesn't work. There is pressure to do the job right, since at the end of every line someone is tallying up the mistakes. "Satisfaction," says Gene Helander, who used to conduct an initial 38-hour training course, "comes from being able to say, 'Well, I didn't screw up today.' "

Time on the line passes slowly for Mrs. Fullbright, especially in the hours after lunch. She tries to make her job more challenging by beating the clock and stuffing her pieces into the board quicker than the person in front of her on the line, giving her a few extra seconds to rest. But after memorizing the specific pattern she is to follow, her thoughts drift to life beyond the line. "All I can think about is that soon it will be 4:30 and I can go home and be with my son," she says. For Mrs. Fullbright, and most of her co-workers, quitting time is the main highlight of the day. Other highlights are lunch and the two 15-minute breaks, at 9:30 a.m. and 2 p.m.

"By the time the 4:30 bell stops ringing, these people are out the door in third gear," says David Beavers, a Datapoint material planner, as he watches the hurried exodus from the factory.

Winding Down

Every other Friday, when paychecks are handed out, there is a mad rush for one of the nearby bars—usually the Pressure Cooker or the Recovery Room, both of which have pool tables and plenty of beer and country music. Some workers used to dash right across the street from the plant to a place called the Number Ten Club, but when the management replaced the pool table with jazz musicians, they went elsewhere. "The place got too civilized," says one worker.

Mrs. Fullbright, however, finds life on the line pretty much all-consuming. Once in a while she'll go to a ballet or symphony performance, but most nights are spent at home. By 10 p.m. she's in bed. "I need a good rest," she says. "If I get up tired in the morning, the boards will put me to sleep."

To Mrs. Fullbright, the computers she helps assemble are machines that will be used in a world far more sophisticated than the one she lives in. She knows a little about those diodes, transistors and capacitors that she handles all day long. But beyond that, the language of computers is foreign. "All I know is that I'm supposed to build the boards," she says. "We go to work at eight, sit down, do our boards, go home at 4:30."

Gary Raffaele, labor-relations and business-policy specialist at the University of Texas, San Antonio, says assembly-line workers quickly learn to tune out anything they don't want to be bothered by. "In order to make it on the assembly line for any length of time," he says, "you almost have to check your mind at the door."

It doesn't take much to get a job on the Datapoint line; just an ability to distinguish between colors and to pass some simple manual-dexterity tests. Entry-level pay is $3.45 an hour—only a dime above minimum wage, but not bad for San Antonio's unskilled-labor market.

Labor unions, which have won greater compensation for assembly-line workers in other industries, have yet to successfully invade the electronics field. No one on the Datapoint lines is eager to talk about unions. Partly, Mr. Raffaele says, this is because most of the workers believe they'll soon be doing something else. "People become interested in unions when they accept their lot," he says. "These workers figure they're not going to be around for a long time, so why care about improving things?"

Since few workers want to make a career out of working on the line, Datapoint has some turnover headaches. Margaret Sterl, a line supervisor, says the women on the stuff lines stay for an average of about 18 months, meaning that a line must be adjusted occasionally to accommodate new, slower workers. "They make their money and go," she says, or they take advantage of Datapoint's various training and promotional opportunities and move up to a better job within the company.

The American Way

Unlike some of their counterparts abroad, who make careers on such lines, American workers often view the assembly line as merely a stopping point on the way up the ladder. "All of these people have a tendency to dream, 'I could have been this,' or 'This is what I'm going to be,' " says Mr. Raffaele. "This is why they never accept these jobs as permanent. That's why somebody who has been there 15 years still thinks he'll soon be doing something better. It's the American way of life."

Even Mrs. Fullbright's mother says, "Annette's sure to be chairman of the board someday."

Mrs. Fullbright may never be Datapoint chairman, but at least she's a company shareholder. The company's stock-option plan is one way the company tries to stir up enthusiasm and loyalty among its workers. Generally, it seems to be working. The factory was buzzing with excitement one recent day when Datapoint split its stock, and the workers all seem to be keeping up with the progress on the company's new headquarters complex. The company-sponsored athletic teams are popular, and several workers wear windbreaker jackets with "Datapoint" written across the backs.

Even the identification badges worn by the workers are appreciated. "The badges make me feel important," Mrs. Fullbright says.

First Names Are Important

James Pruski, overseer of the power-supply and wire-assembly operations knows that the line workers sometimes question their value to a company with over 6,000 employes. So every morning he mingles with them, bantering about sports, the weather, anything familiar to them. "It's very important to them that I know their first name," he says. "It's better than saying, 'Hey you.' The ladies appreciate the interest, and when it comes time to push them a little harder, they're cooperative."

The predominance of women on the Datapoint assembly line wasn't planned that way. But the process demands many minute, detailed tasks, and Datapoint personnel officials say that these are better done by women because women generally have smaller fingers and superior manual dexterity. Besides, says Mrs. Sterl, the line supervisor, "It's not a masculine job. Men panic if we suggest they do this. Two hours and they go berserk."

Ismael Hernandez says he can handle the job; it's working side-by-side with so many women, including his wife, that gets to him. "It's not always so good working around all these women. You have to watch your language," he says while chewing on a salami sandwich during his half-hour lunch break. "Sometimes the ego, man, it comes around and says, 'Hey man, what are you doing working with all these women?' "

Mr. Hernandez swallows hard, telling himself that he needs the money and job experience. Someday, he hopes, he will be a computer technician or engineer. But for now, it's back to the line where another load of circuit boards is awaiting a touch-up. "Sometimes I wonder if it's all worth it," he sighs. "I'm trying to get a degree in electronics so I can move on to something more important. But it takes so long I hope it comes soon."

COMPUTER CHOLER

Many Managers Resist 'Paperless' Technology For Their Own Offices

Machines Force Sharp Shift In Executives' Behavior; Rise in Efficiency Cited

'Will I Look Like a Jerk?'

BY LAWRENCE ROUT

6/24/80

Alexander Pollock has seen the future, and so far he wants no part of it.

The glimpse was provided by the people who are automating the offices at Continental Illinois National Bank & Trust Co. of Chicago, where Mr. Pollock is a vice president. Sitting at his desk in Chicago, he can push some buttons on the keyboard of a computer terminal, and staff memos will appear on a television-like screen. He can respond with his own memos, which will instantly materialize on the screens of colleagues overseas, or be stored for them to retrieve later if their terminals are busy or turned off. And by pressing a few other buttons, he can view bank financial data stored in a computer down the street.

Mr. Pollock can do all that and more, but he doesn't. He hates to type.

"I think most managers—including me, are talkers," the executive says, his computer terminal unplugged and facing the wall. "I would much rather talk than write."

As Mr. Pollock's resistance exemplifies, professionals and executives are being forced to make major psychological and behavioral adjustments as they begin their move into a paperless world. They must get used to, among other things, infallible computers that remind bosses when reports are due, the pressure of always being reachable through a portable computer terminal and the danger of overcommunication. These problems don't necessarily mean users will reject the technology. But they do suggest that the move into the "office of the future" will be costly in human currency as well as dollars.

"We're asking people to change so much, and these are people who have never changed anything in the way they work in the office," says Louis Mertes, a Continental vice president responsible for making the bank-holding company one of the few places that have gone beyond experimentation in applying new office technology.

"Desks" Can Go Anywhere

Still, most people agree that Continental represents the wave of the future. After 15 years of automating the tasks of clerical workers—bank tellers, secretaries and the like—computers are starting to move into the offices of managers and professionals. What executives now typically keep on paper in their desks and file cabinets can be stored in a computer and viewed on a desktop screen at the push of a few buttons; they can send messages electronically, bypassing the frustrations of busy signals and occupied colleagues; and with portable computer keyboards and screens, which can be connected to ordinary telephone handsets, executives can carry their "desks" anywhere.

Communications experts believe it is crucial that executives accept this new way of doing business. Blaming America's slumping productivity on inattention to white-collar workers, they contend that automation can turn that situation around.

"We figure that most managers and professionals spend 18% to 30% of their time doing what we term less-productive tasks—seeking information, seeking people, scheduling," says Harvey Poppel, senior vice president at Booz, Allen & Hamilton, Inc., New York management consultants. "All of these things are reducible through automation."

Automation enthusiasts don't dismiss the human adjustments; in fact, they call them the biggest obstacles. But they also believe that as technology improves, resistance will decrease, and that as more companies automate and problems become clearer, computer makers will design machines better suited to people's needs.

Discussions with executives who use the system, however, and with experts who are studying them, indicate that the problems aren't so easily solved, for the new machines force executives to change radically their office behavior.

Fragile Egos

Those adjustments go well beyond such surface anxieties as fear of the unknown or of electrocution. Stubborn executives like Mr. Pollock may insist that phone calls and dictation are more efficient than typing and that they eagerly await the day computers understand normal speech. But those who observe these executives blame the resistance on something deeper—fragile managerial egos.

"They say, 'I'm not going to use it,' but what they're really saying is, 'I'm scared that I'm not going to be able to use this right, and I'll look like a jerk,' " says Joseph Ramellini, director of advanced office systems at CBS, Inc., which has automated a few experimental offices. He also says executives equate typewriters with low-level tasks. The upshot is a host of excuses for rejection. "They say, 'Can it do left-handed Sanskrit justification?' and when they find out it can't, they say, 'Well, I need that, so I can't use it,' " Mr. Ramellini says.

Typically, though, they do use it. But even when they like it, they soon discover that they must get used to more than new technology. At the offices of the U.S. Army's Development and Readiness Command in Washington, for instance, electronic mail has made message writing so easy that people tend to overcommunicate. Lower-level employes get a kick out of sending copies of notes to high-level executives, a feat accomplished by simply pressing a few buttons.

"I started getting messages I would never have known about," says John Cianflone, a division head. He says that the practice puts "unbelievable" pressure on firstline supervisors, whose bosses suddenly know of all problems in their areas. And while Mr. Cianflone has ordered people to stop sending everything to his attention, others in the office say that terminals are still filled with worthless information, partly defeating their time-saving purpose.

The portability of the computer terminals could also be described as a mixed blessing. Many executives view portability as a major breakthrough, allowing them to work anywhere and any time they want. But it also means they can be reached anywhere and any time, making it difficult to get away from all the interruptions that are part of the daily grind.

No Place to Hide

"There have been times when I would like not to be informed, when I don't want to be reached," says Randy Ivanciw, an Army systems analyst who has a desk-top terminal. "In the past I could have said I was out of the office when the telephone rang, or I didn't get the message. But now the message is sitting there for everyone to see, including the sender. I don't have the chance not to respond."

The ability to tote the office around is "a workaholic's dream," says James Alexander, manager of public services at Continental Illinois, "but it can be addictive to the type of person prone to letting the job overtake him." Mr. Alexander notes that executives are frequently putting messages into the computer in the wee hours of the morning.

Moreover, the "workaholic's dream" can be a nightmare for the workaholic's underlings. "It's bad enough when the boss works 12 hours a day," a middle-level executive at Continental says. "But now he gets up at two or three in the morning and works. He inundates us. I feel like I have to bring the damn machine home just to keep up. And my wife isn't too crazy about that idea."

Even working for a boss who puts in normal hours can be pressured if the boss has a perfect memory. He can get that from an electronic calendar, which lets him view upcoming appointments on the screen, and a "tickler" device, which reminds him when subordinates' reports are due.

When AT&T gave a vice president a follow-up device in his desk-top terminal a few years back, "it caused some real havoc for the people under him," recalls James Burke, a marketing manager at the company's Illinois Bell Telephone Co. unit.

A Structure Is Imposed

He explains that everybody felt under enormous time pressure, knowing that the boss would never forget. Furthermore, "Even when the follow-up was appropriate and the computer automatically dispatched a note to the person who was overdue, it was totally impersonal," he says. "People reacted badly to the machine's doing something that a human being used to do." The experiment, he adds, was dropped.

The turmoil at AT&T, communications specialists say, illustrates perhaps the most disturbing aspect of automation—it imposes its own structure. Managers and professionals have their own way of filing, doling out assignments and reading mail. The computer can considerably narrow that freedom.

John Connell, executive director of the Office Technology Research Group in Pasadena, Calif., gives the example of a marketing manager who tailors each transaction to the special needs of the client. When a computer is introduced, "he learns that there are no exceptions, that all those special deals go by the board," Mr. Connell says. "And he develops an image of technology as structure and constraint."

Similarly, automation specialists commend their machines as reducing the need for meetings. Electronic mail can pass along documents and ideas instantly, they say, and it's a lot cheaper.

"But I like meetings," says one executive at an East Coast concern that has automated some of its offices and cut down on meetings. "It's more than just comparing notes about the budget. There are more subtle things—getting more comfortable with the boss, shooting the breeze with colleagues. Now I've got to figure out a new way to do those things."

That kind of informal communication "can be just as important as, if not more important than, formal communications," says James Driscoll, an assistant professor of industrial relations at Massachusetts Institute of Technology's Sloan School of Management. "Yet can you imagine how difficult it will be to justify a meeting when you can do it electronically?"

Managers also say that available computer systems don't accommodate their work patterns. They rarely sit around reading. Instead, they concentrate on one task for 10 minutes, then another and so on. "If nothing interrupts me for 15 minutes, I get nervous and itchy and start walking around," says John Limb, a department head at Bell Laboratories in Murray Hill, N.J.

But the terminals make it difficult to be interrupted. "The nature of the thing is that you have to look at it in one sitting," says Eduardo Monteagudo, a personal-banking officer at Continental. "I've got to get used to putting aside a block of time."

Opinions differ about where to place the blame for such problems. Vincent Giuliano, an office-technology consultant with Arthur D. Little, Inc., says that people misapply their computers, thinking the equipment they have purchased can be "used for everything."

"The technology is neutral," Mr. Giuliano says. "It can be used to free people if it is used properly. But when it's used improperly, it can be pathological."

Mr. Connell, on the other hand, thinks the fault lies with the computer makers. "Every time we design a system," he says, "we do it on the premise that the people must adapt to the system. I think we have to adopt an ethic that says we adapt machinery to people."

VICTIMS OF THE AX
End of CETA Program Portends Loss of Jobs For Unskilled Workers

Real Work or Make-Work Is Not the Issue to Those Who Get the Paychecks

Five Prepare for the Worst

BY MARILYN CHASE

SAN FRANCISCO   6/17/81

As the chill, first light breaks on a Haight-Ashbury curbside, a street sweeper stoops to gather the gutter's yield of leaves, litter and dog waste. "This job's the best thing ever happened to a poor man," he says. "It's feeding babies. When it's over, I'll be putting cardboard in my little girl's shoes, like my mama did me."

The sweeper will be out of a job by September. He is one of 300,000 employes nationwide—1,400 in this city—facing termination under the Comprehensive Employment and Training Act, as the Reagan team cuts what it considers an ill-conceived and abuse-ridden $4-billion program from a bloated federal budget. The price of economic cure will be steep for some facing joblessness, less drastic for others.

Mounted during the 1974 recession, the CETA Title VI jobs program has played to widely mixed reviews during its six-and-a-half-year run. Designed to prime the economic pump, to enable people to pay rent and put food on the table, and to provide systematic entry into a job market for the hard-core poor, CETA is currently condemned as a trough of make-work sinecures, and as a politicians' pork barrel.

NOT ONLY THE POOR

Urban mayors and other defenders say CETA has built a bridge for the unemployed between chronic welfare dependency and the world of work. But critics note that not all CETA jobs have gone to the poor. Mrs. John Ehrlichman, then wife of Richard Nixon's erstwhile domestic-affairs adviser, was awarded a $10,000-a-year CETA job with the Seattle Symphony. Sports magnate George Steinbrenner benefited indirectly when CETA workers helped refurbish his private box at Fort Lauderdale's Yankee Stadium.

In San Francisco, CETA functioned as "a make-work employment agency," charges a city supervisor and longtime critic, Quentin Kopp. In the mid 1970s Mr. Kopp recounts, 150 CETA positions were allotted to the San Francisco Arts Commission, which at the time had a regular staff of just three persons. "There was no reporting to work, no knowledge by the commission of where these people were."

The jobs program has taken a drubbing from critics on several fronts, and San Francisco's CETA administrator, Eunice Elton, concedes its failures. Still, she expresses pride in what she feels CETA has accomplished. "We're preparing many people for low-level jobs," she says, "but even a low-level job becomes a place you can take off from." While certain CETA slots were "dead-end jobs," she says, "the fact of having showed up for work, of not having gotten fired—that's experience."

JOBS THAT NEED DOING

"CETA has tried to reconcile an enormous mismatch between the low (often sub-7th grade) skills level of the unemployed, and the needs of the employer," she says. "But in some cases, we have been able to train people for real jobs, such as emergency medical technicians and parole aides."

How employable CETA workers will prove to be in the mainstream job market, is a question that troubles the experts. "Socializing people to work is an important first step," says Columbia University economics professor Eli Ginzberg, who is also chairman of the National Commission for Employment Policy. "But we've had a hard time with the second step: moving them into the regular economy." CETA's critics like to point out that only 30% to 40% of CETA workers have a job when they leave CETA. But Johns Hopkins University associate professor Laura Morlock says some 78% are employed two years later.

"Of course, the immediate effect of canceling CETA will be a rise in unemployment," says Ray C. Rist, a congressional program evaluator. "But the long-term consequence will be a heightening of the already-fierce competition for entry-level positions in unskilled work." Employers who have grown dependent on CETA workers may try to keep them on, but without the CETA subsidy, the average worker's chances of retaining his job are slim.

Among the CETA job holders in San Francisco soon to be pushed out of the federally subsidized nest are a mix of hard-core urban poor, Asian and Latin American refugees, and some middle-class youths—all striving for a fix on their futures. For some, the end of CETA means a professional inconvenience; for others, an economic catastrophe.

Leo Shelton

Lean and grizzled, Mr. Shelton, at 55, is the senior member of street sweepers gang number 8, and one of 110 CETA street sweepers in a department of 190. Every morning at 6, he attacks one of the grittiest assignments in the city: Market Street. But by 7:40, he says with pride: "I've already swept as much as a mechanical sweeper could do in one day." In a department plagued with AWOLs, Mr. Shelton does yeoman service.

"This is the first job I've held in 30 years," he says. "You've got to start somewhere and, I figure, this is my start." Before CETA, he served time in Leavenworth, McNeil Island and Alcatraz for bank robbery and transporting narcotics. After his last release, he says, "I was planning another bank robbery, aiming to take enough this time to last me a lifetime or die trying." A friend proposed an improbable alternative: a CETA job. He hooted at that. And then, with great skepticism, he applied.

"I thought they'd never call me, but in four weeks I was working," he says. "That was over a year ago. Now, I believe I can hold down any job." Getting acclimated to work wasn't easy, though. About 90 days into his CETA hitch, "Leo soured," his supervisor says. But some straight talk and a clear-eyed consideration of the alternatives got him back on track.

"If it weren't for CETA, I'd be in jail or dead," Mr. Shelton says. "It's amazing the way this job has turned my life around." His year in CETA has been a year of firsts: He bought his first car, voted in his first presidential election, and plans to marry in June. He rakishly says he hopes to save $100 as a wedding gift so his intended bride, a sober-minded widow, can play the slot machines in Reno. "I never took life too seriously before," he muses. "I was just existing."

When CETA ends, he says, he'd like to shift from asphalt to garden maintenance, perhaps as a city gardener in Golden Gate Park. He can draw on the horticultural training he's gotten in CETA, but he must also pass the city's civil-service exam.

"If I didn't have this jail record behind me, I figure employment would be easier," he says. "But whatever happens, I want no part of welfare."

Rori Reber

Many middle-class children dream of running away with the circus, but CETA paid the ticket for 25-year-old Rori Reber. An unemployed actress, she's the newest recruit into the Pickle Family Circus, an off-beat San Francisco institution. She talks about her $600-a-month CETA job booking engagements and writing publicity for the circus, while a half dozen Pickle performers practice a juggling act in the cavernous abandoned church that serves as a home to this one-ring traveling show.

"I was raised in comfy middle-class surroundings in Palo Alto and I studied theater arts at San Francisco State University, but I guess you take a vow of poverty when you become an actress," she says. She was drawn to the Pickles, she says, because they give a lot of benefit performances for child-care centers and senior-citizen homes.

"This is an organization I feel I could commit myself to long term, but CETA funding runs out soon. One possibility would be for me to go on unemployment until the circus can fund my job," she says. "For me, it's an investment."

The Pickle Family Circus is itself a creation of CETA. Born out of a controversial CETA grant to the San Francisco Arts Commission, the circus was founded by four fresh young performers—all on CETA salaries. Currently, four of its 20 assorted clowns, jugglers, musicians and roustabouts are CETA-funded.

Founder Larry Pisoni—who on stage is Lorenzo Pickle, the clown—for six years drew a $9,000-a-year CETA salary with which he supported a wife and two children. He's sensitive to charges that a CETA circus may seem a fanciful addition to a poverty program but he argues: "Obviously, I'm prejudiced. I think what I do is very important to society." Underlying his philosophy there's a strong family precedent: his grandfather was a vaudevillian for the W.P.A. during the Depression.

Mary Muao

The fifth of 10 children born to Samoan parents, the 23-year-old Miss Muao is a large, coffee-colored, striking young woman who works as a legal-process clerk in the office of San Francisco's public defender.

Before CETA, the diffident Miss Muao drifted in a limbo of poverty, family misfortune and joblessness. A high-school graduate, she was turned down for clerical jobs because of inexperience. Then her mother, a widow living on death benefits, fell ill with heart disease and hypertension, and Miss Muao was needed to tend her. In rare free moments, she used to shadow a local nun who ministers to the Samoan community in her Hunter's Point neighborhood. The nun referred her to CETA. Now with her $330 biweekly check, she pays the family rent in subsidized public housing.

"I thought there'd be an interview, but all I had to do was sign up," she says softly. "I couldn't believe it." Now her workdays in the huge, gray hall of justice begin at 8:15 when she heads for court, reporting on some 60 cases a day. Sometimes she works the front desk, trying to placate restive and often-rowdy clients.

"The experience is good, and I've learned about the law," she says. She contemplates further training for a career in paralegal work, but for now must choose between a salary and school. "I'm afraid if I don't get a job in this field, my skills will fade," she worries.

"Some CETA employes are sitting back, waiting until their time is up, but not me," she says. "When I heard there was a cutback, I applied for a deputy clerk position with the municipal court." Her optimism is shaded by doubt: She still has only a scant year's experience. But her boss calls Miss Muao "a CETA success story, someone who never worked before, and now works overtime."

Sally Eberle

Raised amid plenty on a rice farm in northern California, Miss Eberle is a 26-year-old dropout from the University of California at Berkeley, where she studied comparative literature. The freckled, gingerhaired, six-foot-tall skier was working at a resort in 1978 when a tram accident killed three people and injured others. Carrying casualties down a mountainside in 70-mile-per-hour winds, Miss Eberle discovered her vocation.

"It was so rewarding to help, and it occurred to me that it was possible to get paid for doing that kind of work," she recalls. After 16 hours observing the workings of a CETA ambulance crew, she says: "I knew I had to be a part of it."

Whether called to assist a woman delivering her seventh child in a housing project, or giving emergency life support to an attempted suicide, paramedical cadet Eberle is being trained to serve as the "eyes and ears" of a physician while transporting a patient to the hospital.

But her 2,880 hours of training won't end until November, and CETA funds will run out in September. Earning a gross salary of $367 every two weeks, she doesn't expect it to be easy to put aside enough to survive two payless months. But she'll try. If she stays in the course and gets a job with the city, her salary as a licensed paramedical technician would be more than twice what she is making now under CETA.

Simorn Keovannala

Slight and careworn, Mr. Keovannala seems older than his 32 years. A Laotian refugee, he has faced greater perils than the current threatened loss of livelihood. In 1978, he swam in darkness (to evade Communist guns) across the Mekong river into Thailand, where his family was stationed in a refugee camp—and where his youngest child was born—before coming to the U.S., political freedom, and a CETA job.

Now Mr. Keovannala, his wife and three children call home an olive-drab apartment with barred windows in the city's Tenderloin district, where the drug and flesh trade means children must play indoors. "At first, I was worried and miserable because people say the Tenderloin is not safe," he says. "Then last year, we had a break-in, and the landlord installed better locks."

Rent is $286 a month for a one-bedroom apartment, where the parents sleep with an infant, an eight-year-old son sleeps in the living room, and a five-year-old daughter alternates between her brother's bed and her parent's more-crowded one.

Mr. Keovannala pays that rent with the $360 he makes every two weeks as a CETA child-care attendant in the YMCA's cross-cultural family center. He says his work is gratifying, since it involves helping children of other Indochinese refugees adjust to life here. And he appreciates the half-day English class CETA provides.

But the job bears no relation to his prior work in Laos as a clerk for a Japanese construction firm. Asked what he will do when CETA ends, he smiles puckishly: "Maybe be an auto mechanic?" He doesn't own a car.

"It's hard to say the CETA pay is enough. But we survive," he says. He has applied for public housing. But beyond this, he squeezes his eyes shut and shrugs off any more detailed vision of harder times. "I just have to find another job," he says.

Carolina Research Park Illustrates Innovations In Nation's Work Sites

Changes Are Apt to Spread; Quality of Working Life Looms as Big Issue of '80s

Three Views of the Triangle

BY JANET GUYON

RESEARCH TRIANGLE PARK, N.C.　　　　4/29/81

Stephen Metelits leaves his energy-efficient home in the planned community of Fearrington near here each morning at 7:15. He and another Data General Corp. employe share a relaxing 25-minute auto ride to work through the rolling green North Carolina countryside.

At work, Mr. Metelits (pronounced muh-TELL-its) a 41-year old, $39,000-a-year-manager of computer programmers, wears no tie and can keep flexible hours. He has his own office and computer terminal; there is no waiting in line to get time on the main computer. He can take a portable computer terminal home with him on weekends if he wants to.

His wife, Joy, 40, remembers when the Metelitses moved here from New Jersey three years ago. "When we moved, Stephen said it was like taking early retirement," she says. "Now, he's working harder than he ever has and going to school two nights a week for his M.B.A. He's just thrilled."

Not all employes of course, are as content with their jobs at the many plants here in the park, but this planned amalgam of research and light-manufacturing facilities has had incredible success attracting highly paid, highly educated researchers from all over the world. The combination of progressive, quiet plants plus sophisticated yet small-town living nearby had made the park one of the country's most sought-after workplaces. International Business Machines Corp., for instance, says its site here was once IBM's most popular place for transfers.

Research Triangle is but one example of the innovation that has come to American workplaces during the last decade. In some ways, it also illustrates those to come. Labor experts say that the 1970s were a period of major change in technology and in the composition of the work force. These factors, they say, along with slow economic growth, augur major changes in workplaces in the 1980s.

In fact, American business is more likely to pay attention to the quality of work life now than during any past period, says Jerome M. Rosow, the president of the Work in America Institute, a nonprofit group studying productivity and quality of work life.

"To some extent, the 1970s were a testing time," says Mr. Rosow, who was assistant secretary of labor from 1969 to 1971. "In the 1980s, the quality of working life is going to become a major issue."

DIVERSITY IN WORK FORCE

The reasons are many. The types of people holding full-time jobs changed radically in the past 10 years as more women and members of minority groups entered the work force. Technological innovations such as robots and word processors created new types of jobs, although not necessarily more interesting ones. Labor productivity dropped while costs rose, and surveys show that worker job satisfaction is at its lowest point in more than 25 years. Some experts believe that this is because workers are generally more mobile and educated now and less likely to be satisfied with routine or dirty jobs.

Mr. Rosow believes that companies will be forced to improve working life simply to get these workers to work hard. Innovations in the workplace will be "initiated for bottom-line reasons," he says. "We still have the 'me generation' and the self-fulfillment ethic. When you get these people turned on to the organization's needs, they can make big bucks for you."

RECOGNITION OF CONFLICT

One of the most talked-about changes involves new scheduling that gives workers more freedom as to when they come to work, or whether they come to work at all. Economists predict that rising commuting costs will spur growth in at-home work arrangements while an increase in the number of working mothers will force more flexible work hours.

Other labor experts say that because Americans are more affluent now, they're even willing to take pay cuts in exchange for more leisure and family time. "There's a recognition on the part of some companies that work life and home life conflict sometimes and it shouldn't always be the home life that has to adjust," says Stanley Nollen, an associate professor at Georgetown University's business school. Rudolph Oswald, the director of research for the AFL-CIO, says that organized labor will continue pushing for a 35-hour workweek and for arrangements that permit two people to share one job.

High-technology companies competing fiercely for qualified workers already offer a number of innovative benefits. ROLM Corp., a telecommunications-equipment company in Santa Clara, Calif., just finished a recreation center complete with sauna, steam bath, tennis courts, swimming pool and weights room. As another attraction, ROLM grants employes a 12-week sabbatical every seven years. IBM's computer-programming laboratory, set amid rolling foothills in San Jose, Calif., was specifically designed to make work pleasant for the programmers.

Other innovations are likely to spread through ailing industries such as steel and autos. Financial troubles are forcing them to reexamine the old management system where factory workers simply do what they're told. General Motors Corp., considered a leader at accommodating workers' demands for participation in decision making, is trying a number of approaches. At the GM alternator plant in Albany, Ga., for example, teams of workers meet weekly to discuss job problems and production schedules. Workers regularly travel with managers to help approve purchases of machinery.

Some Albany workers grumble that the union has lost because of this cooperative approach, and they say they can't make any really important long-range decisions in these weekly meetings. But most say that they have more responsibility, and that they enjoy their jobs more, than they would elsewhere.

"I learned more here in two years than I did in 15 up North," says Dale Raymond, who came to Albany from a GM plant in Pontiac, Mich. "Up North, you'd see a supervisor and he'd just ignore you. Here, they'll stand there, shake your hand and talk to you awhile."

Experts believe that all these forces—a more diverse work force, changing technology, demands for worker participation in management, and a sluggish economy—will combine to bring fundamental changes in the traditional adversary relationship between union and management. "American labor is at a crossroads," says Mr. Nollen of Georgetown University. "The old idea that there are always more benefits and wages, those days are over. Workers' expectations and values are different."

Here in Research Triangle Park, there isn't any union labor, and that's one of the state's big selling points. Research facilities nestle in pine-covered hills, but few are visible from the roads that crisscross the park, thanks to strict zoning rules. Tenants can't buy less than eight acres of land and can develop only 15% of the acreage. Big-setback requirements ensure that the park will always have the air of an academic campus conducive to research work.

COMMUTATION BY DESIGN

In some past social experiments, a worker's living area also was planned and owned by his employer. But workers here, by design, commute at least five miles to work from homes in surrounding cities and towns. The park, a 5,600-acre, unincorporated tract, lies between Raleigh, Durham and Chapel Hill.

The research park didn't plan for any residential development, says Ned Huffman, the executive vice president of the Research Triangle Foundation, because "that's the old mill-village concept and you wouldn't want that. You don't necessarily mix your work life with your day-to-day living. It gives you little opportunity for cross-breeding of thought."

While far from a utopia, the park is a good example of an unusually progressive American workplace. Thus, what may be in store for a growing portion of this country's labor force is illustrated by a look at the lives of these Research Triangle workers.

Stephen Metelits

Mr. Metelits worked for IBM, went into business for himself, and worked for a small computer-software company in New Jersey before an ad in a trade newspaper led him to Data General in 1978. Now he supervises 10 other programmers building computer languages.

On his way to the first job interview, he was impressed with mileage signs that marked the distance to the park in both miles and kilometers. He also liked the park's location near a state forest. "One of the most impressive things about this state is it's so green," he says.

He has to drive to work, but "the rush hour is a joke," he says. "I remember living north of Chicago and taking 45 minutes to get 15 miles. Here, the commuting time is 20 to 25 minutes and it's driving time as opposed to sitting in traffic.''

In Data General's modest one-story red-brick building, everyone has his own office, and the offices are arranged in pleasant bays near a windowed conference area. "Our kind of work requires a great deal of concentration," Mr. Metelits says, "It's nice to be able to go into your office and close the door."

EARLY TO WORK

On a typical day, Mr. Metelits gets to work early to make sure the big computers are working. He logs into his terminal to pick up messages from subordinates; the computer system serves both as a text-editing device and an internal office-communications system. He wants to move up in management, so, in a company-paid program, Mr. Metelits is taking night courses toward an M.B.A. from Duke University in Durham. The Duke course is a 25-month, intense program, and Mr. Metelits likes the quick pace.

Living here also is cheap compared with such sun spots as California. The Metelitses found their perfect home for $70,200 in Fearrington, a planned, energy-efficient community near Chapel Hill where the skylighted, all-electric homes have energy monitors that display the cost per hour of the electricity being used at any given time. Last year, Mr. Metelits says, his bill for heating, cooling and lighting totaled $538.60.

"What would make me move?" he asks. "Having to. If there were some kind of economic disaster and the company went out of business."

Coyla McCullough

Mrs. McCullough works at the architectural wonder of the park, Burroughs Wellcome Co., the British drug company. Built in a series of glass and concrete modules, the building's interior is light and airy and the surrounding pine trees are visible from nearly everywhere inside. Contemporary-art selections on loan from the Whitney Museum dot interior walls, and when the assistant curator comes from New York on a consulting tour, employes get a free art lecture.

Like most places in the park, Burroughs Wellcome runs a company-subsidized cafeteria, but at Burroughs Wellcome the Scarsdale diet is available. Another perk: a company-financed van that gets Mrs. McCullough to work from her condominium in Raleigh. It picks her up precisely at 7:24 a.m.

Mrs. McCullough, 45, came here from Massachusetts eight years ago to restructure her life after a divorce. Like Mr. Metelits, she took advantage of the array of educational institutions here: She went back to school and earned a degree in library science from the University of North Carolina in Chapel Hill. That, combined with her degree in physiology from Vassar got Mrs. McCullough a job in Burroughs Wellcome's library, the largest specialized library in the state.

THE LATEST TECHNIQUES

"My work isn't standard library work. It's mostly computer searching," she says. Burroughs Wellcome often sends her to conferences to learn the latest electronic library techniques, and she enjoys a close professional association with other librarians in the park and surrounding universities.

One of her biggest concerns about moving South, she says, was the schools. Her three children were school-aged when she moved, and she feared that they wouldn't get a good education. Now she feels that the schools here were probably just as good for the children as the schools up North. "And my children learned things down here they couldn't have learned in Massachusetts," she says. "They've had much more contact with race problems and the social problems of the world."

Also, she says, "the whole area is a little bit old-fashioned and it's easier to be a good kid. That makes being a single parent easier." Now, on over $20,000 a year, Mrs. McCullough can send one child to college at the University of North Carolina while another has a full-paid scholarship there.

"It's insidiously pleasant here," says Mrs. McCullough. "This area has more Ph.D.'s per capita than anywhere in the country, so they pay for cultural events. I can go to a concert every night."

David VandenBroek

No matter how sophisticated the cultural life or how bucolic the surroundings, however, work in the park doesn't always evoke a feeling of total bliss. Mr. VandenBroek (pronounced VANdenbrock), a small, wiry marathon runner, has been an engineer designing computer programs for IBM since he graduated from college in 1964. Over the years, he says, his enthusiasm for his job has waned, despite his love for the area.

Unlike Mr. Metelits, Mr. VandenBroek, 39, doesn't have his own computer terminal at work and shares a nine-by-12 foot office with another engineer. But his office is in IBM's newest building, where the hallways run along exterior walls so that everyone can get an outside view. "It gives me a better outlook because the outside view isn't reserved for a privileged few," Mr. VandenBroek says.

Still, he wishes that his hours were more flexible and that they were based on work assignments rather than on a strict eight-hour day. Because IBM has so many employes in the park, it rigidly staggers working hours to avoid traffic jams. Mr. VandenBroek works from 7:42 a.m. to 4:12 p.m. (IBM says it plans to begin some flexible scheduling in June, but Mr. VandenBroek doesn't know if he will be affected.)

DULLED AMBITION

Mr. VandenBroek, who earns between $25,000 and $30,000 a year, says his ambition to get ahead at IBM has dulled because "IBM is like a lot of places—how you feel about your job depends on your immediate supervisor." He liked and respected his first supervisors, but later that changed. "To get satisfaction at work, you have to have someone recognize you did a good job. Oftentimes, I felt my opinions were of no order, they weren't important," he says. "I found running gave me more satisfaction."

Now he runs about 90 miles a week, often running 12½ miles home from work. Sometimes he runs at lunch at IBM's nearby recreational area, but IBM discourages that practice because employes are only supposed to take a half-hour for lunch. Mr. VandenBroek says that because traffic in and out of the park has grown, he can't run home on main roads anymore. He worries that the state's plans for encouraging more growth in the park will destroy the easy countrified living he now enjoys.

But on balance, Mr. VandenBroek says, he is happy. He notes that IBM is granting him time off to take his wife, who was recently hospitalized, to doctor's appointments. "Some people who have worked other places may be more pro-IBM than I am just because I don't know how bad it is elsewhere," he says. "Any job isn't perfect. You've got to have a few things in life to bug you."

BUSINESS
Large & Small

Wood-Stove Maker Has Hot Love Affair With Its Customers

Vermont Firm Gives Advice And Holds Annual Picnic; How to Cure Pigs' Worms

BY WILLIAM M. BULKELEY

"The Vigilant"

RANDOLPH, VT.   9/9/81

Many companies figure that they have good customer relations if they can just avoid product-liability lawsuits. Others hope that satisfied customers will spread the word about their products.

Vermont Castings Inc., a maker of wood- and coal-burning cast-iron stoves, generates real affection. The six-year-old company, which has been doubling sales annually, takes considerable pains to keep in touch with its customers. It has managed to preserve the impression that it deals personally with each of them, and most of them seem to reciprocate that personal feeling.

Owners of Vermont Castings' Defiant, Vigilant and Resolute stoves boast about how many friends they have converted to them. When the company asked owners whether they would be willing to show curious strangers how their stoves worked, 3,000 volunteered. At the company showroom in a drafty, long-abandoned plow factory here, a bulletin board is covered with testimonial letters and proud customers' snapshots of installed stoves.

A Picnic for 10,000

One August weekend, some 10,000 people accepted Vermont Casting's invitation to an owners' outing in this town of 4,500 people in central Vermont's dairy region. They gathered in a muddy field in front of the company's two-year old foundry to take plant tours and listen to lectures on wood and coal burning, insulation and stove safety.

Owners came from as far away as Michigan and Texas to enjoy an aging square-dance group, country-fiddling contests and music by a local quartet called "Smash the Windows." The Rotary Club from nearby Bethel sold barbecued chicken, and the Randolph Merchants Bureau vended corn on the cob. Balloonists raised their craft into the misty skies, and champion woodsmen demonstrated their chopping skills. But the prime drawing card for most of the owners was the chance to talk about their stoves and the mystique of solid-fuel burning.

"There seems to be a kind of cult," says James Douglass, a broker of advertising-agency mergers who bought a Resolute for a solar-heated addition on his home in Warren, Conn. "Everybody feels they're members of a club."

Vermont Castings relies on this feeling for much of its success. The company, which sold some 50,000 stoves last year for "more than $20 million," has hardly any retail outlets and sells most of its stoves by mail though some New Englanders come to the factory to pick them up. Customers generally order the stoves without seeing them, based upon recommendations from friends and subsequent telephone conversations with company representatives in Randolph. The stoves sell for $400 to $800.

Company executives glowingly refer to stove owners as "members of the family." And they stress that the company doesn't consider itself just another appliance maker. "When was the last time your refrigerator maker invited you to a picnic?" asks the founder and chief designer, Duncan Syme, who originated the idea for the owners' outing. The company also sends customers a quarterly newsletter.

Vermont Castings isn't universally loved, however. It managed to alienate a number of customers last year when it began taking orders for coal-burning stoves. Although it promised that the stoves, and coal-conversion units for existing stoves, would be ready in time to be installed for the winter heating season, it didn't ship most of them until spring. Nonetheless, few buyers canceled their orders.

Another goof: Last fall the company computer sent a letter to Roland Edgerly of Rochester, N.H., telling him that his stove was ready. He drove to Randolph to pick it up, only to find it wasn't ready after all. The company mollified him by paying for the gasoline for the 200-mile round trip.

Vermont Castings developed almost by accident. Mr. Syme, a Yale-educated sculptor and architect who was living in Vermont, discovered the shortage of cast-iron stoves when he started looking for one during the 1973-74 oil embargo. A natural tinkerer, he decided to build one himself, basing his design on research done for the U.S. government in the 1940s and on information in United Nations pamphlets on wood energy. His stove followed European patterns for airflow control and lateral burning.

Mr. Syme also decided that since the stoves would be going into kitchens and living rooms, they shouldn't look like high-technology miniature furnaces. "We're taking cast iron and making furniture," he says. He developed the stoves so that doors on the front could be left open to let owners watch the fire, providing fireplace aesthetics without the inefficiency. And he decorated the outside with elegantly styled arches.

Start of Business

Initially, Mr. Syme and his brother-in-law, Murray Howell subcontracted the castings to existing foundries and then bolted the pieces together in the abandoned plow factory.

When they started selling the stoves in 1975, demand was so great that a few advertisements in New England periodicals such as Ketchum's Country Journal and Yankee magazine attracted more business than they could handle. The dirt lot at the factory was filled with the trailers and light trucks of do-it-yourselfers coming to pick up their stoves. Today the privately held company employs 420 workers. It evidently turns a tidy profit but won't say how much.

Most of the business management is handled by Mr. Howell, a burly 36-year-old who favors loose work clothes even when he is out of town on business. Before moving to Vermont, he ran a bar and restaurant in Colorado and worked for the real-estate-investment arm of Lazard Freres & Co. in New York. Now he is Vermont Castings' president. "We're the perfect team," he says. "I'm as creative as the sole of my foot, and Duncan is as organized as a bowl of spaghetti."

Rustic Modernity

Despite the carefully cultivated appearance of a small rural business, Vermont Castings managers are proud of their modern business tools. The $5 million foundry was the first in the U.S. to use a vertical recasting method developed in Europe. An IBM computer keeps customer records that track every stove that the company has sold.

While most workers come from this region of steep green meadows and weather-worn houses and barns (the company is already the biggest employer in rural Orange County), most executives at the vice-presidential level boast years of experience with major companies like Texas Instruments and Procter & Gamble. Neil Fox, the vice president for sales, says that to hire him, Vermont Castings topped the $92,500 he earned as executive vice president of GRI, Inc. of Chicago, a direct-mail promotion company. Unskilled entry-level production jobs pay about $5 an hour.

Vermont Castings eschews most of the trappings of success. The offices are uncarpeted cubicles with plywood floors. The furnishings are used steel desks plus tables and bookshelves knocked together out of scrap lumber. At times, hiring has been so pell-mell that customer-service representatives have had to sit on packing crates. There is no conference room. In good weather, meetings are generally held outdoors around a picnic table. In bad weather, they are held in someone's crowded office. Employes wear flannel shirts and jeans and need high boots to wade through the snows of winter and the deep mud in the unpaved parking lot in spring.

Since customers don't have local retailers to call for advice, they call Randolph about such problems as circulating heat to different rooms and eliminating creosote build-up in chimneys. "When you have problems with the stove or with burning, they give good advice," says Leonard Romansoff, a chiropractor from Mahopac, N.Y. At the owners' outing, Mr. Romansoff, wearing a cowboy hat and boots and clenching a toothpick in his mouth, adds that after three years as an owner, "we pass on ideas to them."

New owners seem impressed with Vermont Castings' advice on meeting local building codes and the best way to install equipment in a particular house. "We've had extensive communications and they've been extremely useful. No one has given us the runaround," says Philip McLewin, a tall, lean economics professor at Ramapo (N.J.) State College who is installing a stove in his home in Mahwah, N.J.

The company makes sure owners remember its name by making each a "lifetime subscriber" to its newsletter, a newsprint tabloid that carries such feature articles as "Cast Iron: A Miracle Metal." The article reveals that old auto engine blocks have perfect properties for melting down into stoves.

The newsletter also contains profiles of Vermont Castings employes and detailed articles on Vermont pastimes such as iceboating, fly fishing and maple sugaring. It sometimes contains such tidbits as information on home-brewing beer on a wood stove. Not incidentally, it includes a catalog of accessories that owners can buy, often with the warning that "some mechanical skills are required" for installation.

Use for Ashes

The readers love it. Every issue includes letters and pictures from stove owners such as Marion Arey, 66, of South Thomaston, Maine, who posed in front of the three cords of wood she cut up for 1980. Other readers send advice on subjects ranging from what to do with wood ashes (putting them in pigs' slop eliminates their worms, according to a Louisiana reader) to how to bake stuffed lobster in a wood stove.

The company tries to make sure that its owners feel welcome if they are traveling in Vermont. Depending on the season, the showroom sometimes gives away apples or zucchini, and employes use the showroom to sell the maple syrup that many make in their off hours.

All this seems to be having the desired effect. Muriel Douglass, the merger broker's wife, gratefully recalls that when she and her husband ordered their stove, the company representative insisted that they take a smaller, cheaper stove than the one they asked for, because they didn't need the large one. "I feel about the company the way I feel about a captain in a fine French restaurant," she says. "I know they'll protect me from ordering the wrong thing."

SECOND TIME AROUND

The Attractions of Starting a New Venture Prove Irresistible to Some Entrepreneurs

BY WILLIAM M. BULKELEY

6/9/81

The urge to reemerge sometimes strikes the entrepreneur who started a company, made a success of it and then got bored with day-to-day management. Dozens of executives in such circumstances have left comfortable remunerative jobs in recent years for the excitement and uncertainties of starting over.

"Some people like to climb mountains; others like to start companies," says Philippe Villers, who last year left Computervision Corp., a growing enterprise that he founded 12 years ago, to start Automatix Inc., a maker of robots. "Some people are simply spawners of companies," says Karl H. Vesper, a University of Washington business professor and author of "New Venture Strategies."

REASONS FOR LEAVING

Would-be entrepreneurs are numerous indeed, and not all of them successful, even once. Some 450,000 businesses are started each year in the U.S. says David L. Birch, a Massachusetts Institute of Technology professor who has studied the business population. And each year 400,000 businesses fail.

Of course, people leave companies that they started for a variety of reasons. Some are pushed out when the inventive spirit that launched an enterprise proves inadequate to manage it. Others, who have sold out to bigger companies, grow restive when they lose their proprietary interest. "I want an ownership position, and I can't have that at Exxon," says Dan W. Matthias, who sold his electronic-typewriter company, Qyx, to Exxon Enterprises Inc. several years ago and who, in January, started a business-computer company.

Others still simply prefer smallness. Murray A. Ruben, a co-founder of Data Terminal Systems Inc., left his previous employer, Digital Equipment Corp., because it had become too big. He left Data Terminal for the same reason when it hit $12 million in sales. Now he is running another new company. "I enjoy the entrepreneurial process. It's like being a parent with a child," he says.

VALUE OF EXPERIENCE

Among the best known of the breed is Gene M. Amdahl, the IBM computer designer who founded Amdahl Corp. in Sunnyvale, Calif. The company successfully competes with IBM by making less expensive computers that use IBM programs. Last year, however, Mr. Amdahl resigned from Amdahl Corp., in which he had a relatively small ownership interest, to start another new computer company, Acsys Inc., since renamed Trilogy Systems Corp. "I do like the excitement of starting a new company and operating it," he has said. "What I don't like is the environment of a bureaucracy."

Experienced entrepreneurs bring a great deal of knowledge to new ventures. "We've had a lot of success backing people who have left companies we helped start," says Paul M. Wythes, a partner in Sutter Hill Ventures, a Palo Alto, Calif., venture-capital firm. "I like to find a fellow who's been a founder of a successful company and wants to do it again," Mr. Wythes says.

The high-technology belts around Boston and San Francisco are good places to find entrepreneurs who have left top-level jobs to take on new challenges. Three founders of Boston-area companies who recently made the leap illustrate some of the satisfactions—and the drawbacks—of starting anew.

J. William Poduska

Prime Computer Inc., started in 1971, is one of the spectacular success stories of the minicomputer industry. Bill Poduska, one of its seven founders, played a big part in its success, designing and developing its computers and eventually heading a 450-person engineering staff.

But 20 months ago, at the age of 42, he decided to find something else to do. He had been a member of the MIT faculty, so he considered going back to teaching. He thought about becoming a venture capitalist. He decided to go skiing.

Before he could hit the slopes, however, he

got a call from Sutter Hill Ventures. "Why don't you consider starting your own company?" Mr. Wythes recalls telling him. On Jan. 8, 1980, Mr. Poduska flew to Palo Alto. On the cross-country flight, he sketched out a business plan and "that afternoon we had a handshake deal," he says. "Sutter Hill said they'd raise the money, and they told me to put together a management team."

A month later, Mr. Poduska and two other engineers who had left Prime were working in Mr. Poduska's living room on Apollo Computer's new product. Mr. Poduska says his $34,000 minicomputers, which are connected in networks that let users obtain information from the other minicomputers, are designed for scientists doing complex calculations and for engineers designing products. Their large memories let an engineer change a design on the screen in 1/30th of a second. Some current graphic-display terminals that share the resources of a central computer take up to 25 seconds to do that.

While Sutter Hill raised the initial $1.5 million, Mr. Poduska recruited a management team with broad experience that has made possible sophisticated marketing and planning for growth. Apollo has set goals of profitability by 1983 and sales of $100 million by 1985. Joseph Gal, a venture capitalist who is an investor and director, says, "I've never seen a start-up with fewer problems."

Mr. Poduska says he doesn't worry much about failure, but "if the company fails, you're looking at the reason in the mirror every morning when you shave." Starting a company, he says, "is the most fun I've ever had over an extended period. It's like being on a rocket with the fuse lit."

Philippe Villers

When Phil Villers was a Harvard undergraduate, he told a classmate that his ambition was to run his own company. By 1968, after working at five high-technology outfits, he decided that at the age of 34 he was ready. Casting about for a product, "I had the idea that computer-automated design was ready to go," he says. But "I thought I didn't have enough top management experience to be a good president," he recalls. He called on Martin Allen, who had been a manager at Singer Co. when Mr. Villers worked there, and Mr. Allen took the chance.

"I had the interesting experience of picking my own boss," Mr. Villers says.

Computervision, the resulting company, grew rapidly through most of the 1970s and Mr. Villers' 11.5% stockholding made him a millionaire several times over. But as the company prospered, Mr. Villers, whose forte is product development, found his own role diminishing and his job becoming too easy, he says.

Two years ago, Mr. Villers, who has a master's degree in mechanical engineering, began to study the nascent robotics field for Computervision. And ultimately he recommended that the company start making robots. He says Mr. Allen didn't approve the idea though, because management already was stretched thin just dealing with Computervision's explosive growth.

So Mr. Villers left to start Automatix in the infant robotics field and wooed away several Computervision employes. Meanwhile, Computervision has gone to court, charging that Mr. Villers "wrongfully appropriated" proprietary ideas.

Despite the suit, Automatix evolved rapidly. Mr. Villers brought in three of the nation's top experts on robots and put together an experienced team of marketing and financial managers. In a week of making presentations to potential investors, he raised $5.8 million from such backers as the Harvard and MIT endowment funds, Connecticut General Insurance Co. and several Wall Street brokerage firms. "It's a lot easier the second time," he says.

Automatix already is selling robots, combining robot technology licensed from Hitachi of Japan with its own computer software and electronic eyes. Automatix robots include an arc welder and a materials-handling device capable of visually inspecting and identifying parts on a moving conveyor belt.

Mr. Villers predicts profitability next year and $67 million in sales by 1984. Despite the pending lawsuit against him, Mr. Villers says he is enjoying himself. "The excitement of Computervision 10 years ago is the excitement of Automatix today," he says.

Royden C. Sanders

Roy Sander's name is on two companies. The first fired him in 1975. He recently shepherded the second through Chapter 11 proceedings in U.S. bankruptcy court, where it sought refuge while working out a plan to pay its debts.

Mr. Sanders, 64, is an inventor who dropped out of Rensselaer Polytechnic Institute to develop a radio altimeter he had devised.

Later he went to work for RCA's missile operations and subsequently helped start Raytheon Co.'s missile and radar division. "I decided if I could start businesses for other people, I could do it for myself," he says. Sanders Associates Inc., the company he founded as a defense contractor in 1951, became a leader in defense electronics and radar-jamming devices.

He branched out into commercial operations in the 1960s, making computer terminals, and the company grew large enough to make the "Fortune 500" in 1968. But the terminals didn't keep pace technologically, and Sanders began losing huge sums of money. By 1975, directors were dissatisfied with Mr. Sander's failure to stanch the flow of red ink, and they demanded that he resign.

Today, Mr. Sanders remains optimistic about his new outfit, R.C. Sanders Technology Systems, Inc., although he recently resigned as chairman of this Amherst, N.H., company to devote more of his time to product development as the company's "chief technologist."

He spent three years developing a new computer printer that he says produces an infinite variety of characters—including signatures and charts—by using needles to hit an inked ribbon so as to form contiguous dots.

Despite all his experience, Mr. Sanders concedes he made mistakes of the sort that many first-time entrepreneurs do—mistakes that led to the Chapter 11 filing in May 1980. "We definitely didn't get enough money. And we were definitely weak in the marketing approach," he says. Mr. Sanders financed initial development himself because, as he puts it, "the venture-capital market was pretty grim in 1975." Even after selling stock to the public, however, the company didn't have enough capital to survive the problems that plagued the first generation of printers.

When Sanders Technology's partner and biggest customer, a German firm called Pelikan Werke G.m.b.H., backed out of an agreement to buy most of Sanders's production, U.S. marketing couldn't take up the slack.

For a while, Mr. Sanders sought a company to acquire his own, but recently Sanders Technology raised additional capital from investors and reached a sales and licensing agreement with Xerox Corp. that

Mr. Sanders says will provide the merchandising and financial muscle to get the product to market. He says he is glad Sanders will remain independent. "It's difficult to maintain creativity as part of a big company," he says.

A French-Fry Diary: From Idaho Furrow To Golden Arches

For the Potato That Qualifies, McDonald's Has a Slicer, Sprayer, Drier—and Ruler

BY MEG COX

OAK BROOK, ILL.   2/8/82

Deep within the high-rise confines of McDonald's Corp. headquarters, inside his "war room," Chairman Fred Turner ponders a weighty business issue: the fate of five Idaho potatoes.

The potatoes have been transplanted from their American homeland to a field in far-off Holland. Delicate negotiations with the government of the Netherlands preceded the move; eight months in Dutch quarantine followed before the potatoes could be planted. "God, I hope they didn't die," Mr. Turner exclaims.

Lower-level McDonald's operatives are asked to check. Alas, the news is bad. The five potatoes, estranged from their native land, have fallen victim to a virulent foreign potato virus. Once again, McDonald's Corp.'s costly, 10-year struggle to take its favorite source of French-fried potatoes to Europe has been thwarted.

Thwarted but not defeated. This company didn't get to be king of fast food by taking French fries lightly. The attention McDonald's lavishes on the spindly side order suggests something approaching a corporate obsession.

And why not? French fries currently pour more than $1 billion a year into McDonald's cash registers, nearly 20% of annual revenue. They are the most profitable food served under the Golden Arches. Seven of every 10 customers arriving after the breakfast hour order fries. Says Mr. Turner: "They are the *piece de resistance* of our menu."

All-Season Oil

To keep them that way, McDonald's has spelled out no fewer than 60 specifications a strip of potato has to meet to make it into the frying basket. To frustrate imitators, it has a patent on the precise combination of steps in making its fries. The restaurants even use a special blend of frying oil. Its name: Interstate 47.

Now, frying is important, but what good is it if you don't have a sturdy potato to begin with? At McDonald's the tuber of choice is the russet Burbank. "People think all potatoes are alike, but they aren't," says Bill Atchley, the chief of McDonald's crew of spud scouts. He explains: "A russet Burbank potato has a distinctive taste and a higher ratio of solids to water, which makes for crispier fries."

There are plenty of russet Burbanks in the U.S., but overseas is another matter. Mr. Atchley recently returned from the Philippines, where he spent much of his time on his hands and knees in the dirt trying to teach farmers to plant the right kind of potatoes. "If we can grow these potatoes in the Philippines, we'll learn a lot about how to do it in other tropical countries," he says.

But the big target is Europe. No russet Burbanks are grown there, and the Common Market doesn't allow potato imports. Never mind that the Continent offers several hundred other varieties; Mr. Turner says they are small and yellow and low in solids, producing, he adds with distaste, "small and soggy" French fries.

NO RAIN IN SPAIN

To cure this blight, McDonald's devised a scheme to persuade farmers in Spain to grow russet Burbanks. Spain is due to join the Common Market in 1983, and if by then it is raising Idaho potatoes, Mr. Turner reasons, the species will be "grandfathered in."

Unfortunately, Spanish farmers haven't the urgency about this issue that McDonald's has. "Several farmers planted potatoes and took off fishing for two months," Mr. Atchley complains. "That isn't the way to grow a russet Burbank, which is picky about how much moisture it gets." In Idaho, Idaho potatoes are irrigated.

The five potatoes sent to Holland represented more dashed hopes. McDonald's had persuaded the Dutch to admit the interloper for "observation." They made it through their laboratory quarantine without a suspicious sprout, but they couldn't survive in the underground. (There have been some modest international triumphs, however;

McDonald's did manage to plant russets in Tasmania, and they now supply fries for outlets in Australia.)

Life wasn't so complicated when Ray Kroc bought his first hamburger stand from Mac and Dick McDonald in 1954. The brothers made their "shoestrings" themselves, from fresh potatoes. Mr. Kroc liked them. What he didn't like were the "pale and limp" frozen fries then being introduced.

But the chain of franchises grew. Franchisees came to dread the daily chore of peeling and slicing. Masses of peels sometimes caused awful sewer backups. Finally, Mr. Kroc embraced the frozen French fry. But he ordered company food scientists to invent a better one.

The state of the art in French-fry making today can be seen at the J. R. Simplot potato factory in Caldwell, Idaho, which processes a good portion of the billion potatoes McDonald's uses each year. "Mac fries," like the ones Simplot prepares for other companies, begin their journey on an assembly line, where women in aprons pluck out the bad potatoes. Like the others, those going to McDonald's are chopped, prefried and frozen.

But there are subtle differences. Other fries are blanched, or quick-scalded, in water; McDonald's has its steamed, figuring that water carries off flavor and nutrients. All the fries in the assembly line are prefried, then dried; but those going to McDonald's are dried at higher heat, to make them chewy. The time and the heat are covered by the patent.

Nor is McDonald's indifferent to the amount of moisture that slips away between the frying and the drying. Company food scientists monitor this. They call it "drier-frier weight loss."

Elsewhere on the Simplot production line, other people's fries are dipped in sugar to make them brown better. Mac fries get doused in sugar too, but they are sprayed rather than dipped. Spraying the sugar on makes the fries brown unevenly, the company believes, and that makes them look more natural.

In looks, though, color isn't everything. Fries have to be the right length, too. What hungry diner wants to look into his bag and find a bunch of little stubby fries? McDonald's is ruthless about length: 40% of all fries must be between two inches and three inches long; another 40% must be over three inches; the other 20%—well, it doesn't hurt to have *a few* stubby ones.

McDonald's is convinced all this trouble pays off. It says a 1975 telephone survey showed that Mac fries were the favorite of 70% of those called.

Even some gourmets like them. "I think McDonald's fries are remarkably good," says television chef Julia Child. "They're cooked in extremely fresh fat." Nutritionists tend to be less enthusiastic. Isobel Contento, a nutrition professor at Columbia University in New York, says, "About half the calories in French fries come from fat, there are very few vitamins, and you'd feel a whole lot fuller eating a comparable amount of green vegetables."

Some of the company's rivals in the fast-food business dismiss McDonald's French-fry fetish. "The fry isn't the central attraction at Wendy's," sniffs Ronald Fay, the chief operating officer for that longstanding competitor. In Mr. Fay's opinion, the long, skinny Mac fry appeals mostly to children. "Our customers," he declares, "are older."

But Donald Smith is a true believer. He used to be an executive at McDonald's. In 1977 he defected to Burger King, and he freely admits that he tried to make that arch-rival's fries as close as possible to McDonald's. Exactly how close? "That's hush-hush stuff," says Mr. Smith, who has since become the president of PepsiCo's Pizza Hut division.

Even McDonald's, though, could pick up a pointer or two about the mechanization of French-fry cuisine, Mr. Smith believes. In a Burger King restaurant, the frying basket levitates out of the hot oil automatically when the fries are done. "At McDonald's," Mr. Smith scoffs, "a buzzer goes off. Someone has to be there to *lift* them out."

STEEL BLUES

Trailing the Japanese, U.S. Steelmakers Seek To Use Their Methods

But American Firms Face Some Serious Handicaps; Managers Partly at Fault

A Look at Two Major Mills

BY DOUGLAS R. SEASE AND URBAN C. LEHNER

TOKYO — 4/2/81

It's getting hard to avoid bumping into American steelmen in Japan.

William R. Roesch, president of U.S. Steel Corp., beams out from among photographs of celebrities recently staying at the Imperial Hotel here. At the shrines of Kyoto, a woman tourist turns out to be the wife of an Armco, Inc. engineer studying Japanese steelmaking technology. And during an interview, the head of Japan's steelworkers' union says that later that day he will meet with Samuel Camens, the top assistant to Lloyd McBride, president of the United Steelworkers of America.

The American steel industry needs help. Its plants are old, its profits low and its prospects uncertain. To get that help, American steelmen are turning to the Japanese, the world's premier steelmakers. Practically every major American steel company today has some kind of technical-assistance agreement with a Japanese steelmaker. Armco and Nippon Steel even invested a symbolic $1.2 million in each other's stock. And the U.S. government bases its trigger-price mechanism for monitoring imported-steel prices on Japanese steelmaking costs, on the ground that no one can make high-quality steel as cheaply as the Japanese.

"They're better, that's all there is to it," says C. Richard Rough, general manager of Bethlehem Steel Corp.'s Burns Harbor, Ind., plant. "Their quality and cost are no accident and no figment of the imagination. We ignore them only at our peril."

How did the Japanese steel industry in 30 years become the non-Communist world's largest and most sophisticated while the American industry—the source of much of Japan's early steel equipment and knowledge—fell on hard times?

Important Differences

Conversations with dozens of American and Japanese steel executives, as well as government officials, bankers and steelworkers, suggest some broad conclusions. And a close look at the best steelmaking facilities that each industry has built—Bethlehem's Burns Harbor plant and Nippon Kokan K.K.'s recently completed Ohgishima plant—illustrates some important differences between the two industries.

To some extent, of course, the two industries are products of different historical and cultural backgrounds. Ever since the turn of the century, when a Japanese government report identified steel as "the mother of industry," Japan's steelmakers have held an honored place in their society. That has been especially true since World War II as Japan rebuilt its shattered economy. The steel industry's prestige attracted the best and the brightest of Japan's managers, and the government lavished attention and favors on the industry. The Japanese population's homogeneity and fervent patriotism contributed to relatively smooth labor relations. And the nation's long history of international trade facilitated access to raw materials and markets.

The American steel industry, on the other hand, never enjoyed similar respect. The early steel tycoons—the Andrew Carnegies and Henry Fricks—battled fiercely with the immigrant laborers manning their plants; the resulting legacy of hostile labor relations lingers today.The U.S. government was seldom the industry's ally, and for the past 20 years or so it has often been openly hostile. And many of the managers who brought the industry to its heyday in the 1950s were the same men who ignored new technology and the import threat. In doing so, they set the American industry on a 20-year path of decline marked by closure of several steel mills, sliding efficiency of many more, and one of the worst profit records of any major American industry.

Unpredictable Future

But despite the clear trends of the past two decades, the future of neither country's industry is easily predicted. The Japanese industry, for example, is burdened with too much capacity, a problem aggravated by the increasingly protectionist stance of many of Japan's trading partners and the growing steelmaking capacity in less-developed countries. At the same time, the American industry is hoping for good relationships with the Reagan administration, including more protection from imported steel. What's more, a new breed of steel manager has taken over many of the top jobs in the U.S. industry. These managers are trying to improve labor relations and, at the same time, they are scouring the world for the best technology.

Mr. Rough, the 56-year-old general manager of the Burns Harbor plant, is one of that new breed. The Burns Harbor plant, a 5.5-million-ton-a-year facility, is the nation's newest and probably best full-scale steel mill. But the plant, at the south end of Lake Michigan, is already 16 years old and is showing its age. There are things that Mr. Rough wants for his plant that Bethlehem executives at headquarters can't give him because cash is short. He has pollution problems to solve and an 8,500-man work force less willing to work than it once was. Worse, Mr. Rough frequently is reminded of his competitive position when he sees foreign steel being unloaded from ships at the Indiana state docks less than a mile from his own two big blast furnaces.

To get a better idea of what he is up against and what he can do about it, Mr. Rough in 1979 sent a team of Burns Harbor engineers to visit Japan's newest steel mill, the Ohgishima plant, a six-million-ton-a-year facility built by Nippon Kokan on a man-made island in Tokyo Bay. What they found, says John Straka, head of the technology department at Burns Harbor, "is a steelmaker's dream."

The construction of the Ohgishima plant illustrates two of the Japanese steel industry's characteristics that the American industry hasn't shared—a willingness to invest huge sums in projects that mightn't pay off for years and an almost fanatical devotion to quality. Just building the island on which the plant sits required the movement of more earth than did construction of the Suez Canal. And nothing like the plant's complex computer system, which controls almost the entire steelmaking process, had ever been attempted before. Most remarkable of all is that the whole 10-year project, which cost the equivalent of $4 billion, was aimed merely at replacing most of the aging Keihin Works the NKK operated on the nearby mainland.

Difficult Decision

"The construction of Ohgishima was one of the most difficult decisions anyone in the steel industry ever made," says Haruki Kamiya, a managing director of NKK. But the Keihin Works was steadily becoming less competitive with other steel plants. "Were we going to watch it decay or do something about it? That was the decision we had to make," he says. "So we braced ourselves and did it."

The result is a steel mill that incorporates nearly every possible efficiency. High-pressure gases leaving the blast furnaces turn electrical generators. A computer regulates the flow of energy to every part of the plant. And no human beings are in sight in the vast shipping building, where computer-controlled cranes automatically lift and store huge coils of sheet steel. The steel itself meets the highest standards of purity and tight specifications. And the entire plant is practically pollution-free.

"When a steelmaker dies, and goes to heaven, he goes to Ohgishima," Bethlehem's Mr. Straka says.

The Burns Harbor plant was Bethlehem's solution to a somewhat different problem. In the late 1950s, Bethlehem's major plants were clustered in eastern Pennsylvania and New York State, where they couldn't compete effectively in the burgeoning steel market around Chicago and Detroit. First, Bethlehem tried to penetrate the Midwest by merging with Youngstown Sheet & Tube Co., which owned a large steel mill on Lake Michigan. Only after those efforts were twice thwarted by the government's antitrust objections did the company decide in 1962 to build its own plant.

Major Deficiency

By American standards, Burns Harbor is efficient. Its two large blast furnaces enable it to convert iron ore to molten iron more efficiently than most American mills can, and its three basic oxygen furnaces, which convert the molten iron to steel, have twice set North American production records. But when it comes to getting that molten steel into solid forms suitable for finishing, Burns Harbor comes up shy. Only about one-third of its output is converted to solid form through continuous casting. That process saves large amounts of energy and manpower and produces a higher-quality product compared with the old-fashioned ingot-casting method.

The plant has only one continuous-casting machine, and it wasn't installed until 1975, long after the devices were common in Japan. "In retrospect, you might say it was a mistake" to hesitate so long in putting in continuous casters, one of Mr. Rough's top assistants says. The lack of continuous-casting ability is the Burns Harbor plant's biggest shortcoming and one that isn't likely to be overcome soon. Leon Harbold, the manager of the plant's steelmaking operations, wants another caster more than anything else.

Roles in Society

"Leon keeps saying he wants another caster, but I tell him, 'My God, Leon, that would cost $140 million or more,' " Mr. Straka says. For only an $11 million investment, Mr. Straka figures, the plant would be able to begin a proposed program to maintain its ingot molds in better shape—something he learned about in Japan. The mold-conditioning program would improve the steel products' quality, but it wouldn't do much for energy or labor costs.

Another important difference between the two industries is the way in which they view their roles in society. An example is their differing attitudes toward pollution-control regulations. The American industry has been one of the most recalcitrant. Steelmakers have battled the government and environmental groups in the courts for years and even now are seeking a three-year extension of the deadline for meeting air-pollution standards. The Japanese steel industry, by contrast, moved promptly to meet pollution standards far more rigorous than those in the U.S.

One of the biggest sources of pollution in a steel mill is coke ovens, where coal is baked to drive off many of its volatile elements so it can be used in blast furnaces. The gases emitted by the baking coals are poisonous and are suspected of causing cancer. And because of the way in which American coke ovens are constructed, it's difficult to prevent leaks of such gases.

To reduce pollution, the Burns Harbor coke ovens are being operated at slower speeds than they were designed for. Yet they still aren't complying with environmental regulations, and it isn't certain how much more money would be needed to bring them into compliance. Meantime, the reduced operating rate prevents the ovens from supplying as much coke as the blast furnaces use. About 20% of the plant's coke supplies must be purchased from other Bethlehem plants or other producers at considerable cost. In 1979, when coke supplies were tight nationwide, Bethlehem had to buy coke from foreign producers.

At the Ohgishima plant, coke ovens aren't a problem. Indeed, they are something of a solution. When the plant was being built, NKK purchased from the Soviet Union a process called coke dry quenching. Instead of cooling red-hot coke with a torrent of water, the Ohgishima plant surrounds the coke with an inert gas in a sealed chamber that prevents gas leaks. Furthermore, as the coke's heat is transferred to the inert gas, the gas carries the heat away to boilers, where it is used to help generate energy for the plant.

None of this is to say that Japanese steel managers don't make mistakes. Take, for instance, Nippon Steel's giant plate mill at its Oita Works. The mill can make plates nearly 18 feet wide. When it was built several years ago, the company intended to sell the big plates to shipyards building supertankers. But shortly after the mill was completed, the supertanker market collapsed, and Nippon was left with a mill that can't be used very effectively. The company is considering installing a machine to cut the plates into more usable sizes, but meanwhile it is trying to market the plates as flooring for bridges.

And Nippon Steel isn't alone. The Japanese industry's overcapacity indicates misplaced optimism about the rate at which steel consumption would grow during the past several years. And according to a Japanese banker, only the cautious response of the banking industry kept an overenthusiastic NKK from trying to overhaul the old Keihin Works after the Ohgishima plant was completed in 1978. Such an addition to steelmakers' already-swollen capacity "wouldn't have been the best thing for the industry," the banker says.

GOOD LISTENER
At Procter & Gamble, Success Is Largely Due To Heeding Consumer

Household-Goods Firm Uses Market Research Heavily And Encourages Griping

But a Fling on Fling Flopped

BY JOHN A. PRESTBO

CINCINNATI   4/29/80

One day in 1879, a workman in Procter & Gamble's soap factory here went to lunch and forgot to turn off his mixing machine. When he came back, he found a frothy concoction that he considered throwing out. But he and his supervisor decided that the soap hadn't really been spoiled; so the batch was made into bars and sold.

A month later, consumers along the Ohio River who had ended up with this soap began pestering their storekeepers to reorder, "Give us more floating soap," the merchants told P&G, which traced those particular shipments back to the workman's mistake and determined that air bubbles whipped into the molten soap caused it to float.

Thus, Ivory soap was born. And so also began a dialogue between P&G and its customers that not only continues a century later but is growing tremendously. Giant P&G carefully nurtures this rapport with consumers not to keep the Ralph Naders off its back, but to stay the nation's biggest maker of everyday consumer products—including, besides Ivory, such well-known brands as Folger's coffee, Crest toothpaste, Pampers disposable diapers and Tide detergent. The company promotes these brands with what is believed to be the

LAUNDRY LIST OF MAJOR PRODUCTS

LAUNDRY & CLEANING $3.67 BILLION*

BOLD 3 • CASCADE • CHEER • DASH • DAWN • DREFT • DUZ • ERA • GAIN • IVORY LIQUID • IVORY SNOW • JOY • OXYDOL • TIDE • BIZ • COMET • COMET LIQUID • MR. CLEAN • SPIC AND SPAN • TOP JOB • BOUNCE • DOWNY

PERSONAL CARE $3.05 BILLION*

CAMAY • COAST • IVORY • KIRK'S • LAVA • SAFEGUARD • ZEST • SCOPE • SECRET • SURE • CREST • GLEEM • LILT • WONDRA • HEAD & SHOULDERS • PRELL • CHARMIN • PUFFS • WHITE CLOUD • BOUNTY • PAMPERS • LUVS • RELY

FOOD $2.06 BILLION*

CRISCO • CRISCO OIL • DUNCAN HINES • FLUFFO • FOLGER'S COFFEE • JIF • PRINGLE'S • PURITAN OIL

OTHER $741 MILLION*

INDUSTRIAL FOOD PRODUCTS • INDUSTRIAL CHEMICALS • CELLULOSE, PULP ANIMAL FEED INGREDIENTS • INDUSTRIAL CLEANING PRODUCTS

*Sales for fiscal year ended June 30, 1979

largest advertising budget of any U.S. company. P&G declines to disclose any figures, although Broadcast Advertisers Reports Inc. puts the company's 1979 outlays on television ads alone at $463.4 million.

No Big Secret

"A lot of people think P&G 'buys' its way into the market with big ad and promotion budgets, or has some other secret to its success," says Leonard S. Matthews, president of the American Association of Advertising Agencies and a former executive on P&G ad accounts. "I don't think there's much secret to it. The company simply is tuned in to what consumers want, and it does a good job of making products to satisfy those wants."

To tune itself in, P&G draws heavily on consumers' views, both solicited and unsolicited. P&G considers its consumer dialogue an essential ingredient of its success formula, albeit one usually unnoticed by those who try to dope out what makes the company prosper.

And prosper it does. So far in the 20th century, the 143-year-old company has, on average, nearly doubled its earnings every decade, and in the past 10 years its profit has tripled. In the fiscal nine months ended March 31, P&G's earnings rose 13% from a year earlier to $521.5 million, or $6.31 a share, and its sales climbed 16% to $8.08 billion.

"There's no doubt in my mind that we wouldn't be the company we are if we didn't have our close contact with consumers," a top officer says. "We've never added it up, but I'm sure the feedback we get from consumers saves us many millions of dollars a year."

This consumer dialogue works pretty much the same now as it did a century ago. After P&G heard from consumers wanting more "floating soap," it investigated and found that they weren't merely amused by the novelty. They did a lot of washing and bathing in murky Ohio River water, and the floating bar saved them from groping for submerged soap.

Nowadays, this dialogue is conducted on a scale commensurate with P&G's size. The company is the nation's 23rd-largest industrial concern, and it does business more frequently with American consumers—about 17 million transactions a day, it estimates—than any other corporation.

This year, it will receive and answer upwards of 250,000 calls and letters from customers. Half of these communications will be requests for information, a sixth will be expressions of praise, and a third will be complaints of all kinds, including those about products, ads and even the plots of soap operas that the company sponsors on TV.

But P&G is so hungry for more volunteered comment that it is expanding its toll-free telephone operation to make it easier for customers to contact the company. By year-end, all of P&G's 80 brands, including six in test-marketing, will carry a toll-free phone number on the package or label so that people can call in immediately their thoughts about them. P&G expects that by next year 500,000 customers will have contacted the company.

Much Research

Also, P&G will phone or visit some 1.5 million people this year in connection with about 1,000 research projects; that's up from 250,000 such interviews six years ago. These people are questioned extensively on their likes and dislikes about P&G products including their names, packaging and hundreds of other details. In addition, P&G does an unusual amount of continuing "basic" research into how people go about washing clothes, preparing meals, doing dishes and other household tasks.

Generating this mountain of information is only half the process. It's what P&G does with it that really sets the company apart from the corporate pack. The data is funneled monthly to every major segment of the company—including the executive suite—where it is sifted and resifted for implications for P&G's marketing, advertising, manufacturing and research-and-development operations.

"In our business, we are forever trying to see what lies around the corner," says Edward G. Harness, P&G's chairman. "We study the ever-changing consumer and try to identify new trends in tastes, needs, environment and living habits. We study changes in the marketplace and try to assess their likely impact on our brands. We study our competition. Competitive brands are continually offering new benefits and new ideas to the consumer, and we must stay ahead of this."

Despite all the study, some P&G products have flopped over the years, of course—occasionally because the company didn't listen to consumers as well as it usually does. One such case was a product called Fling. Test-marketed in 1965, it was a roll of disposable, detergent-filled dishcloths made of tough, flexible paper. Even with P&G's ad and promotional blitz, Fling bombed.

"We were so enamored with our technical ability to put dish soap in a paper towel that we didn't research the concept well enough," says Jack Henry, manager of P&G's market research department. "When we went back and did what we should have in the first place, we found people were happy enough with the dishcloths they had. There simply wasn't a need for the product."

Inquiries, complaints and other contacts initiated by consumers are handled by the consumer services department. The basic job of the staff's 60 employes—up from 50 a year ago—is to help keep customers happy. That's important to P&G, which strives to build and hold hefty market shares through brand loyalty.

"If people have a problem with one of our products, we'd rather they tell us about it than switch to a competitor's product or say bad things about ours over the backyard fence," says Dorothy Puccini, head of P&G's consumer services department.

A recent study sponsored by the U.S. Office for Consumer Affairs supports this approach: "Many managers view complaints as a nuisance that wastes valuable corporate resources. However, the survey data suggest that complaints may instead be a valuable marketing asset. . . . Responsive companies were rewarded by the greatest degree of continued brand loyalty."

Slow and Deliberate

As it does with almost everything it tries, P&G proceeded slowly but deliberately with the toll-free telephone program. It started in 1974 with a number on Duncan Hines brownie-mix packages.

"We learned that people in high-altitude areas needed special instructions for baking, and these were soon added to the packages," Miss Puccini says. "We also found that one of the recipes on a box label was confusing, so we changed it. And we spotted a pattern of people complaining that they couldn't get the last bit of toothpaste out of the tube without it breaking; the tubes were strengthened."

As the toll-free phone numbers were put on other products, Miss Puccini and others became convinced they were getting a lot more consumer response, and calming more potentially disaffected customers, than if they had continued to depend solely on people who were mad enough, or had time enough, to write letters.

One call that couldn't have been dealt with by letter came from a woman who at that moment was giving her friend a home permanent with P&G's Lilt. Her friend was hanging her head in the sink and the woman said she had just discovered that the neutralizer which "locks in" the curl and offsets the alkalinity of the waving solution, was missing from the Lilt kit. What to do? Rinse your friend's hair thoroughly, was the answer, apply a solution of one part water to one part vinegar or lemon juice and then rinse again. To compensate the women for the inconvenience, P&G mailed them a coupon for a free kit.

Back to the Plant

But P&G didn't stop there. The Lilt plant that made the faulty kit (identified by a product code on the caller's package) was told of the incident. Plant personnel checked the production lines and inspection methods to determine whether they were at fault—a standard procedure in such complaints. In this case, they found nothing amiss at the plant and concluded that the neutralizer may have been pilfered from the package as it sat on a store shelf.

The company doesn't always get off so easily, however. Last fall, for instance, a spate of calls informed P&G that the plastic tops on Downy fabric-softener bottles were splintering when twisted on and off—raising the danger of punctured fingers. P&G quickly identified the supplier of the fragile caps and found out that the supplier recently had changed its formula for making the plastic in the caps, which in time became unexpectedly brittle.

"Because of our early-warning system, we were able to get to the problem before it became widespread," a top P&G official says. "Most of the bad caps were still at the factory, and we simply replaced them." If the consumer reaction had been monitored less closely, the bad caps could have caused real problems. P&G hasn't ever had a product recall.

Consumers' calls and letters are used in other parts of P&G, too. Testimonials, for instance, are forwarded to the ad agencies, where they are scanned for insights into why people like the product. Several P&G ad campaigns have been based on unsolicited consumer comments.

Ideas Sent In

Consumers also send P&G some 4,000 ideas for new products each year, but nothing much comes of them. To protect against legal repercussions, a separate staff sorts through these ideas and almost always politely turns the sender down.

But the feedback itself sometimes suggests new products. For example, some people caring for incontinent teen-agers and adults said they wished P&G offered a bigger version of its Pamper diaper. P&G took the hint and now is test-marketing adult-size disposable diapers, called Attends, mainly to hospitals, nursing homes and medical-supply concerns.

Many more consumer-generated new product ideas come from the other part of P&G's consumer dialogue, which it initiates by asking questions. Much of this is standard market research, used by most major consumer-goods companies. But P&G goes beyond the consumer-oriented market research and studies consumers' habits. Researchers periodically follow housewives around as they do the laundry, for instance, and note how they sort the clothes, how many loads they do and a myriad other details. Over time, this research uncovers consumer-behavior trends that suggest products to P&G.

During the 1960s, for example, P&G noticed that the average household's loads of laundry increased to 7.6 a week from 6.4 and that the average temperature of the wash water dropped 15 degrees. The reason: Clothes were being made of many more kinds of fabrics, especially synthetics and blends of synthetics and natural fibers, and they all presented different washing problems.

Some of them required washing separately in cold or lukewarm rather than hot water.

So P&G developed a detergent that works in all levels of water temperature and on many different fabrics. Beginning in 1969, it was marketed as Cheer and was aimed at people who wanted one detergent capable of handling almost all their laundry. P&G says Cheer is selling very well.

At least once a year, P&G conducts market research on each of its brands. Frequently, these surveys turn up consumer attitudes that prompt the company to tinker even with its best-selling products— perhaps because consumers don't like something specific about the P&G brand or prefer a rival product. Tide detergent, one of P&G's biggest sellers, has been changed significantly 57 times since it was introduced in 1947, Mr. Harness, the chairman, says.

Sometimes a consumer gripe about one product can't be solved directly, but instead leads to another product. In its Downy fabric-softener research, P&G learned that people disliked having to run down to their washing machine on every rinse cycle to pour in Downy. P&G couldn't solve the problem by changing Downy, but it instead came up with Bounce, a nonwoven rayon sheet impregnated with softener that is tossed into the dryer with the clothes.

CITIES

Small Towns to Urban Centers

Small-Town Revival, Like Most Trends, Bypasses Strandburg

Tiny Hamlet in South Dakota Is Among Many in Nation That Are Slowly Dying

BY LAWRENCE ROUT

STRANDBURG, S.D.   10/7/81

Midafternoon on Main Street: two parked cars, no people. The only sounds are the whir of the fan in the cafe and the rhythmic banging of somebody's broken screen door.

Nearby, 64-year-old Lillie Bergman sits at a table in her two-bedroom house, staring out the window and remembering. "Growing up, this was a real good town, with stores and gas stations, banks and doctors," she says. "We had a couple of hundred people, and the streets were full."

She looks down at her clenched hands and continues. "I hate to admit it, but there isn't much left. Our town is dying."

Strandburg, S.D., has a cafe, a lumberyard and 79 residents. They have heard all about the revival of small towns and about urban America's yearning for a simpler kind of life. But they know firsthand that that hopeful trend masks another one just as real: Many of the tiniest of the small towns are fading away.

"People are misinterpreting the rural turnaround," says Eric Hoiberg, a rural sociologist at Iowa State University. "The headlines talk of a small-town boom without recognizing that the growth is in specific areas. Many places, and particularly the smallest ones, are hurting very badly."

Widespread Decline

Glenn Fuguitt, a University of Wisconsin sociologist, recently sampled 600 towns and found that nearly 40% of those with fewer than 500 residents had shrunk during the 1970s. In the Great Plains, 58% of the sample small towns lost people. This has been happening even though rural and small-town America as a whole grew more than 15% in the past decade, compared with 10% for cities.

The withering away of once-vibrant communities shouldn't go unmourned, in the view of some sociologists. Although only some 1.4 million Americans live in towns of fewer than 500 residents, these tiny settlements, which are among the last refuges from such ills as crime and drugs, offer a way of life to be found neither in larger towns nor on isolated farms.

"When we lose these towns, we lose a lot of the diversity that defines America," says Clay Denman, the director of the Small Town Institute in Ellensburg, Wash. In larger places, he adds, "people don't have as much say about how things get run. And they become more self-centered when they don't work together as much."

For the residents, often elderly, who are left behind, watching stores go under and schools close can be devastating. Last year a resident of Antler, N.D., Harley Kissner, was so disturbed over the imminent closing of the school that he offered nine acres of land to anyone who would move to Antler and send children to the school. (The effort succeeded, at least for now; the number of students doubled to 40, and the school stayed open.)

Slow Fade

Today's dying towns aren't former boom towns that are collapsing as fast as they had swelled. They tend to be places that enjoyed years of prosperity and now are slowly declining, taking as long to die as the people who live in them. "It's the terminal stage for a lot of these towns," says Calvin Beale, a demographer for the Department of Agriculture.

The reasons often are complex. Some towns survive mainly through state and federal money for road repair, fire protection and sewage treatment. A town of, say, 2,000 can afford to hire professionals to go after these grants and meet the qualifications; a tiny village rarely can.

But towns die mainly because they lose their economic reason for being. Villages that once were the center of shopping and entertainment for surrounding farmers began to lose that function as long ago as the arrival of television, of cars and of paved roads to larger communities. The trend continued with the thinning of farm populations and, in many cases, the end of railroad transportation through a town. For many a town the end was ensured when a big highway was built nearby and didn't pass through it. Once a place begins to lose merchants, and amenities, one loss can quickly lead to another.

So it has been for Strandburg. The first thing that strikes a visitor to its dusty main street is the silence. The second is the cacophony of the prodded memories of townsfolk.

Strandburg has plenty to remember. Founded in 1880 by John Strandburg—farmer, surveyor, grain buyer and justice of the peace—the village grew quickly. In the 1930s and 1940s, local people say, the population reached about 250. Trains passed through four times a day. There were big houses, banks, several stores, a gasoline station and a grain elevator. Band concerts and movies filled the streets to overflowing on Saturday nights. In 1949, Strandburg's high-school basketball team made it to the state tournament.

The big houses are still there, but the children who used to fill them have left. "It's hard to remember just what happened," says 77-year-old Richard Carlson, the mayor. "It was one thing after another. You just can hardly believe how fast it was. It doesn't make a guy feel too good to think about it."

Most people say things started to sour after World War II. A lot of young men got out of town, saw places they liked better, and never came back. Improved roads to bigger towns with bigger stores left local merchants struggling.

One of the worst things for Strandburg was the growth in the size of farms as tractors got more powerful and six-row or eight-row farm machines replaced two-row equipment. "I remember when I got married 33 years ago, there must have been 16 farms within two miles," says Luverne Enquist, a farmer. "Now there aren't even eight of us." For Strandburg the change simply meant fewer patrons.

This dwindling of farm population—from 30 million Americans in 1940 to eight million today—has been particularly hard on Midwestern and Plains states that were so heavily rural to start with. The 1970 census found 3.7% of the U.S. population employed in agricultural production, but in South Dakota the figure was 22%.

The Last Train

With fewer farmers coming to Strandburg, a couple of stores closed. Without them, young adults couldn't get jobs or grew bored and moved away. More stores closed. "It's the younger people that support the stores in these towns," notes Harley Johansen, a professor of geography at the University of Idaho. "So the stores suffer a double blow: fewer people and older people."

In 1960 the passenger trains stopped running through Strandburg. "We all went out to watch the last passenger run," recalls Myrtle Johnson, 77, who used to own a general store. "Some of us took the kids for a last ride east and back. It was awfully sad." Seven years later, the freight trains also stopped running.

Then, 11 years ago, the school closed. There weren't enough students. The remaining children got bus rides to a nearby school, but Strandburg was devastated.

"That was the worst," says Mrs. Bergman. "The school provided a sense of community. It was something we took pride in. And the teachers who lived in town had ideas about entertainment. They kept it alive." The school stands empty on a hill overlooking the town, boarded up. The village tried to sell the building for $1 but found no takers.

While all this was happening, some nearby towns that had a population edge to start with were growing stronger. Milbank, 18 miles to the northeast, grew to 4,120 people from 3,727 during the 1970s. Watertown, 30 miles in the other direction, grew from 13,388 to 15,649.

Two Who Left

Lenore Rufer, a 1961 graduate of Strandburg High, moved to Milbank six years ago. She isn't sorry she left Strandburg: "I had enough of that town—driving to work, to play, to get a beer. There's always something to do here. I'm never moving back."

Older residents miss other things. Mary Lindahl, who moved with her husband from Strandburg to Milbank in May, explains that "we were so far away from doctors and stores, and with the roads bad in the winter, we had to move. Here they have 'Meals on Wheels' and neighborly women helping out. We hated to move, but it was best."

Many people who remain, of course, love Strandburg. They have lived here all their lives, and it is home. A four-bedroom house can be bought for about $10,000, and property taxes are lower than in other towns. The nearest thing to a crime in recent years, people say, occurred when children knocked on somebody's door late at night and then ran away.

But the residents often comment that, while life in Strandburg is peaceful, something is missing now. "There isn't much left to make this a community, a family," says Pearl Lundquist, who ran a general store for 38 years.

Mrs. Lundquist and others hang on, sure of the town's demise but determined to postpone it. Robert Johnson, 61 years old, has been the postmaster for 25 years and is eligible for retirement. But if he leaves, the post office will close. So he keeps working.

"I had hoped against hope that we could save this town," Mr. Johnson says. "I still love Strandburg, even if it isn't what is used to be. But I'm afraid it doesn't have much of a chance."

Bisbee Learns What Happens When Boomtown Goes Bust

BY WILLIAM E. BLUNDELL

3/3/81

Small houses cling in colorful profusion to the slopes of the Mule Mountains as they dip into a canyon. There, splendidly built old structures line narrow, twisting streets, giving the town of Bisbee, Ariz., one of its nicknames—Little San Francisco. Another nickname: the Cleveland of Arizona.

Mile-high Bisbee, a former mining town of about 9,000 tucked in the southeast corner of Arizona, is struggling to stay alive as a tourist center. At one point it couldn't even afford to pass on employe withholding taxes to the government and only recently escaped a $500,000 city deficit with draconian budget-slashing. The picturesque streets are dotted with closed stores, some boarded up. In the Brewery Gulch area, weedy, rubbled lots, the walls of old structures on them still half-standing, gape at the passerby.

"The place is deteriorating," says Rex Ganoe, an old woodcarver with a shop in the gulch. Adds Mayor J. Michael Lynn, who recently had to close his Ford dealership, the last auto outlet left in town: "We've lost the people with enough money to buy cars. It's a sad thing for all the businessmen of Bisbee."

In the town's distress there are lessons. Across the West, civic officials are losing sleep over the boomtown syndrome—the sudden strain on town resources, the upsetting social changes, that occur when hundreds or thousands of workers flow into an area to exploit natural resources. But in fixing on that problem, it's easy to overlook another: What happens when the goodies run out?

Bisbee learned six years ago, when Phelps Dodge Corp. stopped mining copper in the area. At one stroke Bisbee lost its industrial base, 1,500 jobs, and any illusions it harbored about the benefits of corporate paternalism.

Not that "Daddy P-D" was a rape-ruin-and-run operator. A

benevolent giant, it built and supported the local hospital (it still covers its deficits), aided the city budget and put up many graceful buildings. If anything, Phelps Dodge may have been too nice for the town's good.

"The company warned us years before that it would probably close the mine," says Don Fry, a jewelry store owner and head of Bisbee's industrial development authority, "but a lot of people just didn't believe it because they didn't want to."

So a dazed Bisbee was psychologically unready for what happened next. First, the real estate market collapsed as hundreds of homes went up for distress sale; at the height of the bust miners' cottages were going for as little as $1,000. They wound up in the hands of two divergent groups sharing only an interest in cheap housing and rural charm—retirees, now 42% of the population, and a smaller but more visible number of counterculturists.

The conservative pensioners and the laid-back younger set sometimes get along like a mongoose gets along with a cobra. Many oldsters have refused to shop in the historic old Bisbee district where the counterculture has settled in, and last year's poetry festival created an uproar that hasn't died down yet. Conservative retirees and longtime residents don't cotton to the poetry or persona of radical guest artist Allen Ginsberg. And they were infuriated by what they considered vulgarity in another author's poem in the festival brochure.

More friction arose when a woman was ejected from the Copper Queen Hotel, a favored tourist stopover, for suckling her infant in the lobby. This only touched off a defiant breast feed-in by others that lasted for weeks. And when Mayor Lynn pledged to purge the streets of "dirty hippies," his car and business were vandalized.

Social tension has been accompanied by economic problems. When Phelps Dodge left, city officials blindly kept spending as if the company was still in town, quickly turning a surplus into a deficit. Reality only set in about two years ago, and the payroll has been cut from 178 to 91, with some employes wearing two or more hats. Jeff Freudenberg, for one, is city clerk, treasurer, public works director and golf course manager. Total city spending is down about 30% from 1977. Some roads are gouged and rutted, and the police must buy used cruisers when the old ones wear out. But the city is in the black again.

Bisbee's future is murky, however. It has been unable to lure a single new industry. Its faltering retail base is lopsided; you can buy wood-carvings and stained glass in town, but many people drive elsewhere to shop for food and clothing. A city-run mine tour brings in tourist dollars, but there are few first-class motel rooms, and most merchants, out of habit or lethargy, don't open on Sundays to take full advantage of the trade.

But Bisbee also has real beauty, a splendid year-round climate, and grit. "This is a town of survivors," says Jean Redmond, director of the chamber of commerce. Using those assets, it has become a center for bicycle racing and last year wrested the U.S. national championships from San Diego. Now the industrial development authority is wrapping up a $750,000 package of grants and loans to transform an old art-deco Phelps Dodge building into a center for meetings and small conventions, including a restaurant and shops.

Bisbee should have tried to diversify 10 years ago, says Mayor Lynn, but was lulled into complacency by the benevolent presence of Phelps Dodge. The company is studying potential for gold and silver in the area but hasn't yet decided on mining again. If it does, it may have to operate in a cooler civic climate. "A town should never, never depend on a single business, and we never will again," says the mayor.

THE OLD HEARTLAND
Elmira Will Never Be What It Used to Be, But Is Far From Dying

Town in Upstate New York Loses Plants and People; Opportunities Still Exist

Reporter Goes Home Again

BY JAMES M. PERRY

ELMIRA, N.Y.   10/27/81

Between 1880 and 1890, this city on the Chemung River in upstate New York grew by 50.4%. There were 48 hotels downtown, some of them respectable, and 67 passenger trains stopped at the three railroad stations every day.

There was history to the place, too. Regiments from George Washington's army destroyed the Iroquois Indian Confederation in a battle here. Mark Twain, summering at Quarry Farm, wrote some of his masterpieces here. At one time, this was the fire-engine capital of the world; later it was the typewriter capital. And because gliders are made here, it still thinks of itself as the soaring capital of the world.

But things just aren't the same these days.

The population, as measured by the 1980 census, is 35,327, down 4,618 from 1970, and even down 345 from Elmira's turn-of-the-century salad days. Now there isn't a single hotel downtown, and the last passenger train went through here in 1970. The typewriter business—it once employed 6,600 people—is gone, and the fire-engine company is owned by an Ohio-based conglomerate. The glider company almost went out of business two years ago.

Elmira, the Cassandras will tell you, is dying.

Something Special

If so, this reporter would regret it. I was born here, and my forebears settled here long ago. The family business, an insurance agency in which my brother is a partner, was founded in 1860.

Elmira is special to me, but it isn't so different from dozens of other small cities that stretch across the old industrial heartland from Massachusetts to Wisconsin. In all the hand-wringing about the problems of big cities in this belt—Buffalo, for example, or Cleveland—the fate of these smaller cities generally has been neglected.

So I came here to see if there is any life in the old home town—and, by extrapolation, in the rest of these towns.

There is, first of all, conventional wisdom to consider. Conventional wisdom says that industry has left these small cities, with their strong unions, for the Sun Belt. Conventional wisdom, especially regarding Elmira, also says that people are "down" on their future. "Elmira seems to think it's always going to lose," says Democrat Stanley Lundine, the district's Congressman.

But, after spending a week here, talking to people and touring the plants and businesses, I think there is good news: Elmira isn't dying; it is changing. It just wore out, and the recovery is slow and painful—and a little depressing, for Elmira will never be the town it used to be.

Sign of Change

Some changes are obvious. The day I arrived, workmen were removing the signs from Sears, Roebuck's downtown store. Sears is abandoning downtown for its new store in the Arnot Mall in Big Flats, halfway to Corning. One of my relatives is so angry about it that she cut up her Sears credit card.

And many of the old factories aren't exactly humming. The one we called "The Eeeclipse"—it was the Eclipse division of Bendix Corp.—employed almost 9,000 people during World War II, making cannons and artillery fuzes. The plant is half empty now, a part of Facet Enterprises, and fewer than 700 people work in it, making auto parts.

Despite the conventional wisdom, though, the Sun Belt was never a factor. Typical of Elmira's trouble is what happened to Remington Rand. In 1937 it was offered—and accepted, for nothing—the old Willys-Morrow plant, which had employed 6,000 workers in the 1920s, making transmissions, universal joints and gears for Overland and Willys-Knight automobiles. My grandfather was a manager at the plant, and I still have a pistol he carried—carried unhappily, for he was a gentle man—during periods of labor unrest. Elmira was a tough labor town.

The Remington Rand plant became the biggest office-machine factory in the world, or at least Remington boasted that it was. But in the mid-1950s, the company began switching production abroad. In 1972, it closed the plant entirely, moving its last operation north to Canada, not south to the Sun Belt.

Conglomerate Units

Other plants remain in operation here, but many of them are owned now by conglomerates, with headquarters far away. Kennedy Valve, for example, has been a local institution since 1907; it is now a subsidiary of ITT Grinnell Corp. of Providence, R.I. LRC Electronics Inc. is a division of Augat Inc. of Mansfield, Mass. American Bridge is part of U.S. Steel Corp.

And what is perhaps the city's best-known company, American LaFrance, the maker of those handsome custom-made fire engines, is a subsidiary of Figgie International, Harry Figgie's personal conglomerate (it also makes baseball bats) based in Willoughby, Ohio.

The president of the American LaFrance Division is Gerald Peters, who comes from Kentucky and displays in his office an autographed picture of former Alabama Gov. George Wallace. He isn't a typical Elmira businessman.

But he knows something about trucks, and maybe he is a lesson for Elmira. He came here, people say, to close down this plant. It was old and shabby and the work force wasn't very efficient.

"You wouldn't believe it," he says, "but they were making fire trucks in *stalls*. People brought the parts to the stalls and they put the trucks together. You couldn't tell which truck would be finished first. It depended on the foreman; if he was tough, he'd cannibalize parts from the next stall. We've got conveyor lines now, and it's a lot more efficient."

They also have a new plant, thanks to hard work over 10 years by the city, the county and the state, and here the story comes full circle. LaFrance is moving production into the old Remington Rand plant, where the Willys-Morrow plant used to be. It has been completely renovated, and Mr. Peters says the fire-engine business is here to stay.

Not just fire trucks, either. Mr. Peters reasons that there is more garbage to be collected than there are fires to put out. So he has taken his plant into the production of what he calls "refuse chassis" and what the rest of us call garbage trucks. When he heard that the Egyptian army wanted 200 trailers to carry tanks, he picked up that contract, too. "We opened the old Lehigh Valley Railroad repair shop in Sayre (Pa.), went out on the street to sign up 40 welders and turned those trailers out in nine months," Mr. Peters says. "You can't sit back these days and just wait for new business."

Others here understand that. Richard Evans is one of the city's movers and shakers and the owner of a roofing business. When business dried up here, he bought a plane and flew off and found business elsewhere. A local construction company, facing the same kind of problem, went off to the Chesapeake Bay area to build a bridge.

What Mr. Peters has done for American LaFrance is greatly admired by local business people, but there is a down side to it.

"When these companies were locally owned they did their business here," says Boyd McDowell II, president of Chemung Canal Trust Co., Elmira's only locally owned bank. "They banked locally. But now American LaFrance banks in Ohio; Kennedy Valve does its business in Rhode Island. And they all 'ride the float,' because the farther away the bank is, the longer they can hang on to their money. More and more, we are learning we have to depend on our local people and our local companies. That's our future."

One of the local companies everyone roots for is Schweizer Aircraft Corp. Anyone flying into the Elmira airport (on the few flights that remain) knows about its gliders. Other aircraft seem to weave through the gracefully swooping sailplanes to reach the runway.

Schweizer was founded by three brothers who began building sailplanes when they were in high school. One of them, William, remains at the helm. Gliders don't sell very briskly these days, though, priced as they are from a knocked-down $18,000 model to a competition special at $40,000. "It's a luxury item," says William Schweizer, who, at 63, still soars in them regularly.

The craze now, he says a little sadly, is for hang gliders. But Schweizer doesn't build them and doesn't want to. The suspicion arises that maybe if American LaFrance's Gerry Peters were running Schweizer, he would be making hang gliders.

Schweizer survives on a more mundane product—a crop-dusting, bi-wing aircraft called the Ag-Cat. For 20 years, Schweizer made the plane for Grumman Corp., until Grumman cut Schweizer adrift two years ago. "We lost 80% of our business and had to lay off more than half of our 550 employes," says Paul Hardy Schweizer, Bill's son and a company vice president. "A big company, one of those conglomerates, would have closed the plant. We decided to tough it out. That's what it means to be involved in a community."

Now, Schweizer has bought out the Ag-Cat business and is back in production under its own name, turning out one plane a week. At the same time, the company hustled new contracts—making wing tips for Boeing's new 757 airplane, cargo doors for Beech's Super King Air 200s, even—in a one-shot deal—the tail assembly for something called the Cyclo-Crane, a cross between a blimp and a dirigible that is designed to lift and transport heavy objects.

"We feel we've made this a solid company that no longer will be subject to economic vicissitudes," says young Mr. Schweizer, who came home to his family's business after working eight years in Seattle for Boeing.

A Continuing Fantasy

Some of Elmira's business leaders continue to fantasize about some great national company's coming here to open a huge new plant and put Elmira back together the way it used to be. Last year, the entire Elmira establishment joined forces to bid for a 1.1 million-square-foot engine plant that was to be constructed jointly by J. I. Case Co. and Cummins Engine Co. The total investment was to be $356 million, and the local community, with the cooperation of local and state government, came up with $150 million in incentives. Elmira's industrial-development agency put in thousands of hours pulling the deal together.

"We understand they looked at 196 sites in North America, and we were one of the three finalists," says Andrew Pazahanick, the development agency's executive director. But as things turned out, space opened up in one of Cummins's own plants in North Carolina, and a new plant wasn't needed. A postscript: Elmira wouldn't have won anyway. Says Cummins executive James Shipp: "It was in the final five, but we had concluded it was too far out of the transportation area for our customers and suppliers."

The fact is that Elmira isn't likely to see another new plant that employs thousands of workers. Unemployment here stands at 8.4%, compared with 7.5% nationally. But significant industrial opportunities still exist.

Not long ago, General Electric Co. left town, closing its foundry that had been a fixture here for decades. But a funny thing happened. Representatives of Trinity Valley Iron & Steel Co. of Ft. Worth,

Texas, deep in the heart of the Sun Belt, came to Elmira to look at the equipment, with the idea of buying some and taking it home. Instead, they bought the foundry and put it back into production. Employment, at 300 people, is back to where it used to be, and orders totaling $20 million are already backed up.

"We're delighted with our work force here," says Thomas Kowalik, a foundry official. "They speak English."

Confidence and Passion

There are successful smaller companies here, and surely they represent the future. The Hilliard Co. employs 175 workers and makes industrial clutches and oil-filtering equipment. It plans to expand. "We're going to make it here," vows Vinton Stevens, the president. Hardinge Brothers employs almost 1,000 workers and makes high-precision lathes and related equipment. "We're happy here," says its president, Robert Bauman. "We aren't moving."

Every city needs people with passion. One such person here is George Zurenda, president of Elmira Stamping Co. It was Mr. Zurenda's idea to convert the old Keeney Theater into what is now the Samuel Clemens Performing Arts Center, with attractions such as the New York Philharmonic Orchestra. The center has given Elmira a much-needed boost.

And every city needs an eccentric genius. Elmira has one in Whitney Powers, who started his company, Powers Manufacturing, in a chicken coop in 1959. He had worked for a glass-bottle maker here for years and saw the need for a new product—an electronic machine to test and inspect glass bottles. He invented one and now he produces it. "It's the American way," he says. "I saw a need and I filled it."

When Mr. Powers found that he couldn't get electronic circuit boards fast enough for his machines, he opened a separate business to manufacture them himself. Now, he says, small-time electronic geniuses from all over upstate New York are coming to purchase circuit boards for their own experiments. "These little guys are out there," Mr. Powers says. "Most of them come out of Cornell. I tell you, one day here, we're going to be the new Silicon Valley."

Now that's the old home-town spirit.

STAR OF SNOW BELT
Indianapolis Thrives On Partnership of City, Business, Philanthropy

Metropolitan 'Unigov' Setup Helps Preserve City Core; A Push for New Job Bases

Domed Stadium for 'Hicks'?

BY FREDERICK C. KLEIN

INDIANAPOLIS   7/14/82

For a long time now, Indianapolis has been to the rest of the urban Midwest what Philadelphia is to New York: The butt of jokes about a dull town with residents to match.

Indianapolis is Indiana-No-Place or Naptown, as in snooze. It is where you spent a week one day, where the cabby tells you that the best place to eat around here is Chicago.

Indianapolisans play the game, too. Novelist Kurt Vonnegut Jr., a native son, said the city watches its annual 500-mile auto race one day and sleeps the rest of the year. Indiana Bell Telephone Co. besmirches the city's reputation for literacy by listing itself in the white pages under "Fone Company," among other ways.

There is a current brouhaha over whether a giant domed stadium a-building downtown should be named the Hoosier-dome, after Indiana's cherished countrified nickname; more than one observer has suggested that the only appropriate name for any professional football or baseball team that makes the stadium its home would be the Hicks.

Holding Its Own

In recent years, though, Indianapolis has done something that few of its putatively more cosmopolitan Northern neighbors can match: It has held its own against the Sun Belt in the war for population and jobs. It has even gained a bit.

Indianapolis isn't claiming victory yet. Its current unemployment rate of 9.5% about equals the national average, and the city itself experienced a population dip to just over 700,000 in the 1970s. But during the past decade it broadened its tax and job bases, and the population of its metropolitan area increased by 5%, to almost 1.2 million, making it the third-fastest-growing region with a million or more inhabitants in the Northeast and North Central states. (Minneapolis-St. Paul and Columbus, Ohio, grew faster.)

More important, city officials believe Indianapolis used the '70s to build a solid foundation for future growth. Its downtown is in the midst of a rebuilding boom that Republican Mayor William H. Hudnut III says will turn the city into an economic "cookie" instead of the "doughnut" other older towns have become. Indianapolis has singled out goods distribution, conventions, sports and scientific products as prime prospects for new-job development, and it is pursuing programs to woo them.

Mr. Hudnut and local businessmen tirelessly tout a "partnership" of government, business and philanthropy, especially the huge Lilly Endowment, that they assert is leading the city to a bright tomorrow. "Some people say an 'elite' runs this town. I don't like that word. I prefer 'leadership,'" says Frank McKinney Jr., the 43-year-old chairman of American Fletcher National Bank, the city's largest. "Over the last dozen years we've developed a process to hatch ideas and bring them to fruition."

Some Dissident Voices

Not everyone is pleased with the way things are going. Residents of some older city neighborhoods—particularly blacks, who make up almost 20% of Indianapolis's population—feel that their interests are being neglected and that they are left out of local decision making.

The most-recent focus of unhappiness has been the 63,000-seat domed stadium. Some here have questioned the wisdom of building such a unit in a city that has no big-league football or baseball teams, have taken exception to its price tag of $77 million (up from estimates of $65 million less than two years ago) and have opposed a 1% restaurant tax enacted to help pay off the bondholders.

"I'm not against progress, but I have difficulty supporting a stadium when our schools are woefully underfinanced and other city services are inadequate," says State Sen. Julia Carson, a black who has represented an Indianapolis district in the Indiana legislature since 1972. She adds, "The mayor and the Lilly Foundation wanted the stadium, so it was built. That's the way things are done here."

Mayor Hudnut is unapologetic about the project. "We're building the stadium downtown, so it will keep business in the city instead of letting it get away," he says. "It's being tied to our existing convention center in a way that it should pay for itself even without a lot of big-time sports events. It's the kind of productive facility that will pay off for everybody in the long run, the kind of thing more cities would build if they could."

The Unigov System

One big reason Indianapolis has been able to do what it has in the last dozen years is its unusual Unigov system, the partial consolidation of city and Marion County government that took effect in 1970. In a single act, the Indiana legislature increased Indianapolis's population by some 250,000 persons and its land area by about 275 square miles, propelling it into the top echelon of U.S. cities (it is 12th biggest in population now).

Enactment of the plan was made possible by the election in 1967 of mayor (now U.S. Senator) Richard Lugar, a Republican, and the 1968 GOP sweep of the Marion County state-legislature contingent. That enabled a Republican-controlled Indiana legislature to ram through without a referendum what York Willbern, a professor of political science at Indiana University at Bloomington, calls "the suburban takeover of a major city."

Unigov is a lot less neat or comprehensive than outsiders may think. Although such functions as zoning, planning, health, parks and capital improvements are handled countywide, Indianapolis retains its previous nine township school districts and separate city and suburban police departments. Three towns within city limits keep the right to elect their own mayors while also voting for the mayor of Indianapolis. The 56 taxing districts in Indianapolis send out 101 different combinations of tax bills. It is a sort of government by cafeteria that allows former suburbs to choose what city-wide functions they will or won't join.

Yet even its detractors say it has brought benefits. The mayor of Indianapolis now is the undisputed chief political executive of the county, with much-expanded powers, and the flight of jobs, taxes and middle-class citizens to the suburbs circumvented. "In most cities, you have a decaying core surrounded by suburbs filled with people who want nothing to do with it," says Prof. Willbern. "Because of Unigov, Indianapolis today thinks and acts like a single political community. The importance of that can't be discounted."

More concretely, Unigov has brought the city a solid line of Republican mayors who have successfully courted corporate business cooperation. Mr. Lugar was reelected in 1971. Mr. Hudnut, a Presbyterian minister and former congressman, won in 1975 and 1979, and he is expected to win a third term next year.

Business involvement in Indianapolis politics is channeled mostly through two groups with close ties to each other: the Greater Indianapolis Progress Committee and the Corporate Community Council. The GIPC is a broad-based organization that studies and recommends solutions to city problems. The CCC, composed of the "chief decision makers" of the largest firms in Indianapolis, places corporate resources behind selected projects.

The other major element in Indianapolis's revitalization has been the Lilly Endowment, whose assets of $763 million at the end of 1981 made it the nation's sixth-largest charitable foundation. The 45-year-old institution, created by the founders of Eli Lilly & Co., the pharmaceuticals concern based here, increasingly has swung its beneficiences to local causes with considerable effect.

Sports Center

Many of Lilly's local grants—to theaters, orchestras, colleges and museums—are typical for large foundations. Decidedly untypical is the money it has poured into capital projects of late. Its largest single gift was $25 million for the domed stadium. It also has kicked in $10.5 million for a just-completed championship swimming and diving facility here, $5 million for the planning of White River Park, a proposed giant amusement and exhibition area just outside the downtown, $4 million for a new track and field stadium and $700,000 for a track for bicycle races.

Indianapolis's drive to become a sports center has already paid off in a number of major national and international sports events. Foremost among them is the National Sports Festival, the annual

Olympic-warm-up competition, set for July 23 to 31. The event is expected to draw 2,600 athletes and about 50,000 other visitors.

The city hopes its push for more jobs in goods-distribution and scientific-products fields will make up for recent job losses in its bellwether auto-parts industry. It believes its position as a transportation center (several railroads and four interstate highways run through town) makes it a natural location for firms engaged in warehousing, transportation and wholesaling. Indeed, it added about 6,000 jobs in those areas between 1975 and 1980.

It is pinning its hopes for a science boom on Indiana University-Purdue University at Indianapolis (IUPUI), an entity formed in 1969 from a jumble of professional schools and extension courses run here by its parent institutions. The university is little known outside this city, and in true Indianapolis fashion it is denigratingly called "Ooey-Pooey" hereabouts. Still, its enrollment has grown to more than 23,000 from 13,000 at its formation, and it is gaining distinction for its medical school and work in agriculture and engineering.

Mourning for the Past

If none of the courses Indianapolis is taking seem particularly new, that is also in the city's character, observers say. "Indianapolis has always sat back, watched what was happening in the rest of the country, and picked what it liked," says George Geib, a history professor at Butler University here. "This was true of its late-blooming industrial development in the early 1900s and its recent moves into downtown renovation and big-time sports. The fact that we're always 10 or 15 years behind the times has given us a permanent sense of nostalgia. We mourn for the past even while we're hustling to catch up with the present."

The old ways survive, too, in Indianapolis's neighborhoods. Some newcomers say it isn't easy to break into the established friendship and family patterns of longtime residents.

"It's basically a lazy town, very Southern in flavor," says Brian Vargas, a professor of sociology at IUPUI and a native of California. "It's a friendly enough place, but only if you've been here awhile. People spend Sundays visiting Grandma or Aunt Susie, not having barbecues with their neighbors. In other big cities where I've lived, the first question you're asked at a party is, 'What do you do for a living?' Here it's, 'Where are you from?' or 'What religion are you?'"

Even this may be changing. Earlier this year, people here were shocked when figures released by the National Center for Health Statistics showed Indianapolis's divorce rate to be the highest of any big city in America.

The Indianapolis Star, the city's largest-circulation paper, headlined its story on the subject "Top U.S. Divorce Rate Baffles Hoosier Experts." Indianapolis residents like to think of themselves as "family-oriented and unspoiled by the excesses of both coasts" the story said, but they "apparently are struggling with the same stresses that beset other parts of the country."

POLITICS

Grass Roots
On Up

'GROUND ZERO'
Town of Pella, Iowa, Talks of Little Other Than Nuclear Attack

Group Favoring Arms Freeze Stresses Atomic Horrors, But Some Ears Are Deaf

Refugees From Des Moines?

BY JOHN J. FIALKA

PELLA, IOWA 4/16/82

What is known here as "the movement" began one day in early February when a black-bordered advertisement ran in the local weekly paper, the Pella Chronicle.

The ad wasn't prominently placed. It ran inside the paper right under an announcement of the "Annual Colorful Cutie Contest" by a local photography studio and next to M.M. "Dock" Dockendorff's weekly gardening column.

But it did have an eye-catching headline: "Wanted: People Who Don't Want to Die in a Nuclear Holocaust."

There were already isolated pockets of nuclear angst growing in this rural, conservative and stubbornly prosperous town of 8,000 people in central Iowa. What that ad provided was the spark, the catalyst that brought parishioners out of some of the local churches, teachers from the town's two high schools, and students and faculty from Central College. Together, they sat down to map out a week of activism designed to teach people about the horrors of nuclear war.

"Ground Zero Week" will begin here and in several hundred other towns and cities across the nation Sunday. Seen from the top down, it is a novelty: a do-it-yourself movement based on mail-order kits drawn from government research on the effects of nuclear weapons.

"In the Mainstream"

"We didn't want to go through existing peace groups," explains Ground Zero's founder, Roger C. Molander, a 41-year-old physicist who served from 1974 to 1981 on the National Security Council staff, advising the White House on nuclear-targeting strategies.

Mr. Molander and his brother Earl, a Harvard Business School professor, set out in the spring of 1981 to establish a new organization composed mainly of people who had never been in a movement before. "We wanted to be in the mainstream," says Roger Molander, who developed the movement from his office in Washington.

A great deal has happened since then. Citizens in over 250 New England towns and members of several state legislatures have passed resolutions endorsing a nuclear-weapons freeze. Activists in California are busy collecting some 500,000 signatures, enough to put the issue on the ballot in November. A growing number of Catholic bishops are pushing the church to take a pro-freeze stance when the bishops meet on the matter in November. The drive is also picking up substantial strength in Congress, where Democratic Sen. Edward Kennedy of Massachusetts and Republican Sen. Mark Hatfield of Oregon are leading a bipartisan effort.

And now, after a year of organizing effort and the expenditure of $300,000 (much of the money, according to Earl Molander, coming from "younger members of the Rockefeller family"), Ground Zero is about to hit the streets in an attempt to reach the nonactivists.

Dramatic Effects

More specifically, on Sunday it will hit the town square here when a small group of people, including Mayor C.B. "Babe" Caldwell, will erect a large sign near Tulip Tower, an imposing red, white and blue structure that is normally used for Tulip Time, Pella's springtime festival of flowers and Dutch folk activity. The sign will say:

"If This Were Ground Zero, a One Megaton Nuclear Explosion Would Totally Destroy Virtually Everything Within Two Miles of This Spot—Instantly."

Seen from the bottom up—from just one of the many cities and towns where it is taking root—the Ground Zero movement may have problems, but it doesn't want for dramatic effects.

Nancy Cannon, a 35-year-old registered nurse here in Pella, sent for a Ground Zero information kit after reading about the movement in a publication of the American Lutheran Church, one of a number of sponsoring organizations lined up by the Molanders. Mrs. Cannon was looking for a social issue that her church, Peace Lutheran Church, could become involved with. But when the kit arrived, she saw she would have to make some modifications.

Symbol of a Threat

The Ground Zero kit contains two "educational" scenarios. One assumes a city large enough to be hit by a one-megaton warhead. (A megaton blast is about 50 times the explosion that caused 75,000 deaths at Hiroshima.) The other, "Post-Nuclear Scenario for Small American Cities," describes a small town that is gradually overwhelmed by burned, irradiated, diseased and starved refugees streaming away from the blast areas. Des Moines, the state's capital, is 40 miles northwest of Pella.

Mrs. Cannon decided she couldn't use the small-town scenario. "I just didn't think people would believe it. It sounded like a fairy tale."

She and other leaders of the local movement agree that Pella probably doesn't fit in the category of cities that would be struck by a one-megaton warhead, but they decided to build their campaign around the Ground Zero marker anyway, using it as a kind of a symbol of the threat that hangs over everyone.

Sometimes this distinction doesn't come across. "Just as a point of information, there is absolutely nothing in Pella that would exist if it (the destruction) went out to two miles, would it?" asked a woman at an organizing meeting at Peace Lutheran earlier this week. Told that nothing would exist, the woman seemed relieved, and said, "Good, that's what I told the teachers."

Teachers and students are a major focal point of the Pella campaign. Helen Boertje, a biology teacher at the local public high school, explains that teaching materials on the effects of nuclear weapons have been distributed to teachers in the city's public and parochial schools from the sixth grade up.

"We're sort of teaching it like Earth Day," she explains, noting that some teachers will give extra credits for students who bring their parents to the central event of Ground Zero Week, a rally and lecture under the Tulip Tower on Thursday night.

Mayor Caldwell, the owner of the Ideal Pharmacy, says that many of the older people in town are skeptical about Ground Zero but that the students are different. "You may think they aren't listening, but they are, especially on this atomic deal, nuclear bombs and so forth," the mayor says.

At Central College, a 1,400-student liberal-arts school run by the Reformed Church, many of the students had already been sensitized on the issue by another group: Physicians for Social Responsibility. It has been distributing a film, "The Last Epidemic," portraying the destruction that would result from a thermonuclear strike on San Francisco.

"It shakes students in a very fundamental way," explains Tom Boogaart, a 31-year-old religion teacher at Central College. "They begin to think about life and death, about the future and children."

Shelly Davis, a 22-year-old senior at Central, says she and some other students set out to dramatize the issue by figuring out how many people in Pella would die from a one-megaton strike on Des Moines. "We wanted to have students with stickers on saying 'I'm dead.'"

The problem was, she explains, that the college physics professor calculated that there wouldn't be any immediate casualties, not even from a 20-megaton blast in Des Moines. "Oh, the water supply here (the Des Moines River) would be contaminated, but we didn't think it would be dramatic enough," says Miss Davis.

Finally the students decided to cover one wall of the college's cafeteria with a map of the Midwest showing large rings around Chicago, Des Moines, Omaha and the missile fields of the Dakotas. "Everyone is bound to have a relative or somebody that is involved," Miss Davis explains.

Fire and Brimstone

Nuclear fire and brimstone have been raining down every Sunday from the pulpit of the Third Reformed Church, a phenomenon that resulted in Jim Cobb, manager of Lee's variety store, being dragged to one of Nancy Cannon's organizing meetings by his wife.

Mrs. Cannon and others in the movement insist that it is purely educational, not political, but Mr. Cobb isn't buying any of that. "A lot of the businessmen here are nervous about it," he confided during a Ground Zero presentation to the Pella Early Risers Kiwanis Club. "Everybody here is anti-nuclear war, of course, but they don't want to see it tied to any kind of freeze."

There were others, too, who were difficult to reach. Several churches have failed to respond. After considerable effort, Mrs. Cannon managed to get all of the town's seven doctors to sign a statement saying they were against the horrors of nuclear war and were for disarmament negotiations. "Some doctors signed it just to get me out of their offices," she says.

Publicity has been a problem. In Des Moines, the movement's organizers are handling it by simulating a nuclear attack and then inviting television camera crews and reporters to ride from "Ground Zero" in a Lutheran church bus while Dr. Bery Engebretsen, primed with horrific infomation from the Physicians for Social Responsibility, conjures up visions of the devastation.

Pella doesn't have a television station. What it has is Yvonne Jirak, 28 years old, who functions as the Chronicle's entire full-time editorial staff. She went to the first Ground Zero meeting and agreed to become a member of the group's steering committee. "Then they said, 'How do we get this into the paper?' and they all turned around and looked at me."

This gave her a conflict-of-interest problem, one that she later explained in a column to the Chronicle's 4,000 readers, saying there were "checks and balances" at the paper that would prevent her from overemphasizing Ground Zero.

Snappy Headlines

Nevertheless, she has managed to get off some snappy headlines: "Nuclear Blast Blinds People 40 Miles Away." And in one column she confessed that she has always thought she would die in a nuclear attack. "When it happens, I just want to gather my closest loved ones around me, tell them I love them and wait to die."

By the time Thursday night rolls around, if there is any lingering confusion about whether tiny Pella could be hit by a one-megaton nuclear warhead, Dr. Engebretsen—the same physician who will lead the bus tour in Des Moines—will arrive here to give further explanations. Dr. Engebretsen, the director of the primary-care unit at Broadlawn Hospital in Des Moines, will deliver the windup speech under the Tulip Tower; and he maintains that during an all-out nuclear exchange, a thermonuclear warhead might hit or fall near Pella because Soviet missiles may not be that accurate.

"I don't purposely set out to try and produce fear in people, although I am aware that that often happens," he explains. "People have the right to know the reality of the situation."

When he finishes describing the horrors, Dr. Engebretsen will advocate something he calls "transarmament," a kind of unilateral disarmament that would replace weaponry with passive-resistance tactics.

And that is bound to set Mr. Cobb's teeth on edge. "If I could express a personal feeling here," he told his fellow Kiwanians, "I feel it (disarmament) would be ineffective. We would have to trust everybody in the world, and this world has been born and raised on warfare."

Finally, there are probably some in Pella who will never get the word. "Anti-nuclear?" responded the plump, smiling woman in the Pella Chamber of Commerce office. "I don't know a thing about that. All I know about is Tulip Time, Tulip Time, Tulip Time."

CITY ON THE MOVE

Mayor Schaefer Guides Baltimore Renaissance With a Personal Touch

*He Cuts Through Red Tape
And Coaxes Executives;
Abandoned Homes Saved*

But Can the Gains Continue?

BY DEBORAH A. RANDOLPH

BALTIMORE 8/27/80

Once he was too shy to call businessmen on the telephone, but nowadays Mayor William D. Schaefer is perfectly at ease twisting the arms of corporate bigwigs.

One day the bigwig was Coy Eklund, president and chief executive of Equitable Life Assurance Society of the U.S. The big insurance company had decided to back out of a planned $20 million investment in a harbor-front Hyatt hotel. When he heard the news, Mayor Schaefer swung into action.

"How dare they!" he recalls thinking. Furious, he telephoned a top financial officer at Equitable's headquarters in New York. The executive brushed him off. Undaunted, the mayor called Mr. Eklund and turned on the charm. He persuaded Mr. Eklund to visit Baltimore. The mayor wined him, dined him and showed him the town. When Mr. Eklund left, he had agreed to make the $20 million hotel investment—and said he would think about committing $50 million more.

Mr. Eklund says it was Mayor Schaefer's "direct participation" that made him change his mind.

Mayor Schaefer has changed many things in Baltimore since he took charge nine years ago. Getting new hotels is just one of his accomplishments. Overall, only his harshest critics would disagree that the nation's eighth-largest municipality is a better place than it was in 1971. And most would agree it is no longer fair to lump Baltimore with genuine urban basket cases such as Newark, N.J., Cleveland and St. Louis.

"When I moved here 12 years ago, Baltimore was a dirty old rundown city next to Washington," says George P. Laurent, executive director of Baltimore Neighborhoods Inc., a nonprofit housing-information agency. "Mayor Schaefer came along and changed things." For instance:

—In a city where bureaucratic red tape cuts only one way, the long way, Mayor Schaefer has circumvented the bureaucracy on dozens of major projects. Special quasi-public bodies have supervised everything from a $21 million aquarium to a $725 million renovation of the city's inner harbor. City councilmen hate the system, but businessmen love it. The mayor "has made Baltimore one of the easiest cities to do business in," says Charles Ackerman, an Atlanta developer who is building a $37 million office tower here.

—In a city that is 55% black and was badly scarred by the 1968 race riots, the Schaefer administration has helped create a highly visible neighborhood renaissance. The city has given away over 500 abandoned houses for $1 apiece to urban homesteaders who promise to fix them up, and has provided everything from mortgage money to a "salvage depot" that sells old door knobs, stair railings and the like at bargain prices. Lately, the city has started selling decrepit old commercial shells for $100 to small-businessmen who have turned them into delicatessens, gift shops, beauty salons and ice-cream parlors.

—And in a city that depends heavily on money from Washington and Annapolis, Maryland's capital, Mayor Schaefer has mastered the art of obtaining such aid. Since 1974, Balitmore has raked in $31 million in discretionary funds from the U.S. Department of Housing and Urban Development. That amount puts Baltimore in fourth place in the nation in receiving these funds.

Recount Demanded

As if to prove that he fights hard for federal dollars, Mr. Schaefer recently demanded a census recount after a preliminary tally showed that Baltimore's population had slipped to 740,000 from 900,000 a decade ago. Census tallies are important because much federal aid is tied to population levels.

It is questionable, however, whether Washington and Annapolis, which together provide 64% of Baltimore's budget money, will continue to play sugar daddy in the 1980s. Both the city's federal aid and the state's, much of which goes to the city eventually, face trimming in line with the new mood of fiscal austerity on Capitol Hill. "They're going to cut back on (federally financed) jobs, cut social programs—all the things that directly affect us," the mayor laments.

The $1.3 billion city operating budget for fiscal 1981 is showing signs of strain, and the mayor may have to scale back some of his ambitious dreams. Already, 50 city employes have been laid off, and water and sewer rates have been raised by 15%.

In the meantime, the mayor's popularity seems undiminished since last November, when he won reelection to a third term by clobbering his opponent, State Rep. Patrick McDonough. Mr. McDonough eked out just 18% of the vote. "Mr. Schaefer has a tight organization," he says, "and he knows the neighborhoods."

Baltimore is a working-class-neighborhood town, and the mayor is very much a working-class-neighborhood creature. A 58-year-old bachelor, he still lives with his mother in the same West Baltimore house where he grew up. He attended local schools and City College of Baltimore and got a law degree from the University of Baltimore. Later he spent 17 years as a Democrat in city government, working his way up to president of the City Council before winning the mayoralty with 85% of the vote in 1971.

Housing quickly became the administration's top priority. Back then, hundreds of Baltimore's distinctive row houses had fallen into decay as middle-class families fled from the city for the suburbs, leaving in their place poor families who couldn't afford to keep the neighborhoods up.

"Something needed to be done before the blight spread further," the mayor recalls.

The city more or less stumbled onto the row-house rehabilitation plan: When the Nixon administration put a moratorium on new federal housing in 1973, the city scrapped plans to demolish a block of row houses and decided to rehabilitate them instead.

Initially, the city gave away 25 houses for $1 each, providing 6% loans from a city bond issue so that homeowners could refurbish their bargain castles. The idea caught on and spread to many sections of the city—along the developing waterfront and in scattered sections of East and West Baltimore.

The $1 houses even drew people who work in Washington, D.C., 42 miles away. Christopher Pierson is one refugee from the astronomical housing prices in the nation's capital. (By one estimate, 3,000 persons commute from Baltimore to Washington every day.) "I heard about what they were doing in Baltimore, and I was interested," says Mr. Pierson, a printer at a Washington insurance company. He fixed up his house with a 7%, $30,000 loan from the city.

Some Black Leaders Upset

The homesteading program has riled some black leaders. "The mayor's priorities are out of whack," says Robert Cheeks, executive director of the Baltimore Welfare Rights Organization. He and other blacks charge that the program has brought many middle-class whites into the city only by forcing out thousands of low-income blacks.

The mayor "should be more concerned about the people already living here and not on attracting new ones," Mr. Cheeks says. It is true that many poor blacks have left the city, but the Schaefer administration denies that they are forced out and notes that those who can't afford to renovate their homes can get assistance from the city to relocate within Baltimore.

By and large, the mayor is popular among blacks. His political machine is built on neighborhood civic groups—black and white—and much of his popularity is built on neighborhood visits. He frequently drives around town at odd hours to check out potholes or trash dumps. "I get some of my fun riding around the street looking at alleys on Saturdays and Sundays," he says.

During his drives, the mayor takes copious notes, turning them into acerbic memos to his aides. A recent one to the public-works director read as follows: "I saw trash (in a certain East Baltimore alley) stacked above my head. If you haven't seen it yet, may I suggest you get your eyes examined? I want action!" Then he drove past the site a few days later to check up. The trash was gone.

Ignoring the Council

If the mayor browbeats his staffers, he frequently does his best to ignore the City Council. He has established more than 20 quasipublic agencies to run those big projects. The special agencies pay their top managers some 25% to 33% above city wages, and the agencies aren't accountable to the council.

"It would take too long if we had to hold hearings on every project," the mayor says. "We are strangled with red tape."

Critics have lambasted the special agencies, calling them a "shadow government." Thomas Waxter, a city councilman, says that "there should be political checks on the fact that (Mr. Schaefer) can just set up these things" without council or voter approval. Mr. Waxter recently co-introduced a bill that would require the bodies to publish full budgets and submit them to the City Council for approval.

Apparently the mayor doesn't take the criticism very seriously. After the Baltimore Sun ran a series of stories on the "shadow government," Mr. Schaefer showed up at a gathering of business leaders dressed in a black cape and top hat that recalled "The Shadow" of comic-book and radio fame.

Harborplace and Coldspring

Many residents seem unconcerned, too. All they see is a grubby downtown being transformed into a modernistic amalgam of glass, brick and steel. They also see the new expressways, the new public-transit systems, and the complete renovation of the so-called Inner Harbor. Last month they saw the opening of Harborplace, a glass-enclosed cluster of specialty shops and restaurants on the harbor.

One of the most ambitious projects of all is a $200 million "new town within the city" called "Coldspring," about four miles from downtown Baltimore. Publicly financed but privately developed, it will ultimately house some 12,000 residents on a 375-acre tract of land. It is designed to attract young middle-class homeowners and renters in an effort to shore up the city's tax base.

The big question now is whether Baltimore can continue such grand dreams in the face of cutbacks in state and federal financing. Mayor Schaefer vows to go on building. "Redevelopment gives our people jobs," he says, "and we've got to continue."

Brash B.T. Collins Handles the People For the Brown Camp

He Provides Common Touch For California's Governor; Bullwhip Thrills the Kids

BY CARRIE DOLAN

SACRAMENTO, CALIF. — 7/19/82

It is a Tuesday night and a former Green Beret is telling dirty jokes in the California Capitol. He has a hook arm, a big mouth and a lot of friends.

Across the hall, his boss, Gov. Edmund G. Brown Jr., is intently watching a slide show on solar energy near Tibet.

Their styles couldn't be more different, but their relationship is surprisingly effective. B.T. Collins is Jerry Brown's chief of staff, which is something like having a bourbon chaser after a cup of herbal tea. Mr. Collins is a 41-year-old, rusty-haired Republican who didn't even vote for Gov. Brown the first time he ran. He hates indecision, Jane Fonda and filtered cigarettes. But he loves his job.

People in California government say Mr. Collins is an invaluable asset to a governor not known for his common touch. While the governor wrestles with esoteric political concepts, Mr. Collins drinks with the Capitol crowd and sends birthday greetings to everyone's children.

"Everybody thinks Jerry Brown is a flake," says Mr. Collins, "but he's just so far ahead of his time. His mind is so full of ideas it's like a dump truck. So he handles the issues and I handle the people."

'The Science of Irreverence'

Mr. Collins handles them in a way most bureaucrats wouldn't dare. In an arena where most people watch every word they say, he never gives his a second glance. "He practices the science of irreverence," says a state senator. Mr. Collins calls the State Assembly a "(obscenity) day-care center" and a short staffer "Tattoo." Jacques Barzaghi, the governor's shiny-bald director of administration, finds it amusing when Mr. Collins calls him "pinhead."

"People feel bad if B.T. doesn't give them a name," says Alice Lytle, California's black director of state and consumer services. She finds Mr. Collins "absolutely charming" even if he has introduced her as the "governor's colored maid."

Although he lost two limbs in Vietnam, Mr. Collins has no patience with pity. When State Director of Rehabilitation Edward V. Roberts, himself a paraplegic, is wheeled around the Capitol grounds, Mr. Collins yells, "Get off the street, you cripple, you're depressing everybody in sight." Mr. Roberts, a close friend, says, "That's just B.T.'s way of saying he doesn't accept the old stereotypes about the disabled. He loves to shock people."

The governor's staff certainly got a shock when Mr. Collins burst in last October. His predecessor, now running for the State Assembly, had a polished, cautious style. Mr. Collins runs the show like a cross between a platoon and a saloon. He delegates much responsibility and wants prompt results. "There are two kinds of people," he says. "The quick and the dead. You have to make a decision and live with it." He relies heavily on his deputy, James Burton, whom he calls a "commie" because he has a beard. "A commie is anybody with a beard or a master's degree in sociology or who doesn't agree with me," explains Mr. Collins.

His office door is open to a steady stream of staff and sarcasm. "How about getting me some coffee?" he bellows out to his assistants. "Get it yourself," they reply. "Hey, I would, but I got an arm and a leg blown off in the war," he says. There are bottles of aspirin and Midol on his desk for those who complain too much. On a recent night, local reporters wanted to ask him questions after hours. The staff advised against it. Mr. Collins invited the reporters in, gave them information and vanilla wafers, then asked them to "please get the hell out of my office and write the (obscenity) truth for a change."

When grade-school children came to tour their State Capitol one day, the six-foot-two Mr. Collins stormed into the hall, waving his hook and the bullwhip he keeps in his office, and thundered, "Why aren't you in school?" An assistant to the governor recalls, "It made their trip."

B.T. (for Brien Thomas) does obnoxious things loudly and nice things quietly. He is the Sacramento Valley blood-bank chairman and a regular donor, as "payment" for the 39 pints he used after his injury. He keeps a list of about 300 birthdays, anniversaries and other dates that are special to friends, so he always remembers to call. After Terry Thomas, the deputy legislative secretary, had a big fight with the governor, Mr. Collins plunked two dozen roses on her desk and said, "I just want you to be happy here."

An apt political practitioner, the bachelor chief of staff dines in the Capitol cafeteria and sometimes drags his boss along. "It's good for him," Mr. Collins says. "People love it. They think the governor doesn't eat lunch or drink beer or pick his nose like anybody else."

His colorful comments make him a popular speaker at official functions and assorted taverns. A recent Monday night found Mr. Collins in a San Diego bar, downing Scotches and soda till last call and telling about the time he and other Army paratroopers dropped into the 1965 revolution in Santo Domingo. By 10 the next morning, he was delivering a much-applauded address to the 62nd annual convention of California Veterans of Foreign Wars. "He's the kind of man we need in politics. He doesn't give any double talk," remarked Walter W. Thompson, an ex-marine from Modesto.

Some Aren't Charmed

Not everyone is charmed by Mr. Collins's style. Shortly after he came on board, two agency heads resigned. Pearl West quit as youth-authority director after Mr. Collins canceled a conference she planned on juvenile delinquency. Al Loeb resigned as mental-health director when Mr. Collins killed public-service announcements aimed at aiding homosexuals.

At one point, Mr. Collins himself offered to quit. Last November, a Los Angeles Times reporter accompanied him on his routine bar rounds, then wrote about his remarks that the governor "is out on Uranus" and needs "to wash his hair." The resulting flap caused Mr. Collins to offer his resignation. But Gov. Brown refused it and ended up using the incident to inject some humor into his usually stoic style. Speaking on government austerity, he said he had saved the state a lot on shampoo.

"The only reason B.T. gets away with what he does is that he acts the same around everyone," says H. L. Richardson, who has been a Republican state senator for 16 years. "He's consistently outrageous, but he is consistent." (Demonstrating that, he addressed this reporter alternately as "kid" or "bimbo" or "the mouth.")

The Insecticide Drink

During the Medfly battle, he pulled his most-publicized stunt. Mr. Collins was then director of the California Conservation Corps, a state program hiring young people for environmental work. Corps members balked when he ordered them to pick tons of fruit that had been sprayed with the insecticide malathion. In an effort to prove that it was safe, he gulped an entire glass of diluted malathion.

He attracted attention in other ways when he took command of the CCC program in 1979. He gave it a slogan—"hard work, low pay, miserable conditions." A former corps member says, "He got down on us right away. He was part John Wayne, part Dizzy Dean and part Baretta." Recruits had to rise at 5 a.m., run two miles, work eight hours and take classes three nights a week. They were told to vote and give blood, and men had to sign up for the draft. Mr. Collins's standard line to the "troops" was, "You know I don't care about you. I don't care about your happiness. I just want a lot of hard work."

Those who survived his program saw through his macho talk. "He just says he doesn't care, to rile you up," says Sherri Johnson, 21, who was a Woolworth's cashier before joining the CCC two years ago. "He forces you to exceed your limits. The discipline really changes your life."

Mr. Collins, who was raised in New York, could have used that discipline in his younger days. He flunked out or was thrown out of three colleges before joining the Army in 1963. In Vietnam, an Army buddy recalls, Mr. Collins took a dislike to those military clergymen who stayed away from the action and delivered encouraging words to soldiers headed for combat. Registering his protest, the buddy says, Mr. Collins would disrupt services by loudly reading pornography outside the chapel.

Months in Hospital

His second tour of Vietnam ended in 1967 when a grenade he was lobbing exploded prematurely, costing him those two limbs and nearly his life. "He had one of the worst injuries in the ward, but he was a one-man pep rally," says Dr. Richard M. Sullivan, who worked at the military hospital where Mr. Collins spent 15 months recovering.

He went on to Santa Clara law school, where a stern and beautiful professor once chastised him before the class for not being prepared. When she asked if he had anything to say for himself, he replied, "Yes, ma'am, I'd just like to say that's a particularly attractive sweater you're wearing today." A former classmate recalls, "Even the professor had to laugh. B.T. has always had the ability to bring out warmth and humor, even in the most unwilling subjects."

Some say that's exactly why he's important to the governor. And if Gov. Brown manages to become Sen. Brown this November, he wants to take Mr. Collins to Washington. "We're a good team," says the governor. As for Mr. Collins, he wants a reporter to believe he is through with politics and plans to "run guns to the Falkland Islands" when his job ends.

But those close to him say he won't refuse a request from the governor, to whom he is fiercely loyal. "If the governor goes to Washington, B.T. will be the first one at the airport with his bags," says the bald Mr. Barzaghi, a friend of both men. "He'd love it," says John E. Dugan, the director of the CCC. Adds State Sen. Richardson, "In Washington, he'd just have a bigger bunch of bars to hit."

THE POWER BROKERS
A Registered Agent Helps Saudis Fathom And Sway Washington

But Fred Dutton Is Criticized By Some Fellow Liberals; Hottest Issue: Awacs Sale

Leaking Memos to Himself?

BY KAREN ELLIOTT HOUSE

WASHINGTON 3/29/82

The evening is something out of the Thousand and One Nights.

A handsome Saudi prince is leaving town. A Senator, a former governor, the chairman of the Joint Chiefs of Staff and a dozen of Washington's most powerful reporters assemble to say goodbye. They gather in a fabric-draped room designed to re-create the intimate allure of a harem. As they dine, drink and debate late into the night, a nubile young black woman serenades the prince with an old favorite, "My Way."

This fairy-tale evening offers a glimpse of one of Washington's master power brokers at work. He is Frederick Dutton, a lawyer, liberal Democrat and hired consultant to the government of Saudi Arabia.

A balding gnome with an irrepressible "hee, hee, hee" chuckle, Fred Dutton has been a Washington insider since he arrived in 1961 as a 37-year-old aide to President Kennedy. Already, he had served as chief of staff to California Gov. Edmund Brown. In the ensuing years, he worked in the campaigns of liberals such as Robert Kennedy, George McGovern and Arthur Goldberg and practiced a little law. Nothing very lucrative.

Then, seven years ago, the Saudis hired him on the recommendation of Rawleigh Warner, the chairman of Mobil Corp., a Dutton client. So now he sells his expertise and access to one of the world's most conservative regimes. The Saudis pay him and his lawyer wife, Nancy, so well—$400,000 last year alone—that he has only a few other clients, among them International Telephone & Telegraph Corp.

Mr. Dutton is one of an estimated 1,000 registered agents working here for foreign nations. These men and women occupy a special niche among Washington lobbyists: They lobby for specific changes in U.S. tax laws, immigration policies, import restrictions and so on to benefit their foreign clients. They must register every six months at the Justice Department. But, with exceptions such as Libya's controversial hiring of Billy Carter a couple of years ago, they rarely attract public attention.

What distinguishes Fred Dutton from the others is that he isn't just a foreign-interest lobbyist but a public-policy strategist. So involved is he in mapping Saudi political strategy toward the U.S. that he has established himself as *the* Saudi representative in this country.

"I don't know anyone else who does quite what Fred does," says Clark Clifford, the Washington lawyer and former Defense Secretary who until recently represented Algeria.

What Mr. Dutton does is much more ambitious than winning on any single issue—even one as important as last year's successful fight to sell Awacs radar planes to Saudi Arabia. He tries to teach the Saudis the inner workings of this alien political system so they can manipulate it to achieve their ends. Because they lack a domestic lobby such as American Jews provide for Israel, he coaches them on how to use powerful Americans ranging from top businessmen to even the President to do their lobbying for them. He also tries to take advantage of his many press contacts.

Being so close to a foreign nation would seem to pose difficult questions about how to balance your client, your country and your conscience. "Many of these people are motivated chiefly by loyalty to the dollar," says Joel Lisker, former chief of the Justice Department's foreign-agents registration unit.

Some of Mr. Dutton's fellow liberals privately say he has "sold out" to the wealthy Saudi monarchy. And although professional lobbyists for Israel don't question his loyalty, they criticize his tactics. "I've been involved in a lot of political fights in my day," says Thomas Dine, executive director of the American-Israel Public

Affairs Committee, "but I never saw anti-Semitism used as he did in the Awacs debate. It was abhorrent."

Mr. Dutton denies that there was any anti-Semitism in his Awacs efforts. And he scoffs at criticism by liberals that representing a foreign government raises serious questions about divided loyalty. "There's a lot of hypocrisy in liberals; they like blacks but not Arabs or Africans," he asserts. "If we can't learn to live with the Saudis, how can we learn to live with the rest of the Third World?"

Because by nature the Saudis tend to be vague and indecisive, Mr. Dutton is largely self-propelled. Sometimes he is summoned to Riyadh. But more often—at least four times a year—he goes there at his own initiative to commune with the younger, Western-educated princes and through them get a whiff of what's on the rulers' minds.

Relaxing in their homes during dinners and televised soccer games, he listens, observes and then shares gossip and insights into American politics. From these informal sessions emerges a mutual sense of direction.

At the heart of Mr. Dutton's strategy is his recognition of the central role of the media in shaping public policy. His contacts with journalists are unusually wide and his credibility unusually deep, and he exploits those ties to promote himself and his clients.

For instance, when the Carter White House sought to portray the Saudis as supporting the Egyptian-Israeli peace treaty and contended that Saudi Crown Prince Fahd's cancellation of a visit here in 1979 was due to illness, Mr. Dutton made sure that the media knew the real reason: Saudi unhappiness with the treaty. To the discomfort of presidential spokesman Jody Powell, it was Mr. Dutton's version that dominated news accounts.

"We were sandbagged," Mr. Powell says. The Saudis hadn't told the White House the real reason for the cancellation because they didn't want to offend the President.

More recently, Mr. Dutton used the press to launch the slogan that came to dominate last fall's Awacs debate. With President Reagan's proposed sale of the radar planes in deep trouble in Congress, Mr. Dutton told a newspaper interviewer, "If I had my way, I'd have bumper stickers plastered all over town that say 'Reagan or Begin?'"

The slogan caught on—achieving his goal of crystallizing the issue of whether a foreign leader such as Israel's Menachem Begin should have a veto (through mobilizing pro-Israeli support in Congress) over the American President's decision to sell Awacs.

Mr. Dutton's friendship with the press dates to the 1950s when, as a young California lawyer representing obscure sewer districts and city councils, he began a political column in the Los Angeles Times. Historian Arthur Schlesinger noticed the column and recruited him for Adlai Stevenson's presidential campaign—and launched Mr. Dutton's career in politics. Since then, he has cultivated journalists. To his frequent dinner parties come Washington Post Executive Editor Benjamin Bradlee, New York Times Washington Bureau Chief Bill Kovach, columnist Joseph Kraft, NBC-TV anchorman Roger Mudd, CBS-TV diplomatic correspondent Robert Pierpoint and others including this reporter.

A Popular Source

He rarely calls journalists, but he's so full of gossip and ideas that they call him. "If Fred were to start writing wills and trusts tomorrow, I'd still want to see him," says Sander Vanocur, ABC-TV's diplomatic correspondent. "He's the only guy I know who leaks his memos to himself."

Says Mr. Dutton: "I've lasted because I have credibility. I criticize the Americans, I criticize the Saudis, I criticize Israel. It's just my style to be frank."

His detractors suggest that his credibility often is selective, that he is more interested in enhancing his reputation for candor than in being loyal. "He's candid so long as it's in his interest," a longtime acquaintance says. For instance, after Mr. Dutton resigned as Gov. Brown's chief of staff to join the Kennedy White House, word began filtering back to California that President Kennedy considered the governor indecisive. When a Brown staffer accused Mr. Dutton of being the source of derogatory stories about his former boss, he recalls Mr. Dutton responding, "But I've got to be honest."

While Fred Dutton is attentive to the press, he is also solicitous of his Saudi clients. He recently gave Petroleum Minister Ahmed Zaki Yamani, a believer in astrology, a "moon clock" that records a 25-hour day based on the rising and setting of the moon, not the sun.

Helping the Prince

Prince Bandar, son of Saudi Arabia's influential defense minister and a favorite of the crown prince, also gets special attention. Without charge, Mr. Dutton has helped Prince Bandar with legal transactions ranging from the purchase of several homes to giving his car to a friend.

Because Mr. Dutton lacks access to the traditionally remote senior princes who run Saudi Arabia, his links with the younger, Western-educated princes and ministers are all-important. Besides Prince Bandar, his most important connections are Prince Saud, the foreign minister, and his brother, Prince Turki, the director of intelligence.

At their homes in Riyadh or around Europe, he holds tutorials on American politics, policy disputes in the Reagan administration, and such things as the mind and motivations of Ronald Reagan, whom Mr. Dutton knows well from his own days as a member of the California Board of Regents while Mr. Reagan was governor. To create camaraderie, the tutorials sometimes have the quality of bull sessions, including typical "men talk " about women.

Before Secretary of State Alexander Haig met Crown Prince Fahd last September in the Spanish town of Marbella, Mr. Dutton flew there to brief Prince Bandar, who briefed his uncle. The topic was Awacs. Similarly, in December, Mr. Dutton met with Prince Bandar in Geneva before Secretary Haig's meeting with the prince there.

Advice Often Ignored

Mr. Dutton says his clients often ignore his advice. He says he urged the Saudis not to ask the Reagan administration to sell Awacs—thus sparking a fight in Congress and leaving the White House with a sense that America had done Saudi Arabia a favor. "I felt we should be fighting in the Executive Branch for policy decisions in the Middle East, not for military hardware," he says.

When the Saudis went ahead, he warned that the fight in Congress would be difficult because an American President's wishes don't prevail as easily as do those of a Saudi king. Sure enough, the sale narrowly escaped Senate disapproval last October, by a 52-to-48 vote, exactly the margin of victory Mr. Dutton had predicted in a rare memo to the Saudis six months earlier. "Your value is enhanced if you say a Mack truck is coming at you and it does," he says of his warning to the Saudis.

He didn't lobby with either administration officials or lawmakers. He did meet with Democratic Sen. John Glenn of Ohio at the Senator's request but left the lobbying to the Saudis themselves. "The client is better informed," he says, " and besides most of these guys on the Hill haven't ever met a Saudi, so they need education not at an informational level but at an attitudinal level."

Administration Prodded

His major role in the Awacs fight appears to have been prodding the Reagan administration to ever greater lobbying efforts on behalf of the Saudi sale. "When I felt they were stalling, I told the Saudis," he says. To rectify matters, he helped Prince Bandar, the real Saudi lobbyist, prepare talking points for several meetings with the President, his counselor, Edwin Meese, Secretary Haig and a host of Senators. He helped target the Senators who might be moved by a visit from the Saudi prince and also suggested what arguments might be most persuasive.

He also advocated a lobbying role for big business. "Business is basically cowardly," he says. "They make money off the Saudis, but they want to keep their heads down in a controversy. I don't think they ought to get away with that."

Many Saudis agree. So Prince Bandar summoned a number of chief executive officers here and politely suggested that they lobby with their Senators to "support President Reagan" in his Awacs decision. Business support was heavy but not so decisive in the Senate vote backing the sale as was Mr. Reagan's own lobbying.

Because Mr. Dutton doesn't do much lobbying personally but rather does most of his talking to his clients, he has avoided major conflicts between himself and liberal friends who back Israel. And the former antiwar activist and opponent of U.S. arms sales rationalizes his client's huge purchases of U.S. arms by arguing that America can't rightly terminate arms to the Saudis without doing that to Israel too.

Mostly, Mr. Dutton maintains that he has been spared hard choices between his client and his country because Saudi Arabia is an ally of the U.S. As such, he argues, Saudi Arabia deserves the same opportunity to shape U.S. policy that Israel enjoys. "There's nothing disloyal," he says, "about helping a friend of America."

CAPITOL HILL STRAYS
Spiritual Descendants Of Old Sam Maverick Enliven the Congress

*A Mixed Bag of Politicians—
Reformers and Rogues—
Thrive on Independence*

They Wear No Man's Brand

BY DENNIS FARNEY

WASHINGTON   11/12/81

One dreary afternoon, as the House of Representatives debated plant patents for hybrid okra, the tousle-haired figure of Rep. John Burton materialized to transform boredom into chaos.

The San Francisco-area Democrat seized the microphone with a question—a serious one, he insisted. Might not the proposed changes in plant-patent law lead to bureaucratic meddling in human reproduction?

Not "unless the gentleman can extract a fetus from okra, celery, peppers, tomatoes, carrots or cucumbers," answered a non-plused Rep. E. "Kika" de la Garza, the Texas Democrat who managed the legislation.

"I could do that," Mr. Burton replied airily. "In fact, I have seen it done. It was in the gentleman's district."

A fleeting expression crossed Mr. de la Garza's face. It was the expression of a man who stumbles into a nightclub and, inexplicably, finds himself playing straight man in a comedy act. The irrepressible Mr. Burton moved on to a discussion of genetics.

The Quipster

"If you cross a potato with a sponge, it takes a lot of gravy," he informed the House. "Or if you cross a rooster with a rooster, you get a cross rooster. But I think we are talking about something more serious here."

John Burton was being serious, in his fashion. "My style, whatever it is, is more effective than charts and graphs," he says. Through humor, he says, he is "often able to get to the heart of a piece of legislation and kick it in the ass." The plant-patent bill passed anyway. But that style, whatever it is, makes Mr. Burton part of a declining breed in Congress: the maverick.

Mavericks go their own way. The term originated with Samuel Maverick, a 19th century Texas rancher who refused to brand his cattle; thus, unbranded strays came to be called mavericks. Political mavericks also wear no man's brand. The term became firmly embedded in political folklore with the arrival in Washington of Samuel Maverick's grandson, Maury Maverick Sr., an outrageously independent Texas Congressman in the 1930s.

Legend has it that one fine Sunday morning Maury Maverick, an outspoken liberal, showed up at a straight-laced Episcopal church in San Antonio. "Why uh, Mr. Maverick," a woman parishioner greeted him sweetly. "I'm so happy to see you here. I've just never wanted to believe all those stories that you're a Communist."

All That Gossip

"By the same token, madame," Mr. Maverick replied, "I've never believed all that gossip that you're nothing but a street whore."

Modern-day mavericks, rarely so breathtakingly blunt, are a mixed bag. They include free spirits, loners, idealistic reformers and rogues. They tend to be their own worst enemies. They often walk fine lines of principle that only they discern. They often champion foredoomed causes. Yet, stubbornly, they refuse to change. Probably they couldn't change if they wanted to.

Henry Gonzalez, the volatile, crusading Democrat from San Antonio, a man who knew Maury Maverick, says it best:

"*Cada hombre tiene su tema.* Every man has his own peculiar theme. *Cada chango a su mecate.* Every monkey to his own swing."

And it is true. Even the dullest members of Congress, including the old men who regularly fall asleep at committee meetings, do have themes uniquely their own. Even in this increasingly homogenized Congress, where more and more members look like bank clerks, each member does have his own peculiar obsessions. What sets the mavericks apart is that their themes are more peculiarly peculiar.

The Mime's Muse

John Burton's theme is impertinence. One day last year he was watching a fellow member speak on television. With the sound turned down on his office television set, Mr. Burton could see the guy waving his arms and moving his lips, but he could not hear the words. All at once, Rep. Burton had an inspiration.

The next day he gave a speech of his own on the floor. He had interviewed the economic advisers of all the presidential candidates, he told the House, and he could confidently outline a three-point program for reviving the economy.

"Number one," he announced. His mouth continued to move. He flailed his arms. But he emitted no sounds. "Number two," he said clearly. Speaker Thomas "Tip" O'Neill leaned forward, straining to hear. "Number three. . . ."

"You just have to have fun here," says Rep. Burton, whose GOP opponent in 1980 threatened to use videotapes of such antics as campaign commercials. "Otherwise, this place would be bloody awful."

Andrew Jacobs's theme is flinty independence. " 'Cowards die many times before their deaths,' " says the Democrat from Indianapolis, who quotes Shakespeare often and easily. " 'The valiant never taste of death but once.'

"Usually sooner."

The 49-year-old Congressman came close to dying a political death at the start of this Congress when he refused to vote with his fellow Democrats on a party-line motion. The vote was on whether to shut off Republican debate so that the majority Democrats could get on with the business of organizing the House.

Mr. Jacobs voted with the GOP. (Philosophically, he opposes attempts to limit debate.) The next thing he knew, an irate Richard Bolling, the chairman of the powerful Rules Committee, was suggesting that Speaker O'Neill strip him of his committee seniority, purge him from the prestigious Ways and Means Committee and banish him to "Siberia," the District of Columbia Committee. But the tempest blew over after Mr. Jacobs wrote the Speaker justifying his vote.

"Evidently," observed Mr. Jacobs, triumphantly, "being in favor of democracy does not violate Democratic principles after all."

A Taste for Mr. Symington

If all of this makes Mr. Jacobs sound stuffy, nothing could be further from the truth, as a visit to his office establishes. There, below the sign, "Smoking Prohibited Under Penalty of Cancer," is a red doghouse. It is a memorial to the late C5, the dog that "grew like a government contract."

C5, a Great Dane, was named after the Air Force cargo plane of cost-overrun fame. Around the Capitol this hulking dog is best remembered for biting then-Congressman James Symington on the hand as Mr. Symington was heading for an elevator. An aberration, everyone supposed. But three years later, Mr. Symington showed up at an office party that Mr. Jacobs was throwing for the dog.

Mr. Symington offered C5 a bit of cheese. C5 ate the cheese, then bit him again.

"He was a hound of heaven," says Mr. Jacobs fondly.

Colleagues tend to accept mavericks more easily if, like Mr. Jacobs, they offset their principles with a certain zaniness.

Thus, even though his fellows tend to dismiss him as somewhat ineffectual, they have warm feelings for California Democrat Fortney "Pete" Stark, a white man who once attempted to join the Black Caucus.

There is a similar amused tolerance of arch-conservative California Rep. Robert Dornan, who is known for his hoarse-voiced tirades on all manner of subjects. One liberal Democrat savors the day that the Republican Mr. Dornan—who, incidentally, is a nephew of the late actor Jack Haley, the Tin Man in the "Wizard of Oz"—launched into an impassioned defense of the B1 bomber.

Past is Prologue

"He insisted on starting with the overthrow of the Russian Duma in 1917," the Democrat recalls. "He ran out of time, so I yielded him five minutes. That got him up to the bombing of Tripoli, or somewhere, in 1944. We tried to help him, but no matter how much time we fed him, he never made it past the '50s."

Congressmen generally are less amused by members who are opinionated, outspoken—and deadly earnest. That is a pretty good description of Oregon Democrat James Weaver, a tireless battler against nuclear power and the timber interests.

"I have kept the idealism of my youth, it being all I have," Mr. Weaver has written. He suspects it is inherited: His great-grandfather was the 1892 Populist nominee for president, James B. Weaver.

But Mr. Weaver's stubborn idealism can be another Congressman's pain in the backside. Last year in a futile attempt to block a big Northwest power bill, Mr. Weaver stalled by introducing 73 amendments, including one that took 90 minutes to read on the House floor. In the end, the bill passed despite him.

A Vanishing Breed

Mr. Weaver has won some battles, notably a series of fights to create wilderness areas, but he concedes that to be a maverick is to be lonely. "The most unusual thing about us," he says, "may be how few of us there are."

Life in Congress also can be lonely for Rep. Gonzalez, the modern heir to the original San Antonio maverick. To visit the 19-year congressional veteran is some experience. A big man with an outsized face, he paces back and forth, switching from English to Spanish, brilliantly impersonating politicians living and dead. His legislative performance, also outsized, has put some of his colleagues in a state of wonderment.

In 1977, Mr. Gonzalez angrily resigned as chairman of a special House committee investigating the assassinations of President Kennedy and the Rev. Martin Luther King. He quit following a bitter war of words with his top committee aide. The Congressman labeled the investigation hopeless because "vast and powerful forces, including the country's most sophisticated crime element, won't stand for it."

Baying at the Moon

Mr. Gonzalez can become obsessed with an issue, unable to let it go. In 1979, a federal judge was murdered in San Antonio, and the Congressman suspects that organized crime was involved. Over and over, he has risen at the end of the day to address a near-empty chamber on the subject. In one such late-night speech, at 2:10 a.m., he allowed that the exercise might be "like a coyote out in the brush howling for the moon and really making no difference at all." Yet he can't stop.

" 'Henry, why are your handing your enemies a stick to beat you over the head? Why do you want to do that, Henry?' " he says a cohort once asked him.

His answer is this: "We need outspoken members, not intimidated ones. What we need most is *forceful* language, not weaselly, mealy-mouthed talk (with) members flying under false flags."

Anyway, insists Mr. Gonzalez, he *does* tone down his statements, he *does* hold himself in check. "If I really said what I liked to, what my inner voice tells me. . . ."

RENEWED HOSTILITIES

Design of Proposed Memorial to Vietnam Dead Is Reopening War Wounds Meant to Be Healed

BY ANDY PASZTOR

WASHINGTON   2/17/82

To some, it is a masterpiece of modern architectural design: somber, simple pieces of black granite eloquently displaying the name of each American killed in Vietnam.

To outraged critics, it is a "disgraceful dark ditch," a stark, embarrassing monument wedged in the ground to mock the war and demean the victims it is supposed to honor.

Nearly a decade after U.S. troops left the battlefields of Southeast Asia, a new fight is taking place over plans to build a Vietnam War Memorial on the Mall here. A number of veterans' groups and politicians are up in arms over the memorial's unconventional design—two low, sloping walls of black granite joined in the shape of a V.

What is at stake, though, goes far beyond aesthetics. Conceived as a symbol of national reconciliation, the proposed monument instead has reopened many of the divisions and deep psychic wounds that tormented this country during the Vietnam war.

"The thing that really tears me up inside," says Lloyd Unsell, an oil-industry lobbyist who is a leading fund-raiser for the project, "is to see guys who fought side by side (in Vietnam) start yelling at each other about the shape of the monument." The arguments, Mr. Unsell warns, "could sidetrack our plans, and there may never be any memorial."

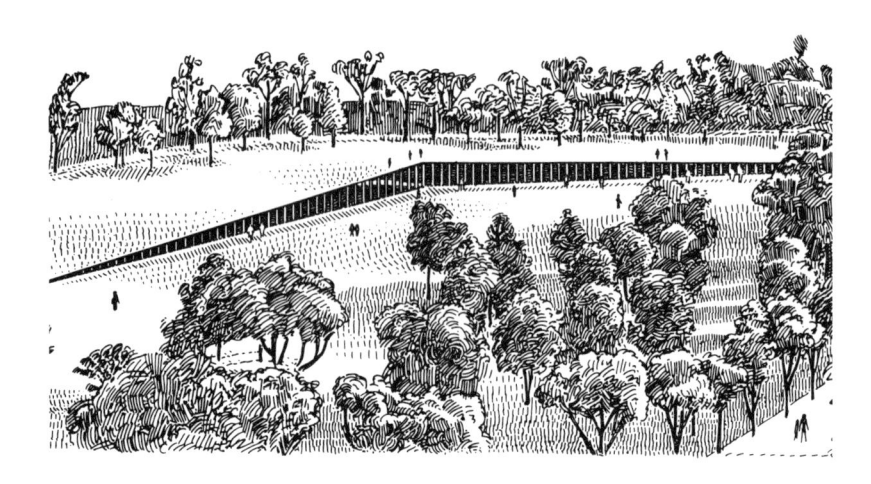

Not Simple

That would be an ironic blow to Jan Scruggs, a 32-year-old former infantryman who was wounded in the war and who has led the drive to erect a memorial since 1979. "Too bad it wasn't a simpler war," he says. "Then we could put up a heroic statue of a couple of Marines and leave it at that."

With feelings running high and the ground breaking that is scheduled for next month still not certain, that doesn't seem like a bad idea to the memorial's most vehement critics. Rep. Don Bailey, for example, a Pennsylvania Democrat who was decorated four times during a 15-month stint in Vietnam, insists he would rather see nothing built than go along with the "bitter, anti-government message" of the current design.

The monument's sponsors went out of their way "to make sure there isn't any reference to the war as a just cause," Rep. Bailey asserts. "The suffering of veterans," he argues, "shouldn't be used to satisfy the views of the draft dodgers and Jane Fondas of the world."

Such acrimony was hard to imagine in the summer of 1980, when Congress with much fanfare set aside two prime acres in Constitution Garden, between the Lincoln and Washington monuments, for a memorial commemorating the more than 57,000 Americans who lost their lives in Vietnam. A heady list of dignitaries rallied behind the plan. They ranged from former President Gerald Ford and retired Army Chief of Staff Gen. William Westmoreland to anti-war leaders such as former South Dakota Sen. George McGovern.

The monument, according to its sponsors, would transcend any "political statement about the war or its conduct." It was to be a "place of healing," a common ground where supporters as well as opponents of the war could remember the courage and weep over the sacrifice of all those who served and died.

Richard Radez, a New York banker who engineered the fund drive that has raised more than $5 million so far, argues that a primary goal of the memorial must be to avoid glorifying the war or the reasons behind it. "It has to be a reflective statement," he says, "a warning to think about the cost the next time our government gets into such an adventure." But the first hint of divisiveness emerged almost before the ink on the controversial design was dry.

Maya Ying Lin, the Yale University architecture student who beat out 1,420 other competitors last May to determine how the monument would look, immediately began feuding with some of the sponsors. She wanted only the names of the dead, carved in letters less than three-fourths of an inch high, to appear on the two highly polished, receding walls. Directors of the memorial fund, worried about adverse public reaction, eventually overruled the designer and included plans for a highly visible inscription on the face of the monument praising the "devotion to duty and country" of those who died in the conflict.

But that decision didn't stop the increasing chorus of complaints from individual veterans and some (but not all) of the country's largest veterans' organizations. And some members of Congress have joined in the protests. Last month, Rep. Henry Hyde of Illinois and more than two dozen other Republican lawmakers wrote a blistering letter to President Reagan arguing that the design "makes a political statement of shame and dishonor." They demanded an entirely new approach to building the monument, one "less intent on perpetuating national humiliation—no matter how artistically expressed."

Is the 'V' a Peace Sign?

Even Ross Perot, the Texas millionaire who has championed the monument for years and donated at least $170,000 to the cause, is having second thoughts. He is thinking of financing a survey to determine just what the more than 2.5 million Vietnam veterans think of the design. Mr. Perot concedes that a lot of verterans believe the monument "is trying to bury any positive feelings or references to the service" they performed.

Some critics go much further. They say the proposed dark stone is inappropriate because it reminds them of the traditional black "pajamas" worn by the Vietcong. Others see the V shape of the memorial as suggestive of the two-fingered peace sign flashed by anti-war demonstrators.

Stung by the complaints, officers of the memorial fund have tried desperately to come up with last-minute modifications. After heated discussions with representatives of a half-dozen veterans' groups, the memorial's board of directors agreed to place an American flag somewhere on the site. And the board intends to commission a realistic, larger-than-life statue of a soldier that would stand on a pedestal nearby.

All the changes need the approval of Interior Secretary James Watt, who also has to certify that backers have collected enough money to finish the project once construction begins. So far, Mr. Watt has shied away from wholeheartedly supporting the proposal. But several aides say he is likely to allow work to start later this year with the stipulation that design details be negotiated among interested parties.

Legion Supports It

Jack Flynt, the national commandant of the American Legion, believes a compromise can be reached. The Legion is one of the veterans' groups backing the proposed monument, and it has pledged $1 million toward the work. Mr. Flynt says of the divisiveness that "people are simply trying to jump on a political bandwagon" by raising questions about the design at this late stage.

Paul Thayer, the chairman of LTV Corp. and the honorary head of the corporate fund drive, calls the criticism "a little too late and a little too strident" to kill the project.

Still, the internecine squabbles bother many participants, including Gen. Westmoreland. "Sure, I would like to have the words 'worthy cause' somewhere on the memorial," says the former commander of U.S. troops in Vietnam. But considering the residue of anger left over from the war, the general says, "I'm satisfied it's a dignified and simple design . . . that will blend handsomely with the rest of the Mall."

To Mr. Scruggs, fighting doggedly to save his dream, the design "isn't anti-war or pro-war. It is a great work of art chosen by a jury of leading architects in the largest design competition ever held in America." But there is plenty of bitterness in his tone, too.

When Mr. Scruggs started out singlehandedly to raise money for the memorial, he vowed to avoid corporate contributions. "The companies that made hundreds of millions of dollars (of profits) off the war shouldn't be asked to put up the money," he said at the time. "I don't want to see the memorial become a captive of the military-industrial establishment."

He has been forced to change his tune. More than 20% of the estimated $6 million to $7 million needed to build the monument is expected to come from private industry. And Mr. Scruggs clearly is relying on pressure from some board rooms to persuade the government and balky veterans' groups to support the memorial.

In the past, similar bitter arguments about monuments here have faded from the public's consciousness without a trace. Probably few of the millions of visitors who flock here each year to marvel at the Washington Monument are aware that more than 125 years ago supporters of the Know-Nothing Party took over the half-finished obelisk and prevented workmen from reaching the site in a protest against the politics of the monument's backers.

Nevertheless, there is a surrealistic element to the current debate. Sometimes the two sides appear more like bitter adversaries negotiating an end to the drawn-out Vietnam war than former comrades in arms. Only instead of the shape of the table, the argument is about the shape of the monument.

Asked about the status of talks between the monument's critics and supporters, a spokesman for Virginia Sen. John Warner, who set up the negotiations, has a response reminiscent of the extended maneuvering to end the war: "The talks are at a very delicate stage," the spokesman says. "A fragile agreement has been worked out. From the perspective of diplomacy, it is important to establish it more firmly . . . before making any public comments."

CRIME

On the Streets and In Corporations

ON THE WATERFRONT
New York Fish Market Points Up a Pattern Of Extortion and Fear

Thefts and Illegal Payments Found by Investigators; Wrong Carmine Got $300

Wrecking of a Bar-and-Grill

BY STANLEY PENN

NEW YORK 4/14/82

Extortion of businessmen by racketeers is an old story in New York. An FBI official here says, "it isn't uncommon for us to go to a businessman who tells us, 'Of course I make payoffs. That's the way to do business in New York.'"

But businessmen, because of fear, generally refuse to bring charges. "I don't have a hell of a lot of sympathy for them," says the FBI official, Kenneth Walton, deputy assistant director in New York. "If all the legitimate businessmen stood up in a united voice and cooperated and testified, the problem could be eradicated. Realistically, I didn't expect that to occur."

A prime example of the extortion, and the fear, is provided by the Fulton Fish Market in downtown Manhattan. Wholesalers there have long been victimized by organized crime, according to evidence produced at four successful criminal prosecutions last year in Manhattan's federal district court.

The picture provided in court is graphic: undercover payments, stolen fish, the shooting of a witness and the reluctance of wholesalers to complain to the authorities. Why the reluctance? Because wholesalers assume that the Mafia has greater power than the federal government, said Assistant U.S. Attorneys Daniel H. Bookin and Andrew J. Levander in a recent presentencing report.

"Frightened to Death"

Thus, one wholesaler, Alec Messing, was asked by a federal grand jury if he gave protection money to Carmine Romano, a former union official and alleged crime figure. Mr. Messing chose to go to jail for three months and pay $60,000 in contempt-of-court fines rather than answer.

In attempting to justify his refusal, he told the grand jury, "I am afraid of what will happen to my wife, my children, my grandchildren and my business. Threats have been made against me if I answer your questions truthfully." He added, "I am frightened to death."

The Fulton Fish Market, next to the East River, is in a shabby two-block area just north of the Wall Street district. It is the largest sales outlet of its kind in the U.S. At 5 a.m., when most New Yorkers are asleep, the market comes alive as retailers from New York, New Jersey and Connecticut start doing business with some 60 wholesalers. Last year, the wholesalers at the market grossed about $325 million from the sale of 168 million pounds of seafood. Thanks to the successful federal prosecutions, they probably got to keep more of their profits than they did in past years.

Since 1975, federal investigators said in a presentencing report, the wholesalers have shelled out $700,000 to Fulton Patrol Service, a protection racket, controlled by Romano, an alleged member of the Genovese crime family. The wholesalers have made the payments, the investigators say, so that their businesses won't be wrecked.

Daily Thefts

Despite the payments, federal prosecutors and investigators charged in court, thousands of pounds of fish purchased by the wholesalers are stolen from crates every day by unloaders employed at the market. Some of the unloading companies' profit, prosecutors have said in court, is kicked back to Romano.

Retail merchants, who drive to the market to buy their fish, often must pay fees to concessionaires for parking in the public streets around the market. Certain concessionaires kick back some of their profit to Romano, the government has said in the presentencing report. Retailers who won't pay fees risk damage to their vehicles and theft of their fish. The retail price of fish reflects the payoffs made at the Fulton Fish Market, federal investigators say.

Federal prosecutors have charged in court that Romano, together with his brother Peter, exercised a stranglehold on the Fulton Fish Market through control of Local 359 of the United Food and Commercial Workers International Union (AFL-CIO). Carmine Romano was Local 359's secretary-treasurer from June 1974 to May 1980. Peter Romano then took over the job, while Carmine Romano became the $650-a-week administrator of local 359's welfare and pension funds.

Brothers Convicted

The market would have a hard time operating without Local 359's 700 members. They unload fish from trucks, serve as sales clerks for wholesalers, and deliver fish from the wholesale stalls to the waiting vehicles of the customers.

Some of the corruption has evidently been cleaned up. Carmine and Peter Romano were convicted in federal court last October of racketeering, acceptance of illegal payments and other charges. Carmine drew a 12-year prison sentence and $20,000 in fines and now is in jail. Peter got an 18-month sentence but is free on bail. They are appealing their convictions.

Besides the Romano case, Local 359 was fined $200,000 in federal court last year after it was tried and convicted for taking payments from wholesale dealers. In another action, 11 wholesale companies pleaded guilty to making illegal payments and received suspended sentences.

The convictions seem to have halted, for the time being at least, certain illegal payments made by the wholesalers. No longer are wholesalers each giving $300 in Christmas gifts, and they have stopped "renting" cardboard union-shop signs from the union at $25 a month.

But the investigation continues, according to U.S. Attorney John S. Martin Jr. The government, in court papers, says that the Internal Revenue Service has uncovered "massive tax evasion" by the Fulton Market's unloading and parking firms.

Louis Martine, Carmine Romano's attorney, denies government charges that Romano belongs to the Mafia, or that he gets kickbacks from unloading and parking companies. Mr. Martine says a false picture of Romano was painted by prosecutors. "He is one of the best-loved men" at Fulton Fish Market, Mr. Martine says.

The attorney points to some 350 letters of praise for Carmine Romano sent to the federal court by businessmen and workers in and around the Fulton market. "It is quite a remarkable tribute to the man," Mr. Martine says. (Federal prosecutors contend that some businessmen who publicly praised Carmine Romano confided to the government that they fear him.)

Those who sent character references for Carmine Romano included John Hightower, president of the South Street Seaport Museum in the Fulton market area. In his letter last year to the federal court, Mr. Hightower depicted Romano as a "enormously positive force in the Seaport area." Romano "is needed here," Mr. Hightower said, urging that charges against him be dismissed.

In a phone interview, Mr. Hightower said that Romano had helped to protect the seaport museum, which has been vulnerable to vandalism and break-ins. "I can only assume," Mr. Hightower says, "that he told members of the union not to break into the museum."

Since the crackdown by the federal government, Local 359 has been under the trusteeship of its Washington-based international union. Carmine has been removed from the welfare-pension funds, and Peter is no longer Local 359's secretary-treasurer. Robert Funk, associate general counsel of the parent union, says the trusteeship won't be lifted until Local 359 is "operating properly."

Little Help

The transcript of the Romanos' criminal trial, together with court documents connected with the trial, make clear that the wholesale dealers gave little help, if any, in the federal probe of the Mafia at the Fulton market. Wesley Walker, who took part in the investigation as an agent for the U.S. Labor Department, told in court of sitting in the prosecutor's office with a group of wholesalers before the trial. "Nobody wanted to be the first person to testify," Mr. Walker said. "Some were highly nervous. Some were shaking. Their voices were cracking. One or two cried."

Wholesalers don't mind discussing their business problems: They worry that consumers are being scared off by the rising price of fish, and they grumble that they are being bypassed by some big retail chains that buy their fish direct from shippers. But wholesalers won't talk about the Mafia. They give the impression that, despite some problems, the rough-and-tumble at the Fulton Fish Market is clearly preferable to some antiseptic office job.

David Samuels, who graduated from Syracuse University with an accounting degree 10 years ago, sells fish at the market for a company his grandfather founded more than 50 years ago. Clad in heavy work clothes to protect against the damp and the chill, Mr. Samuels says he enjoys his work and the people around him. "This place is a real melting pot," he says. "You have the good, the bad and the ugly."

Under oath in court, wholesalers defended their actions on the ground that they had to stay on good terms with Local 359. One fish wholesaler, testimony showed, tried to hide a payment by treating it as an expense for repair of a boiler. Many simply shrugged off the payments as a fact of life. But Frank Bearese, of Finest Fillet Co., said he got "sort of a sick feeling in my stomach" in making his Christmas payment.

Their timidity at the trial of the Romanos may have stemmed from the gangland-type shooting in April last year of Anthony D'Andrilli, part owner of a company that unloads fish at the market. Mr. D'Andrilli, a government witness, had been forced to testify by court order against his partner, Nunzio Leanzo, and his testimony led to a perjury conviction of Leanzo. Shortly after Leanzo was sentenced to two years in prison, Mr. D'Andrilli was shot by two gunmen in ski masks outside the Local 359 office at the Fulton market. Despite being shot in the neck, face and head, he survived. His assailants haven't been found.

Carmine Romano used others to solicit and collect illegal payments from wholesalers rather than accept them himself, according to court records. This led to a highly embarrassing incident for John Morrison, bookkeeper for a Fulton Fish Market wholesaler.

As Mr. Morrison told it in court, his boss said to him, " Here is $300, give this to Carmine like we did last year." Mr. Morrison thought that his boss meant Carmine Romano. Finding Romano at a bar near the fish market, he handed over the money. "Thank you," Romano said. "You aren't a reporter from the New York Times, are you?" Mr. Morrison said he wasn't, and Romano "put it in his pocket," Mr. Morrison said.

Mr. Morrison's boss was greatly upset to learn that the money had been given to the wrong Carmine. According to a federal investigator, Mr. Morrison "became afraid to go to work and quit his job." His former employer says the reason he left his job was that the employer had a surplus of bookkeepers and that Mr. Morrison decided to enter the "computer field." Mr. Morrison couldn't be reached for comment.

Patrol Service Still Used

Although wholesalers may have halted some questionable payments at the fish market, they continue using Fulton Patrol Service to protect against thefts, according to federal prosecutors.

In court testimony, at the Romano brothers' trial, John Pontebbi, a Fulton Patrol official, said his company collects $2,700 weekly from a group of wholesalers in the two main Fulton market buildings, known as the "old" and "new" buildings.

Among supervisors hired for Fulton Patrol was Anthony O'Connor, a former official of Local 359. "I figured (that) in case (O'Connor) knew people that is robbing us, or stuff like that, he could help me get the fish back," Mr. Pontebbi said. O'Connor, indicted with Carmine and Peter Romano, failed to appear for trial; he is a fugitive from justice, according to the government.

Mr. O'Connor's replacement was Michael S. Petrillo, who is "big"—six feet tall and "fat"—Mr. Pontebbi said. "I mean real, real heavyset," Mr. Pontebbi added. Asked what Mr. Petrillo did for his $350 a week salary, Mr. Pontebbi said, "Nothing."

Another supervisor of Fulton Patrol is Vincent Romano, brother of Carmine and Peter. Last year, Vincent Romano pleaded guilty in Brooklyn Supreme Court to a charge of promoting illegal gambling. He received a $5,000 fine. This month the U.S. attorney announced that Vincent Romano had been indicted on charges that he inflated assets of his wholesale fish company to get bank loans and defaulted on the loans, owing more than $110,000. He hasn't yet pleaded to the charge.

A watchman hired by Fulton Patrol was one Richard Reuter, Mr. Pontebbi's brother-in-law.

"Does he steal fish?" Mr. Pontebbi was asked at the Romano brothers' trial.

"I would say yes, sir."

"Is he still on your payroll?"

"Yes, sir," Mr. Pontebbi said.

"In fact, do you think he can help himself from stealing?"

"No, sir, he can't."

"He is a compulsive stealer?" the prosecutor asked.

"No, sir, I told you before he's nuts."

"He's nuts?"

"Legally nuts," Mr. Pontebbi said.

"And he steals fish and you can't stop him from stealing fish?"

"You can't stop him from doing anything, really."

"How long has he been on the payroll?"

"Since my wife put him there."

In a presentencing report, Mr. Pontebbi was identified as an unindicted co-conspirator in the Romanos' case. Fulton Patrol wasn't charged with any wrongdoing. Mr. Pontebbi testified in court that he didn't do anything wrong and denied the government's allegations that Carmine Romano is Fulton Patrol's boss.

A story told in the court transcript shows that one time the Romanos got their comeuppance from a little businessman in Fulton Fish Market. The Romanos were furious and got vengeance, but they also lost face.

As told in court testimony and documents by Prosecutor Bookin, New York Police Sgt. Joel Pierson and IRS Supervisor Anthony Carpiniello, the story went like this:

Carmine Russo, uncle of Carmine Romano and a former business agent of Local 359, sold his Carmine's Bar & Grill to one Joseph Paterra several years ago. Mr. Paterra paid about $35,000 for the place.

In about late 1980, Mr. Paterra was offered $120,000 for the bar-and-grill. The Fulton market area is currently undergoing redevelopment, and property values have soared.

Mr. Paterra decided to sell. Carmine Russo was furious. Vincent Romano, his nephew, informed Mr. Paterra that he musn't sell to anyone except to Carmine Russo for the $35,000 that Mr. Russo got. To underscore his point, Vincent Romano and an unnamed individual beat up Mr. Paterra.

Mr. Paterra wasn't to be bulldozed. He went to his brother, Dennis "Frankie Harlem" Paterra. Frankie Harlem, according to Prosecutor Bookin, is connected with the Genovese crime family.

Frankie Harlem arranged a "sitdown" in East Harlem with organized-crime bigwigs. Result: The Romanos were told to lay off, and Mr. Paterra was permitted to sell his restaurant to a married couple, Piera and Vincent Molini, according to law-enforcement officials in the presentencing report.

The Romanos were embarrassed. They struck back, not at Mr. Paterra but at the new owners.

On Jan. 21 last year, at about 10 in the morning, Carmine Romano and some companions destroyed the premises of Carmine's Bar & Grill, Prosecutor Bookin said. They smashed windows and a mirror, broke tables and chairs, threw food and liquor all over the floor, destroyed cigaret and coffee machines, and tore a stove out of the wall.

So the story goes. Mr. Molini, who was there at the time, informed authorities he hadn't any idea who wrecked his restaurant or why. No charges were filed.

THE POT TRADE
Dealing in Marijuana Can Mean Big Money—But Also a Life of Fear

Joey Takes In $2,000 a Week But Frets Over 'Crazies'; How Arthur Slipped Up

Danny's Ambush in a Motel

BY DAVID J. BLUM, LAUREL LEFF, ROGER LOWENSTEIN AND STANLEY PENN

7/16/80

John Edwards's daily business deals have become rather boring to him. "It's like selling lettuce or broccoli. There are some exciting moments occasionally, but most of the time it's unbelievably tedious," he says.

John is a marijuana dealer in Chicago and has been one for 10 years. (His name and those of the other marijuana dealers mentioned in this story have been altered, for obvious reasons.) He began when he was a 15-year-old high-school student—as he puts it, "a wild adolescent in a wild place at a wild time," revolting against his upper-middle-class upbringing and smoking marijuana as a "social statement."

Today, he doubts whether social statements still exist. He is still selling marijuana, but he has made peace with his family and has embraced the middle-class living style he once shunned, occupying a comfortable apartment in one of Chicago's more pleasant neighborhoods. As a cover, John works a few hours a week for a friend repairing foreign cars.

Once in a while he thinks of getting out of the marijuana business;

someday he would like to write a novel. But right now the money is coming in so smoothly—more than $20,000 a year, tax free—that he dismisses the idea. One deterrent to breaking away is that he has acquired a taste for cocaine, so, he says, "a lot of my money goes right up my nose."

The end result of John Edwards's teenage revolt against the establishment could be considered ironical: He has become a cog in another system—one based entirely on self-interest and the profit motive—that moves over 10,000 metric tons of marijuana a year into the hands of an estimated 16 million steady users.

Nobody knows for sure how many people are engaged in this vast, loosely structured marketing system, but the estimates start at a low of 150,000 and build from there. The supply chain generally originates with the smugglers who bring pot in from Colombia and Mexico in bales. Thereafter, it is packaged and repackaged by a horde of anonymous wholesalers, middlemen and dealers in ever-smaller amounts—pounds, half-pounds, ounces, half-ounces, $5 "nickel bags"—until finally it may even be sold as an individual cigaret, or "joint," on a street corner or in a school lavatory.

Laurence McKinney, a Cambridge, Mass., business consultant who began researching the marijuana-distribution system 15 years ago when he was a student at the Harvard Business School, believes that at any one time there may be as many as a million people involved in some form of marijuana transaction. "A common practice, a carry-over from college days, is that someone will buy a pound of grass and then split it up at cost among his friends," Mr. McKinney says. He puts the number of "pound dealers," who are in the business for profit more or less full time, at 300,000.

The market for marijuana has undergone a radical transformation and enlargement in the last two decades. Many pot historians trace the origins of today's wide use to the participation of college activists in the "freedom marches" in the South for integration during the 1960s. The collegians borrowed the practice from black field laborers and brought it back to their Northern campuses, where it soon became a fad and then much more than a fad.

Now, pot has lost its connotation of long hair and Ivy League activism and has been increasingly accepted by young office and blue-collar workers. On the broad plaza of New York's World Trade Center, brokerage clerks and stenographers openly share "tokes," or puffs, from their marijuana cigarettes while they take in the sun during their lunch hours. And in New Jersey, a recent survey of suburban high schools found the highest percentage of pot users to be in vocational schools rather than in higher-income areas.

"This broadening of the social base of users has undoubtedly been an important element in the move to decriminalize possession and use of marijuana," comments the privately financed Drug Abuse Council, which in a report this year predicts that if America's youth and young adults maintain the attitudes they now have, "we can expect to find an increasing acceptance of marijuana in the years ahead."

Nevertheless, by federal edict, marijuana remains a Class I "controlled substance," which puts it in the same category as heroin and LSD: drugs officially classified as having no accepted medical use and a high potential for abuse. Moreover, there is widespread fear by parents that marijuana creates "apathy" among their children and is a steppingstone to more dangerous drugs, although medical evidence indicates that marijuana, by itself is nonaddictive. Reflecting these public pressures, arrests for marijuana violations by state and local police recently have averaged well over 400,000 a year, double the number in 1970 and 10 times the annual figure in the supposedly riotous mid-1960s.

Thus, while possessing small amounts of marijuana has been legally condoned in broad parts of the country, selling it remains as illegal as ever. The resulting scarcity and surreptitious nature of the drug probably mean that dealers like John Edwards—and "Joey" and the others to be mentioned later in this article—will continue to make big money even though it means living life "at the edge," in constant fear of arrest or something worse from the very tough people who have positioned themselves at the heart of this vast trade.

Joey

Walk along the garish, honky-tonkish block between Seventh and Eighth Avenues on New York's 42nd Street and the chances are you'll see Joey. He is there six days a week (with Sundays off), nearly always lounging in front of the same store.

He is 20 years old, one of the youngest pot peddlers on the block. Joey blends in with the street. He has an Afro and a mustache, wears blue jeans, sneakers and a pullover. You would think he was just waiting around for a friend unless you heard his soft call: "Yo, yo, nickel bag."

Joey sells pot in three sizes—half-ounce bags that retail for $20 to $25 each; tiny bags for $5 that yield six to 12 joints; and single joints for $1. He also sells three joints for $2.

If he wanted to, he could sell bigger amounts—quarter-pound and half-pound bags. That would be a lot easier than selling small amounts to 30 customers a day. But Joey is no fool. "Guys would think I have big money because I could afford such big purchases, and they'd rip me off," he says.

Joey generally won't sell to strangers, unless they are black or Puerto Rican. To Joey, a white male stranger is a potential cop. He has plenty of regular customers, although he doesn't know them by name and doesn't want to. "Everything strictly business," he says.

Joey knows only two kinds of pot—quality and commercial. Commerical is cheaper, $50 a pound less than the quality kind. What's the difference? "Commercial gives a bad smell on the breath. Quality has a better look, better taste and better head." Joey won't sell commercial, he says.

He charges customers roughly twice what he pays for his marijuana. In a peak week his sales total $2,000. That leaves $1,000 clear. Isn't that big money? "Not so big," Joey says. "Sure, we don't pay taxes. But look at the fines I got to pay. Every time I'm busted, it's a $50 fine or two weeks in jail." Joey says he has paid $1,000 in fines since he began selling a year ago.

Joey moved to New York from Puerto Rico two years ago. He had four legitimate jobs. He couldn't hold them because at first his English was bad and he couldn't understand instructions from his bosses. He began selling marijuana after he had been put in touch with a wholesaler. The man sold Joey a quarter-pound on credit because Joey didn't have the money to pay for it. As soon as Joey sold the pot, he paid the wholesaler. Now he has a relationship with the man; they trust each other.

Joey likes the business—it's better than working for a boss. But the hours are long and the winters are hard. He gets so cold standing on the street all day that Joey wears two pairs of long johns under his trousers and several pairs of socks.

Joey must always be on guard for the "crazies." These are drug addicts who come by and suddenly start fights. You never know, he says, when one will pull a knife on you. Another fear he has is of people with cameras who conduct an odd type of extortion on the street's pot peddlers. "They say, 'Give me money and I'll give you the picture,'" Joey says. "When somebody with a camera comes, I turn and look the other way."

Uniformed cops don't hassle Joey. It's the plainclothes ones who are the nuisance, he says. Joey never knows when they'll bust him.

"Worse, they seize your herbs (marijuana). So you get fines to pay and you've lost your herbs," he says.

Someday, Joey says, he will quit the racket—probably when his oldest son grows up and gets old enough to ask his father what he does for a living. Meantime, he says, he lives a comfortable life. "We eat good—beefsteaks and chicken," he says. And at Christmas, he and his family fly back to Puerto Rico to see the relatives.

Arthur Sewell

Arthur Sewell grew up in one of Los Angeles's sprawling, affluent suburbs, the son of religious but not fanatic parents. He attended a prestigious Western university and then went to law school. "Everything about Arthur's background indicates he would be the straightest person in the world," comments a friend and former college roommate.

There's one difference, however: Arthur deals in drugs. Or rather did, until he was busted not long ago. Like most dealers, Arthur sold everything from marijuana to LSD. ("I never sold heroin," he notes somewhat defensively.) His annual income—$40,000 tax free—was enough to permit him to dabble a bit in real estate.

In his mid-30s, Arthur has a professional look, with short hair and a neat beard. He dresses conservatively—by California standards, at least—in a plaid shirt and corduroy pants. His renovated Spanish-style house is decorated with antique furniture and oriental rugs. He is a registered Republican.

Arthur didn't set out to become a drug dealer. After he flunked out of law school, he moved through a series of dead-end jobs. Then an odd thing happened: His personal drug dealer became a devout Mormon and wanted to move to Utah with a clean slate, so he offered his business to Arthur. Like a young internist buying into the practice of an established physician, Arthur paid his former dealer for a list of about 30 regular customers, a complete drug inventory, the names and numbers of six suppliers to restock the inventory, a ledger of debits and credits, and even an answering phone.

Arthur served an elite clientele in Los Angeles's wealthiest enclaves. He describes them as "business people, very well-to-do, with nice homes." One owned a chemical company and lived in a house "bordering on a mansion"; another, a bachelor attorney in Beverly Hills, drove a Rolls-Royce. Arthur added a few friends of his own to his client base.

When a customer wanted to buy some drugs, he left a name or a number on Arthur's answering phone. Arthur returned the call and took the order. "It was like a high-class grocery store," he recalls. "You'd say, 'I'd like a lid of grass, a tab of acid, six uppers and two ounces of cocaine, please.' It's a very urbane way to do things." Arthur even made home deliveries.

Arthur always tested the product personally. "If I had a good time and found it enjoyable, everybody else seemed to. If I smoked a joint and didn't get high enough, I wouldn't buy it. I had a lot of fun sampling the wares. That's a nice fringe benefit of being a dealer—you're loaded all the time."

He marked up the price as much as 200%, but his clients didn't seem to mind as long as the quality was there. Arthur discounts the myth of Colombian marijuana, supposedly one of the most potent varieties: "I think it's all Mexican, but by calling it Colombian you can get a higher price." His average order was for about $100. Most people paid cash, although Arthur happily accepted checks.

While Arthur's customers were upper-class, his suppliers weren't. "The wholesale end of the industry is full of pretty seedy characters—a lot of crazies, real addicts, very pathetic people," he says. They seemed to have plenty of money "and always had expensive cars—Cadillacs and Datzun Zs," he adds, "but they were very paranoid, very suspicious." Some of them carried guns all the time.

Arthur finally slipped up when he took on a new customer who he says was paid by the police to inform on him—"a real down-and-out street kid who would ruin someone's life for $100." The police arrested Arthur when he went to meet the informer to complete the sale. During his trial he exaggerated the extent of his drug and financial problems, making it seem that he was forced into dealing by the pressures of his habit. Arthur received a rather lenient sentence—probation and a fine.

Arthur is still on probation and making a living speculating in real estate. He doesn't plan to go back to dealing drugs, although he uses them frequently. He professes no guilt feeling. "I provided a service to the community. People are always going to get drugs anyway," he says.

Danny

Danny, a drug wholesaler, has had some years when he made several hundred thousand dollars, but he doesn't seem to be enjoying his affluence. He is 33 but looks a worn 40, with a pale, gaunt face, a lean frame draped in a tan safari suit and stringy blond hair that hangs to his shoulders.

Danny buys marijuana in the form in which it is shipped from Colombia, in 20-to-80 pound bales, that cost him roughly $300 a pound, or $400 if the pot is especially good. Danny picks up his load outside Manhattan. Then he drops off quantities that range from a pound to 10 or 20 pounds with various customers, or "fronts," mostly in the East Village section of Manhattan where he lives. If all goes well, Danny parts with the commodity in a matter of hours, at a profit of $10 to $15 a pound.

When the supply is plentiful, as it is currently, Danny cuts prices by 10% or so. Last year, however, when there was a "famine," he made an easy $50-a-pound profit on one lot of 1,200 pounds.

Yet Danny probably worries more than most businessmen. "This is a tricky business," he says, "because so much can go wrong."

Take the time Danny drove to a motel in New Jersey on a tip that he could buy cheap, high-quality marijuana. Instead, he was ambushed by waiting gunmen. Or the time Danny purchased 900 pounds of pot that contained "a huge seed pocket." Danny's suppliers wouldn't take it back, and he says, "I wound up with 40 pounds of seeds."

Once he was indicted on what he says was a false charge of drug smuggling, but he wasn't convicted. Another time, a gang stole $30,000 of marijuana from one of Danny's fronts. The front is paying Danny back in painful $500 installments.

"There aren't any standards in this business," Danny says. "When they say they're giving you a kilo, you'd better weigh it yourself to make sure it's 2.2 pounds."

Danny's biggest worry is that his fronts won't repay him. "All it takes is for two or three pounds to default, and you've lost the profit on an entire bale," he says.

Danny has earned enough money selling marijuana to invest in other enterprises, such as a rock-music club and an underground newspaper. But he has also lost large sums in "bad deals." He probably could afford to live in a better neighborhood than his run-down block, but "anonymity," he says, "is the key to surviving in this business."

RANDOM RAGE
How a Park Mugging Led to Impulse Killing Of a New York Lawyer

Crimes Without Motive Rise, And Often Defy Solution; But a Manhunt Pays Off

'Hit Men' and 'the Wild Boys'

BY STANLEY PENN

New York City police detectives (L to R) Juan Crosas-Medina, Nicholas Guarriello and Gennaro Giorgio.

NEW YORK 11/9/82

On a Saturday evening a little more than a year ago, attorney Patrick Kehn and his companion, Mary Murphy, were strolling at sunset through an isolated section of East River Park in lower Manhattan. As Miss Murphy later told the grand jury, the first hint of trouble was the sound of running feet behind them.

With only this fleeting warning, the couple suddenly found themselves surrounded by three youths, who forced them to sit down on a bench hidden by shrubbery from the six-lane Franklin Delano Roosevelt Drive adjacent to the park.

"They wanted money," Miss Murphy, an employe of American Broadcasting Cos., says in testimony. "They weren't speaking in complete sentences, just chattering."

The victims handed over all their cash—$170—plus Miss Murphy's gold neck chain and wristwatch. As their assailants fled, Miss Murphy recalls, "I turned to Patrick. His eyes were (bursting) out of his head." She knew he had been beaten with a baseball bat, but was as yet unaware that one of the youths had plunged a hunting knife into his chest and abdomen.

Random Violence

Shouting for help, Miss Murphy could see no one around. After vainly trying to flag down passing motorists, she ran frantically through the park to an overpass spanning the FDR Drive and then past dingy buildings until she found a pay telephone and called police. A short time later, 38-year-old Mr. Kehn, a tax and estate specialist at a big Manhattan law firm died on an operating table at Bellevue Hospital.

For increasing numbers of Americans, the word "crime" has come to mean the particularly terrifying sort of random violence that cut down Mr. Kehn: a split-second, chance encounter with a stranger that erupts into horror. It is the kind of crime for which there is scant defense, and it is on the rise nationwide, according to the Federal Bureau of Investigation. A generation ago, police say, most killers knew their victims and had motives for their acts. Now, they say, killers often murder at random, without specific motive.

Such "impulse killings" not only defy explanation, they also frequently defy solution. With victim and killer strangers—and without a motive—initial leads are often nonexistent, and the trails to follow seem limitless. These obstacles were present in the Sept. 26, 1981, slaying of Patrick Kehn, yet the detectives investigating the case eventually found the killer.

This is the story of their four-week manhunt, one that led through the housing projects and abandoned tenements of Manhattan's Lower East Side into an urban netherworld inhabited by kids known only by street names like "Hulk," "Caz" or "White Boy." It is a world where fear, suspicion, braggadocio and sudden violence prevail and where neighborhood gangs—"Hit Men," "Wild Boys," "The Ball Breakers"—offer what passes for authority. In this milieu, muggers brandish 12-inch knives known as "007s" and derisively refer to their victims as "geese."

Mr. Kehn's murder was one of a record 1,826 homicides in New York last year, a 63% increase from 1970. According to Kenneth Conboy, a New York City deputy police commissioner, a major factor in this rise is the sharp upsurge in senseless impulse killings—many of them committed by youths. "We have 12-year-olds, 13-, 14- and 15-year-olds committing the most brutal, stupefying cruelties," he says.

These lawless youths are driven by what Mr. Conboy terms "instinctual fury" to commit brutalities. "Talking to a kid charged with murder is a chastening experience," he says. "Someone, ostensibly a human being, is snuffing out a life without remorse or concern."

Exploring the City

Such offenders are highly unpredictable. According to experts on criminal behavior, Mary Murphy and Patrick Kehn acted prudently by obeying their attackers and offering no resistance. But Robert Panzarella, a professor of police science at John Jay College of Criminal Justice in New York, observes that prudence is no guarantee of safety. Inexperienced muggers may panic and lash out, he says, and some muggers have reported feeling scorn for "overly compliant" victims, whom they then kill or injure "out of a sheer feeling of disgust."

That Mr. Kehn and Miss Murphy were strolling at sundown in a high-crime neighborhood suggests that they were victims of their own trusting natures as much as anything else. Mr. Kehn, a native of the Syracuse area who had come to New York City in 1979 to join the big law firm of Shearman & Sterling, and Miss Murphy, the manager of ABC's literary-rights division, had been in the habit of exploring the city on weekends. "We were walking the perimeter of New York," Miss Murphy says. "We had completed Brooklyn, the Bronx and Queens. We had gone into a lot of Staten Island. We had never had a frightening experience."

Then, inexplicably, in an isolated playground. Mr. Kehn was killed. Detective Nicholas Guarriello of Manhattan's Ninth Precinct was assigned to investigate, aided by Gennaro Giorgio and Juan Crosas-Medina, detectives attached to a Manhattan area task force. At the outset, they lacked both a motive and a useful eyewitness description. Miss Murphy, frightened and distraught, couldn't furnish a description. "She was hard to talk to, outside the fact that they were dark and young," Detective Guarriello says.

Police did find a business card belonging to Mr. Kehn at the scene of the stabbing. On it were partial prints of two fingers—not Mr. Kehn's. The prints were useless until suspects emerged, but later they would help clinch the case.

The murder was front-page news in New York, and tips started coming into the stationhouse almost immediately. Two days after the killing, a Hispanic woman phoned the Ninth Precinct suggesting that police try to find a youth known as "Chico," who, the woman said, had boasted in the neighborhood of muggings he had pulled off.

Evidence quickly began to pile up against "Chico." Detective Guarriello says: "A kid we found in an abandoned building claimed that 'Chico' was bragging that he ripped someone off and may have killed him." That knifing supposedly had occurred on the day of Mr. Kehn's slaying.

Police went to a precinct file of neighborhood youths with arrest records that is cross-indexed according to nicknames, real names and even tattoos. From it they plucked a photo of "Chico," whose real name is Luis Guzman. Then 16 years old, he was a gang member and a resident of a housing project near the crime scene, and was repeatedly in trouble with the law.

A jogger who had been in the park around the time that Mr. Kehn was stabbed placed Mr. Guzman near the crime scene. A youth who said he had seen Mr. Kehn fall, his shirt bloody, also said he had spotted "Chico" nearby.

Mr. Guzman was arrested Sept. 30 and indicted for murder by a grand jury. It seemed that a major part of the case had been solved. But Mr. Guzman, it turned out, wasn't involved in the Kehn killing.

Almost from the start, one detective had doubts about Mr. Guzman's guilt. "Something didn't sit right," the detective says. "On the one hand, he kept denying he'd been in the park, although we knew he had been. On the other hand, he'd been so up-front about (his) cutting people, stabbing people and doing robberies (in the past) that somehow I felt he hadn't done this one." Even so, police kept Guzman in custody to await trial.

The day after his arrest, a friend of Mr. Guzman's came to the precinct house insisting on Mr. Guzman's innocence. He said he had been in the park with his girlfriend and had witnessed the stabbing.

The detectives, who refer to this youth as "Hulk 2" to distinguish him from another neighborhood "Hulk," let him talk without interruption. "We don't say anything," Detective Giorgio says. "But we know his story isn't right," mainly because details he provided didn't jibe with known facts. When the officers confronted him with these inconsistencies, "Hulk 2" admitted that he was lying and claimed he knew who was involved in the killings. He alleged that an acquaintance known as "Speedy" had said to him of the Kehn killing: "You see the papers? I did that. Me and my boys."

"Hulk 2" led detectives to "Speedy's" place, where he lived with his grandmother. "Speedy" wasn't home and wasn't found during a patrol of the neighborhood. Detectives instructed "Hulk 2" to inform "Speedy" that he was wanted for questioning.

"Speedy," whose real name is Miguel Molina, came into the Ninth Precinct the next day. A slightly built, black-haired native of Puerto Rico, he was then 19 years old and was listed as a student at a Lower East Side high school. Detective Guarriello says of him: "A nice-looking boy, but not too bright upstairs."

Mr. Molina, the product of a broken home, had been arrested earlier in 1981 for criminal possession of a loaded revolver. He pleaded guilty and got five years of probation, according to court documents.

Mr. Molina denied having anything to do with the Kehn crime, though he said he had witnessed it. He had been alone in the park and hidden in the bushes, he said, when he saw two Hispanics and a black youth corner Mr. Kehn and Miss Murphy. Mr. Molina, who at first agreed to take a lie-detector test and then backed down, said he thought the killer went by the nickname of "Polo" or "Peelo."

The police were skeptical of Mr. Molina's contention that he had only been a witness. "He knew too much," Detective Guarriello says. "He had all the details—who stabbed who, what Miss Murphy did, who ran where."

Nevertheless, Mr. Molina was permitted to leave and go home. "So far, we had nothing to implicate him," Detective Giorgio says. "We let him feel comfortable in the situation. We said to him, 'Keep in touch.' "

Shortly thereafter, Mr. Molina told detectives the killer's nickname was "Leepo."

In retrospect, detectives figure that Mr. Molina didn't think they would catch up with "Leepo." Mr. Molina knew, but didn't tell detectives, that "Leepo" had by then fled New York. He had gone to Charleston, S.C., to stay with a sister.

While searching in vain for "Leepo," police talked to a housing policeman who said that a youth living in one of the projects near East River Park went by the name of Leo or Leopoldo; possibly he would turn out to be "Leepo."

The housing cop led detectives to Leopoldo's apartment, where they learned that his last name was Siao-Pao (pronounced Say-poe), that he was dark-skinned and 5 feet 10 inches tall, and that his Chinese father and black mother were both dead. What they still didn't know was whether Siao-Pao was "Leepo."

Although Mr. Siao-Pao had an arrest record, his arrest sheets, for some unaccountable reason, didn't contain his photo or fingerprints. However, Detective Crosas-Medina, using the police-department computer, found that Mr. Siao-Pao, now almost 21 years old, had once applied for a job as a school-crossing guard, a job for which applicants are fingerprinted. Mr. Siao-Pao's application also contained his nickname—"Leepo."

The case began to fall into place. The police fingerprint lab concluded that Mr. Siao-Pao's prints matched those found on Mr. Kehn's business card. Then, an arrest sheet on Mr. Siao-Pao containing his photograph was found in a lower-Manhattan courthouse. Mr. Molina, shown the photo of Mr. Siao-Pao, identified him as "Leepo," according to detectives.

Although detectives were unaware of Mr. Siao-Pao's whereabouts, they devised a scheme to flush him out. They told a member of his family in Manhattan that he should show up in court for a prior petty crime in which he had been implicated. The ruse worked; Mr. Siao-Pao, unaware he was a suspect in the Kehn killing, returned to New York, where he hid out in a Brooklyn martial-arts academy.

Police were tipped to this hideout by a Vietnamese grocer for whom Mr. Siao-Pao had once worked. After detectives "sat" on the building for 16 hours, they seized Mr. Siao-Pao when he entered at 3 a.m.

After being told of the evidence against him, Mr. Siao-Pao gave a written confession to the police and a similar, videotaped statement to the prosecutor, Gregory Waples, a Manhattan assistant district attorney. In his confession, Mr. Siao-Pao says he was in East River Park looking for someone to rob when he came upon Mr. Molina and "Sammy," whose real name is Samuel Jimenez. Mr. Molina held a baseball bat and Sammy the branch of a tree. The three youths decided to rob Mr. Kehn and Miss Murphy, who had just walked by.

Pointing his knife at the couple, Mr. Siao-Pao said: "Don't nobody move." At some point, according to Mr. Siao-Pao's confession, Mr. Molina warned Mr. Kehn, "Don't look at my face, otherwise I'm gonna hit you." Mr. Molina, for some reason was greatly upset by Mr. Kehn and beat him over the head with his bat. "(Molina) was acting just crazy," Mr. Siao-Pao says.

Mr. Siao-Pao contends that he attempted to separate Mr. Molina from Mr. Kehn. Explaining how the knifing occurred, he says that with knife in hand, "I pushed the guy (Mr. Kehn) back on the bench. Then from the time I pushed him back to the bench, he ain't move."

Before fleeing across the FDR Drive, Mr. Siao-Pao noticed Mr. Kehn's blood on his knife. He cleaned it off and the next morning, flung the weapon into the East River. (Police divers later searched for, but never found, the knife.)

The youths split the victims' cash, Mr. Siao-Pao says he sold Miss Murphy's chain to a jewelry store for $16 and her watch to someone on the street for $7. Altogether, they netted less than $200.

Later, Mr. Siao-Pao sought to suppress his confessions by maintaining in court that his request for a lawyer was ignored by detectives and that he was wrongfully hit by a detective in the station house when he fell asleep. Detectives denied his charges. Judge John C. Leonforte refused to throw out the confessions, noting that Mr. Siao-Pao, in his videotaped statement, had expressly said he hadn't been threatened. Nor, the judge said, had he mentioned to the prosecutor that his supposed request for an attorney had been turned down.

Mr. Siao-Pao decided against a trial and pleaded guilty to murder. In September, he drew 18 years to life imprisonment, which means he must serve 18 years before he is eligible for parole.

Mr. Molina confessed to a murder charge after he was implicated by Mr. Siao-Pao. He is serving 15 years to life. Mr. Molina's last statement to Detective Guarriello was: "Can I continue my boxing career while in prison?"

Samuel Jimenez, the 16-year-old lookout for Mr. Siao-Pao and Mr. Molina, received a sentence of 40 months to 10 years as a juvenile offender after he pleaded guilty to attempted murder and robbery.

The murder-robbery charges against Luis Guzman in the Kehn affair were dropped. But after his arrest, police discovered he was a fugitive from a juvenile facility where he had been serving time for a 1980 robbery. Mr. Guzman is serving a term of one to four years for that robbery.

Mr. Kehn was buried in the Syracuse area, where his mother still lives and where, at Syracuse University, he had received his bachelor's, master's and law degrees. Father Thomas F. Guyder, the pastor of St. Joseph's Church in Camillus, N.Y., officiated at the funeral service. In his eulogy, he quoted some lines that Mr. Kehn, an amateur poet, had written in a notebook that was found in his law office. "He mentioned," the pastor says, "that life is strange, and sometimes something quickly comes to an end."

problem. Many husbands, of course, relish the role of career coach. Others, however, resent their wives' success—or are simply jaded. One husband complained bitterly to Harvard's Mr. Powell: "I can't stand it! She is so enthusiastic."

For Mr. Graubard, whose wife is advancing fast in her airline career, such problems are all too real. The 59-year-old lingerie manufacturer eagerly anticipates retiring to Arizona in three years, but knows his wife will need convincing. "After a while you feel you've done this for enough years," he explains. "But she is just starting. She says, 'What am I going to do with myself?' "

Intense strains can occur just as easily when both spouses are pressing forward in their separate careers. In Frank Glickman's case, a taut relationship snapped. His wife's decision to leave a job in publishing for a career in clinical psychology was the pressure point. Her new profession demanded more of her time. Mr. Glickman, who runs his own graphic-design firm, was working harder, too—driven by the financial pressures of a new baby and a newly purchased home. The result was that after 10 years of marriage, the Glickmans separated for six months.

"The wire got to be as tight as it could," says Mr. Glickman, now happily reconciled with his wife, of that period. "I didn't retrench because of financial commitments. She couldn't retrench because of professional commitment. The breaking point was the marriage. That was the safest place to tamper."

Mr. Glickman isn't alone in feeling that it's sometimes safer to retreat from a marriage than to thrash out the painful conflicts associated with a wife's new career. Many men are ill-equipped to grapple with the emotional ambiguities of an evolving relationship.

"Men find it incredibly difficult to talk about feelings," says Marjorie Shaevitz, the co-director of the Institute for Family and Work Relationships in La Jolla, Calif. "They live lives of quiet desperation and isolation."

Indeed, their silence on the subject is sometimes heartbreakingly eloquent. Asked about the adjustment he underwent when his wife returned to work, a New York oil executive begs off with the excuse of a heavy workload. Finally, after a long, still moment, he says quietly: "Look, I'll be honest with you. It's just too painful for me to talk about it."

POVERTY CYCLE
Welfare Mother Begets 3 Welfare Daughters, Perpetuating Life Style

Teen-Age Pregnancies Keep Family in Harlem Poor; Avoiding Rats in Kitchen

A Son's Escape Into Service

BY JULIE SALAMON

NEW YORK 8/10/82

Life has disappointed Juanita, and she hadn't asked for much. As a child, growing up in North Carolina, she had modest dreams: "I imagined a home. I imagined me and my kids out working together to make ends meet."

At age 16, she was pregnant. At 22, she had had five children. At 28, she began to collect welfare. Her three daughters, Juanita hoped, would do better than she had done.

They haven't. Two gave birth before they were 18; her youngest daughter, 16, is pregnant. They all are unmarried. "I had so much I wanted them to have, even knowing I couldn't get it for them," says Juanita, now 38, as she pulls her granddaughter to her lap. "I wanted them to try to get ahead. Now there are the babies to take care of. Welfare has gone to my daughters from me."

Unwed teen-age mothers like Juanita's daughters seem most vulnerable to the snare of dependence. Such young women often drop out of school when they have children, thus losing one of their best chances of escaping unemployment and the dole. Their children are likely to know only the life of welfare recipients.

Mothers and Children

The problem is growing. The most recent census data show that there were 262,700 births in the U.S. to unwed teen-age mothers in 1979, up 44% from a decade earlier. Many of these women and their children are likely to live on public assistance indefinitely. In households receiving Aid to Families With Dependent Children payments, about 60% of the women were teen-age mothers, according to the Urban Institute, a Washington research concern. In non-welfare households, only 35% of the mothers were teen-agers when they had their first babies.

"The likelihood of being in a welfare family and begetting a welfare family is very strong," says Susan Berresford, a researcher on teen-age pregnancy at the Ford Foundation. "If the pregnancy happens when you're a teen-ager, your fate is essentially sealed."

Some teen-agers have babies to increase the money they get from welfare. But, sociologists say, far more have babies for other reasons. They are ignorant or fearful of birth control. They may live in poverty-stricken areas where unwed motherhood isn't uncommon. They sometimes just want something to give them hope for the future. In almost every case, though, the babies arrive without a great deal of planning on the part of teen-age girls who have only a vague idea of how motherhood will change their lives.

From Parent to Child

Juanita and her two oldest daughters, Carlene and Addie—all of whom agreed to be interviewed at length provided the family's surname wasn't disclosed—offer some understanding of how welfare dependence is transferred from parent to child.

From the time Juanita's daughters were little girls, circumstances were pushing them toward unwed motherhood and continuing life on public assistance. The school system didn't provide the direction their parents failed to give them. Their father left home when they were small. Their mother was old-fashioned and afraid of birth control for herself and for her daughters. On the Harlem streets where the girls grew up, welfare, unemployment, teen-age pregnancy, drug-dealing, petty theft, and violence aren't at all unusual.

Opportunities for escape are dimming for Juanita's daughters and for many teen-agers in similar circumstances. Federal financing for job training, family planning, day care and sex education programs is being eliminated. "Almost everything that's aimed at helping these girls get off welfare is being cut," says Patricia Dempsey, the Harlem director of Project Redirection, a two-year-old Ford Foundation program, which, using existing government and community services, tries to help get teen-age mothers back into school and to counsel them about jobs, birth control and child care. "Without help, they'll use their youth and energy to sell drugs, to hustle, to prostitute—and they'll still be on welfare," says Miss Dempsey.

Marriage and Family

Juanita was born to working parents. Her mother was a housemaid; her father, who died when Juanita was six, was a day laborer. When she was 16, she became pregnant by a 28-year-old man. The two were then married. After their second child was born, he moved the family from North Carolina to New York, where he found work.

The marriage was never peaceful. Her husband yelled at Juanita, she says. He hit her and cheated on her. Still, he provided for his family and loved his children enough that they speak tenderly of him and often visit him at his home in Brooklyn. Ten years ago, Juanita went to court and had him removed from the house.

The wages she earned as a cleaning woman didn't pay the bills, so Juanita began to collect welfare. In 1976, she quit working because her blood pressure was high and because her salary was a deduction from her welfare check, anyway.

For her, living on welfare is boring, depressing and nerve-racking. Her monthly allotment of $776, including child support, provides for a household of five. Monthly rent is $226 for a shabby ground-floor apartment on a street where half the buildings are sealed up with cinder blocks. The living-room furniture consists of a sagging couch, a chair, a fish tank, a table, a television set and a milk crate used as a coffee table. There isn't a carpet or drapes or a lamp shade, and the walls have holes. Juanita is afraid to venture into the kitchen because the rat poison she put there doesn't seem to work.

Her luxuries are a cable-TV hookup and occasional dinners at a nearby Chinese restaurant that accepts food stamps.

The moral code Juanita was taught in North Carolina—that unwed mothers got married or were shipped out of sight—didn't equip her for Harlem. She says that shortly after she moved to New York, she ceased attending church because the minister allowed an unmarried woman who had just had a baby to pass around the collection plate.

"She was unclean," says Juanita, shaking her head. "The preacher would get up and preach about cigarettes but wouldn't preach about a woman having a baby out of wedlock. Here, everything was turned around."

When Juanita decided to stop having babies, she had her Fallopian tubes tied. She didn't discuss sex with her daughters and, fearful of side effects, discouraged her oldest daughter from taking birth-control pills when she asked for them. Now, Juanita has two illegitimate grandchildren, and her youngest daughter is pregnant. "I feel ashamed," she says. "This lady above me says, 'What's that lady do, just sit there and let her kids have baby after baby?'"

Adolescent Pastimes

Her youngest child, a 15-year-old son, is distressing her, too. He has been arrested for "token scooping," taking subway tokens from turnstiles. His sisters say he spends too much time smoking marijuana and hanging out on the corner.

Her one source of pride, she says, is her older son, Carlos. He joined the army three years ago and earned his high-school diploma. "Carlos has the ambition," she says, smiling for the first time while discussing her children. "He tells his sisters they should leave the kids here and join the service. They *should* do that, rather than get stuck sitting in the same position as I am."

At 20, Juanita's oldest daugher, Carlene, dressed in blue jeans and a T-shirt, looks like the lanky basketball-playing tomboy she wishes she still were. "I wish the clock would go back," she says, staring past the soap-opera characters on the small television set in front of her. "I loved my kid life. I wish I'd never grown up."

Carlene's adult life has little to recommend it. She lives on the fifth floor of a Harlem walk-up tenement with her 2½-year-old daughter, Tracy. The bathroom is in the hallway. Her building is adjacent on one side to a liquor store and on the other to a candy store where marijuana and other illicit drugs are sold at night. Random killings on the street aren't unusual. Welfare pays the bills.

Hopeless Future

She is well spoken and streetwise but doesn't see herself going anywhere good. "I feel like I haven't made it in life and like I'm never going to make it," she says.

Carlene dropped out of school in the ninth grade, before she became pregnant. She recalls a third-grade teacher who paid attention to her; then, Carlene's school attendance was perfect and she was on the honor roll. But, in junior high school, Carlene drifted away and no one noticed.

At age 16, she began to date Wayne, the young man who ultimately fathered her baby. "He held off until I was 17 before we had intercourse," she says. "I figured he loved me." Shortly before Tracy was born, Carlene moved in with Wayne and his mother. Their income came from welfare and Wayne's bootlegging of liquor.

For a while, things went well. "When I brought Tracy into the world and I was laying with her in my arms, Wayne came into the room and we both started crying, we were so happy," she recalls. Seven months later, the two fought over Carlene's frequent visits to her mother. She pulled a knife, and he pointed a gun. The police came. Carlene took Tracy to her mother's house. A court forbade Wayne to come around anymore.

The Ideal Life

At home, Carlene quarreled with her mother, who pushed her to try for a job, to finish school, to forget about Wayne, who Juanita thought was best gone anyway. In January, Carlene took Tracy and got her own apartment and her own welfare budget. She passes her days dreaming, watching soap operas. Her best fantasy is a replica of her mother's. "Ever since I was small I dreamed of getting married, having a nice house, having kids, having a good job," she says. "I dreamed I'd have this guy, and we'd talk out our problems, and he wouldn't walk out."

Carlene says she wants to finish high school and go to work, but she forgets to show up for meetings with job counselors. She worked eight hours a week at a fast-food restaurant for a short time, but her pay barely covered bus fare. She is too old for job programs for teenagers. And she can't resist the street. Almost every evening she drops Tracy off at her mother's, then goes dancing or to bars. She says she must relieve the boredom of the days she spends waiting for the check to come. "That's not a good feeling," she says. "But that's what it's about."

When 18-year-old Addie, Juanita's middle daughter, became pregnant at age 16, it upset Juanita, and the rest of the family thought it must be a joke. Tall, slender and pretty, Addie has an air of innocence about her. Giggling, she describes herself as her friends and family do: Miss Goody Two Shoes.

A dreamy girl, Addie isn't a fighter by nature, but she is fighting hard to pull herself out of welfare. She didn't drop out of school until after she had given birth to her son, Markees, now 16 months old. While she was pregnant she was recruited by Project Redirection, where counselors helped her enroll in a Comprehensive Employment and Training Act (CETA) job program and a high-school equivalency course.

In school she had been a loner. She refused to smoke "cheba," or marijuana. Shyness and a slight speech impediment keep her voice at a quiet mumble. When other children took to the street, she clung to home, spending long afternoons on the stoop or watching TV.

Though many of her friends and her older sister were having babies or abortions, she wasn't interested in the details of sex. In the 10th grade, she began to play hooky. She met a boy named Charles, and one spring afternoon she became pregnant, "I didn't know how to prevent it. It was the first time for me and I got pregnant like that," she says, snapping her fingers.

Now, Juanita takes care of the baby as Addie travels through a world populated by social workers who give her pamphlets on birth control (which she practices now) and exhort her to be on time. Her days are exhausting, traveling by bus to school in the morning and then by subway to a CETA job at a day-care center in the afternoon. She attends a CETA job-counseling session once a week and irregularly goes to childcare classes at the YMCA, as Project Redirection requires her to do.

But Addie reads at a fifth- or sixth-grade level, and she is painfully shy and monosyllabic with strangers. "I'm afraid Addie is going to get caught in a rut," sighs Carmen Rivera-Torres, the director of the CETA program that Addie is in, and that is to be eliminated in September. "All she can bank on is that someone will recognize she's a good worker. She's dependable. She calls when she can't come in. She brings notes from the doctor when her baby is sick. I've got smarter kids in the program who won't do that."

Lessons in Self-Reliance

In class and in group counseling sessions, Addie sits on the edge, watching. At one CETA training-class, a lively young black instructor lectures 30 teen-agers, including Addie. "The savior isn't coming. No one's coming to make our lives better. In the '60s it was different. Well, you're in the 1980s. Unemployment for us is said to be 50%. You have to egg yourself on."

Addie gazes off into space. After class, as she stops at a store to buy a rat trap for her mother, she explains that she's worried about whether Charles will get a job, about the baby, about whether she will ever get off welfare.

Later, she excitedly discusses her plans for the future, when she will be earning money. "I'll buy my baby clothes, toys, a nice room with furniture. I'll get myself clothes, furniture. I'll buy my mother some furniture," she says. Her baby, she declares, smiling, will be a "big businessman" when he grows up, "important" and "famous."

She is still very much a teen-ager and her weightiest burdens alternate in her mind with deciding what shirt to wear. Her jeans are always neatly pressed, and she changes hair styles almost every day. She takes pains to match the color of her shoes and blouses. She moons over Charles, whom she says she will marry someday. She likes horror movies and eats pizza slices and hot dogs for lunch. She giggles frequently.

No Nonsense Mother

Her childishness abates when she is with her baby. At a visit to a hospital clinic pediatrician, she answers the doctor's questions decisively, without her usual apparent slight bewilderment. The baby is often sick with colds and flu—from sleeping in a drafty room, Addie thinks.

As she leaves the clinic, carrying the baby and sipping a Coke, Addie murmurs: "I'm afraid I'll lose him. I'm afraid he'll die."

Addie often expresses the notion that she's jinxed. Though she is optimistic that through hard work she will obtain her high-school degree and a job, her conversation is laced with vague fears that some outside force will interfere with her efforts. "Everytime I love something, every time I'm happy, it's taken away from me," she says. "Every time something good's going to happen, it doesn't happen."

Her older sister, Carlene, wishes she were in Addie's shoes, bolstered by teachers, social workers, and some sense of hope. Observing that children now are becoming pregnant and dropping out of school at ages 12 and 13, Carlene offers this assessment of her own daughter's future. "I figure she's got a one-in-a-million chance of doing better than her mommy."

THE DISPOSSESSED
Homeless Northerners Unable to Find Work Crowd Sun Belt Cities

They Gather in Tent Towns And 'Cardboard Camps'; Scavenging for Survival

Soup Kitchens and Suicides

BY GEORGE GETSCHOW

"They's movement now. People movin'. We know why and we know how. Movin' cause they got to. That's why folks always movin'. Movin' cause they want somepin better'n what they got. An' that's the on'y way they'll ever get it."

—John Steinbeck,
"The Grapes of Wrath," 1939

HOUSTON — 11/12/82

Some 30 miles from the center of this sprawling Sun Belt city, on the banks of the San Jacinto River, is a community that came into existence some six months ago. It now has about 250 residents, most of whom came from other states, and is continuing to grow week by week.

Its name is found nowhere among real-estate ads. Indeed, it has no official name. Neighbors, however, call it Tramp City U.S.A. because its residents sleep in tents, cook on campfires and collect aluminum cans for a living.

Those who live here deeply resent being called tramps. Most are displaced families from depressed Northern states who have lost their jobs, exhausted their unemployment benefits and trekked south in search of work, only to find such work is no longer available. "We have no job, no money and no place else to go," says William Loveall, whose family drifted to the tent community from Detroit two months ago after their real-estate business collapsed and their savings evaporated.

Dire Straits

Stirring a pot of beans simmering on his campfire, Mr. Loveall surveys the poor and tattered people around him and discusses reports that local merchants and homeowners regard the tenters as a collection of ne'er-do'wells. "A lot of locals think we love it out here," he says. "They don't realize just what a fix we're in."

Across the U.S., tens of thousands of families and indivduals are in a similar fix. Not since the mass economic distress of the Great Depression, which drove the nation's destitute into tin-and-tent towns called Hoovervilles, have so many working-class people suddenly found themselves in such dire straits. President Reagan has urged the 11.6 million Americans who are officially unemployed to "hang in there" until the economy recovers. But many of the nation's jobless have nothing left to hang onto.

A recent report by the U.S. Conference of Mayors says thousands of families have been evicted from their homes and are living in cars, campgrounds, tents and rescue missions. The report notes that federal welfare programs that would have once kept such families afloat have been sharply cut back and adds that many more of the nation's "new poor" will spill onto the streets after the 26 weeks of their unemployment benefits expire.

It is a situation that is affecting towns and cities across the country. In New York, officials say the city's five public shelters, now jammed with 3,700 people, won't be able to accommodate the 1,500 more expected this winter. In Detroit, a new 45-bed shelter was filled the first night it opened. In Cleveland, Depression-style soup kitchens that once catered to skid-row loners have been revived and expanded to serve whole families.

Bitter Harvest

But nowhere is the ugly specter of the homeless poor more shocking than here in the Sun Belt, which is reaping the bitter harvest of unemployment from all over the country. "I swear it looks like 'The Grapes of Wrath' around here," says Virginia Cuvillier, director of Houston's Travelers Aid Society. In the last 12 months, the society has seen 22,000 transients, mostly from Indiana, Ohio and Michigan.

Lured by tales of unlimited employment opportunities and the refuge of warmer weather, the jobless are streaming into the "promised land" in groaning jalopies, packed with bedsprings and babies, in numbers that may exceed even the highest estimates of 50,000 a month. But in an ironic twist from the '30s, when tens of thousands of Okies fled their barren farmlands in the dust bowl for fruitless vineyards in the West, today's migrants are mostly Northerners headed for the now-sputtering oil fields of Oklahoma, Texas, Colorado and other states.

In Galesburg, Ill., for example, a city of about 35,000 hard hit by an epidemic of plant closings and layoffs, there are at least 900 vacant homes. "Hundreds of families packed up and headed for the oil fields," says Howard Martin, the director of Galesburg's Salvation Army. "They get there and find that the jobs have dried up, but they can't return because they have no homes or jobs to return to."

'Don't Come Here'

Some Sun Belt cities have been trying to put out the message that the area no longer is the land of opportunity they once boasted about. "We now say to the unemployed people from Michigan, Ohio and Indiana, 'Don't come here, we don't have jobs,' " says Clyde Cole, director, of the Tulsa (Okla.) Chamber of Commerce.

But for many, the message doesn't get through. Tulsa now has several thousand transients stranded in campgrounds or under bridges. Downtown Denver has filled up with so many homeless people that they have begun overflowing into the prosperous suburbs of Lakewood and Arvada. And even in a smaller oil town like Abilene, Texas, whose population is about 104,000, there may be 5,000 people living in tents, abandoned buildings and cardboard boxes, says June Benigno, executive director of the Abilene mental-health association.

Outside Houston, the community called Tramp City U.S.A. was organized with the help of the Rev. Ray Meyer, a local preacher, and is located on state property. With assistance from six volunteers, Mr. Meyer retrieves food that has been discarded by grocery stores and vegetable stands, cleans it up and delivers it to the tent people. Residents provide their own tents.

Newcomers to the community are welcomed by Barbara Tolbert, recently appointed "town greeter" by Mr. Meyer because she and her four children have been residents for four months and she knows everyone well. Mrs. Tolbert offers the new arrivals some food, finds them a space to set up housekeeping and even helps them enroll their children in school. She also gives them a manual entitled "How to Survive in the Out of Doors," written by Mr. Meyer.

A typical newcomer is Dave Johnson, who lost his job and home in

Gary, Ind., after the steel mill that employed him shut down. He arrived in Texas with his pregnant wife, Donna, two children and high hopes of finding work. "At home, all you ever hear about are all the jobs down here," he tells Barbara Tolbert. She replies: "I hate to disillusion you, but"—she points to a parking area filled with out-of-state license plates—"That's what everybody else here heard, too."

The problems facing these homeless legions in the Sun Belt grow apace with their numbers. Not the least of those problems is the frontier philosophy pervading much of the region that "you take care of yourself and your own," says John Hansan, executive director of the Washington, D.C.-based National Conference on Social Welfare. Because of that attitude and because the Sun Belt hasn't faced widespread unemployment and poverty before, Mr. Hansan says, public and private philanthropic agencies to help the poor and needy are in desperately short supply in many Sun Belt cities.

And the supply is getting shorter; some cities in the region are closing down private shelters, hoping the homeless will go away.

Phoenix, Ariz., for example, in the past year has condemned three shelters and several soup kitchens and has passed a slew of ordinances that, among other things, make it a crime to sleep in the parks at night or lie down on the sidewalks during the day. The reason for those actions was to make room for downtown renewal projects and to insure that "panhandlers and derelicts," as many citizens call them, wouldn't spoil the success of those projects.

The Arizona Republic, Phoenix's morning daily, and many of its readers supported the city's actions. "We Didn't Tolerate Prostitutes, Why Tolerate Bums?" the newspaper asked in an editorial headline. A letter to the editor from a reader made this observation: "If a stray dog is found wandering the streets, it is picked up and put to sleep. Unfortunately, we cannot put these 'human animals' to sleep, but we surely should not support and encourage their way of life."

According to Louisa Stark, a Phoenix anthropologist, the city's cold shoulder has pushed many of the city's 3,300 homeless out of private shelters and public parks into jails or "cardboard camps" outside the city. Wallace Vegors, assistant park manager of Lake Pleasant Regional Park, a county facility about 30 miles from downtown Phoenix, says that "lots" of people "are permanently camping" in the park and in the surrounding desert.

Others have settled on federal land near the city of Mesa, 17 miles from Phoenix. James Forrest, assistant director of the Mesa Chamber of Commerce, says the city has asked the federal rangers to get the homeless campers to move out, "but they chase them out one day and they come back the next." He adds: "As long as they don't bother anybody, we don't do too much about them."

The problem will doubtless worsen as Phoenix pushes ahead with its downtown redevelopment, Louisa Stark says. As new offices and shops replace cheap hotels and apartments, she says, "more and more people are becoming homeless because they can't find anything else they can afford."

Ambitious urban-renewal projects in southern California are also shrinking the supply of cheap housing. "Lots of longtime indigents are landing on the streets, but so are a whole new class of people—families from Michigan and Ohio that are flooding into the area," says Michael Elias, who operates a family shelter in Orange County.

There is little public sympathy for the county's 15,000 homeless, Mr. Elias says. The city of Irvine, for example, recently voted to build a $3.5 million animal shelter for stray pets. "But the city won't donate a dime for the homeless," Mr. Elias says, "because they see them sleeping under bridges and assume they must be bums."

Little Compassion

Even in Houston, a relatively prosperous city in the heart of the Bible Belt, there is little compassion for the growing horde of economic refugees pouring in from out of state. Kay White, a social worker who has been criticized within her own church for using church funds to aid destitute transients, says: "A lot of churches will help their own people, but as far as the Yankees go, they aren't welcome."

Joseph Williams, a laid-off landscaper from New York's Long Island, knows the feeling. Stranded on the steps of the Catholic Charities relief agency with his wife, Cornelia, and their four young children, Mr. Williams, a Catholic, says the family has no shelter for the night. The agency, he says, told us if we were foreign refugees they could help us; otherwise we'd have to go someplace else. But where can we go? We don't have a car or money to pay for a hotel room. There's no work, and there's no family shelter here." (There is one free shelter for men; it's so crowded that it has to turn away as many people as it can take in. The other shelters charge as much as $5 a night, an impossible sum for many.)

So after dark, when the downtown has been deserted by those more fortunate than they, the homeless drift in, filling the parks and fighting for space in abandoned buildings. One dilapidated downtown building is so full, in fact, that its tenants have hung home-made doors with padlocks to protect their occupancy.

The increasing presence of these ragged vagrants panhandling on the streets and loitering in the library (where they go to clean up and read their hometown newspapers), has aroused fear and anger among downtown shoppers and office workers. But the police say there is very little they can do about the situation. "How can you control it?" asks Patrolman Thomas Joyner. "The city is overflowing with these people, and it's getting worse every day. Besides, it's kind of hard to crack down on them when all they're trying to do is survive."

Patrolman Joyner adds that "there's been an upswing in petty crime in the downtown area," such as stealing food from grocery stores and breaking into vending machines. "If someone doesn't have a job or any money, and they've got families to feed," he says, "they're going to steal if they have to to feed them."

The problem is particularly acute here and in other Texas cities because what welfare assistance there is in the state is limited to "unemployables"—and most homeless adults, regardless of their circumstances, are considered employable. Furthermore, the homeless can't even get food stamps because they don't have a local address. "It's a horrible Catch-22," says David Austin, a professor of social work at the University of Texas. "Many of these homeless people are half-starved, yet they aren't eligible for stamps."

One such "employable" is Ronald Larson, a 30-year-old plumber from Chicago who a few months ago lost his job, his car, his savings and, finally, his home. His family moved in with relatives, and he hopped freight trains looking for work. Now he finds himself standing in a church-sponsored soup line in Houston with 200 other homeless men, women and children, suffering from hunger and depression and staring into a future that he sees as hopeless. "If it weren't for my family," he says, "I probably would have pulled the trigger long ago."

Some of Houston's homeless survive by scavenging garbage bins in the back of fastfood chains. Others sell their blood at prices of about $7 to $10 a pint. Two such donors are Kenneth Harris, a 48-year-old laid-off hotel manager from Portland, Ore., and his wife, Mary. "We can't find work. We don't qualify for any assistance. So what else can we do?" asks Mr. Harris as he stands in a waiting room with at least 300 other donors. To survive, he says, he has sold his car and even his wife's wedding ring. He adds: "My blood is all I got left."

The plight of the homeless has caused some to turn their children over to county welfare agencies. "It really pulls at your heart to see these parents give up their kids in order to provide a better life for them," says Carl Boaz, who runs Harris County's Child Welfare Emergency Shelter.

Violent Behavior

Others turn to alcohol, violent behavior and even suicide. "They see new skyscrapers and shopping centers going up, and they think there's plenty of work here," says the Rev. George Grant, a minister from nearby Humble who has dealt with five suicides in a local tent community. When the homeless don't find work, Mr. Grant says, they react like a little child who has planned a magnificent birthday party but no one shows up. "It just blows them away," the minister says.

Another source of anxiety for the homeless is the threat of local vigilante groups who chase them off with shotguns and sirens. With local unemployment rising, Mr. Grant says, the vigilantes fear that they too might come to share the fate of their tent neighbors.

In "Tramp City U.S.A.," residents constantly feel the disdain of the local population. Some children refuse to go to school, having been called "river rats" by their more prosperous peers. Many of the families have also refused to go to church after one family in the community was turned away at a local parish for wearing dirty clothes.

The Rev. Ray Meyer tries to bring the Gospel to the homeless. But it isn't easy, he says, explaining: "These tent people are mostly middle-class people who've suddenly lost everything they've worked for, and they're angry at God." So rather than preaching, he sings songs, accompanying himself on his guitar. "Trouble has tossed you here and there, so now you don't even care," he sings. "You look for help at every place, but now there isn't anywhere else to go. Ah . . . but it seems like you're living in so much hell."

LEISURE AND THE ARTS

"The Hook": Songs of Pain and Double-Dealing

BY MICHAEL L. KING

DAYTON, OHIO 7/24/81

The short black man, nattily dressed in a gray suit and white hat, waits unobtrusively in a rear doorway at Gilly's night club here.

Onstage, a casually attired five-piece band finishes its second tune before an inattentive audience. Then, Deacon Jones, the young organ player, makes the introduction; "Ladies and gentlemen, the godfather of the blues, Mr. John Lee Hooker."

The youthful white audience springs to its feet, shouting and applauding. In short, measured steps, the man they call "The Hook" saunters forward and takes a seat on stage. Placing a guitar across his lap, he surveys the audience without acknowledging its ovation.

In a deep, resonant voice, the singer-songwriter launches into a song about the inadvisability of clinging too tightly to the past. "It serves me right to suffer: it serves me right to be alone," he sings in a mournful wail reminiscent of a New Orleans dirge. "Because I'm livin' in a memory, a memory . . . in a memory that's gone by."

The song is vintage Hooker. It's crafted like an essay, concisely stating a thesis and then expanding on it. His voice huddles within a very limited range, little more than an octave. Yet as he repeats phrases and melody lines, he varies the notes ever so slightly, creating a raw, improvisational effect.

As he performs, he sits almost motionless on the stage, except for rhythmically raising and lowering the heel of his left foot. That stillness helps lock in the audience's attention on his words. He sings every song as though he lived it and by singing it transcends the pain.

The crowd of about 300 sits spellbound for the next hour and a half. They snap their fingers, rock back and forth in their chairs, and periodically shout out approval: "All right!" "Sing it!" "I deserve to suffer!"

John Lee Hooker is a relic from the classical blues era of the forties and fifties. His songs relate tales in such an intimate and spirited manner that audiences feel as though they are reading a diary. He is more popular than ever before. "I've got way, way more fans than I used to have," Mr. Hooker says.

He was sitting in a backroom at Gilly's and seemed to be a man ill-at-ease talking about himself. Squirming a bit in his metal chair, he often chuckled, sometimes stuttered and professed not to have "an ego," saying "I never like for people to put me on the top shelf. What's important is that I've got all the young audiences listening to me now."

Depending on whether one believes Mr. Hooker or his associates, the musician is either "about 55" years old or nearly 75, which is more likely. At age 14 he left Clarksdale, Miss., and headed north to make his fortune in the music business.

Unlike many other blues singers, he didn't leave home to escape poverty. "My daddy was pretty well off," he remembers. "He had a lot of land and cattle. But that wasn't the life I wanted. I wanted to play music. And I just up and ran off."

He worked briefly in an auto plant in Detroit before signing a contract with a small record company. For the next 20 years he traveled the "chitterling circuit" of sleazy beer joints on the wrong side of innumerable, nameless towns. Mr. Hooker would stir his all-black audiences with tear-stained songs of loves that went wrong, lives ravaged by poverty and families torn apart because of loose women and strong drink.

Then, he'd encourage them to dance away their cares while he played a brand of upbeat music he called "boogie," which later was recognized as a precursor of rock and roll and many variations of jazz. Boogie songs were cheerful and triumphant. They didn't always have a message; the only essential element was a hammer-like beat that made audiences want to get up and dance. And in the ultimate epicurean gesture, he punctuated his boogie with rhythmic belching sounds.

Mr. Hooker pumped out almost 100 albums from the late forties to the early sixties, and he dominated the blues world as no one had since the turn-of-the-century tours of Gertrude "Ma" Rainey. He last made a recording five years ago, and may never make another, he says. "It ain't exciting to me. I got enough out there to last me a lifetime. People will never forget me."

By the early sixties, interest in blues was waning. Younger blacks came to regard blues as monotonous renditions of the stereotypes they wished to escape. Other blacks simply found the blues depressing.

So Mr. Hooker packed his gear and moved to England for two years. There, he was revered by concert goers and up-and-coming young musicians alike. Mr. Hooker followed many of those young musicians back to the U.S. and on their coattails embarked on his second career spent primarily in front of affluent white audiences. His popularity grew vicariously as Mick Jagger and the Rolling Stones, the Beatles, guitarist Eric Clapton and other musicians claimed him as an inspiration. His signature guitar licks have become the staple of rock and jazz.

Frank Tirro, dean of Yale University's School of Music, says blues had a "tremendous influence" on modern popular and jazz music. Within the last 20 years blues has "filtered its way back into the mainstream" of American music as artists of earlier periods have been rediscovered, he says.

John Lee Hooker was perhaps the most important blues artist of the late forties and fifties, says Jon Goldman, who teaches modern music history at Case Western Reserve University in Cleveland. "He influenced a lot of white guitarists and singers. His style is heavily rhythmic, but not very melodic."

Many recent fans don't realize that Mr. Hooker had a thriving career years ago. For example, Kaye Richards, a 30-year old suburban Dayton housewife at Gilly's one recent evening, thinks that "the 1960's created the blues." She has been a devoted fan of Mr. Hooker's since 1970, she says. "Although I am white, he is the king. I'll be listening to him when I'm 50."

One reason why she may be still listening 20 years hence is the "poetry" of Mr. Hooker's music. There are, of course, countless songs about hard times and unrequited love, but most of them merely tug at the emotions. Blues, on the other hand, tell realistic and unvarnished stories aimed straight at the heartstrings. And Mr. Hooker seems to write and sing these stories better than most.

Many in his audiences see themselves in every downbeat Hooker lyric about hard times and double-dealing. "Baby, that's my story," says Richard Reid, a 49-year-old air-conditioning repairman. "He's putting my life into music."

Though Mr. Hooker seems genuinely grateful that so many people are paying money to see him do what he likes most—sing and play the guitar—he does think it sad that so many blacks have turned away from the blues. "That's the only real (American) music there is," he says. "Blues is the roots. Everything else comes from the blues. This is just a fad for the young whites."

But no matter who is in the audiences, he says, "the blues is gonna live on. When the world was born, the blues was born. Everybody's got problems; everybody's got heartaches. And that's the blues." Specific problems come and go, but human misery is constant. That's why "blues is just like old man river, it keeps on rolling," Mr. Hooker says.

The Texas 'Fandangle' Replays a Proud History

BY EDWIN WILSON

ALBANY, TEXAS   7/7/81

About 125 miles due west of Fort Worth, in the heart of Texas cattle country, lies Albany, population 2,400. The land around here is low, rolling hills covered with fern-leafed mesquite trees and buffalo grass. On most of the ranches nearby—hardly noticeable among the mesquite— oil pumps move silently up and down. The oil means a lot to the financial well-being of the ranch owners but it is not what they talk about. The activity that formed the people here, and that still obsesses them, is raising cattle.

A prime example of the real thing in working cattle ranches is Lambshead, still run by the family that settled it in the 1850s and so authentic that it has been used several times in "Marlboro country" cigaret advertisements. One day late last June cowboys Lee Condor and Harry Swedlund were rounding up cattle in the Valley Pasture at Lambshead; that night they performed in a local outdoor drama called "The Fandangle."

Staged here each year on the third and fourth weekends in June, "The Fandangle" may well be unique in American participatory theater. In song, dance, pantomime and narration, "The Fandangle" tells how the original families settled in the area ("Build the barn first, then the house," says one settler), fought the Indians and hunted buffalo. (Any negative aspects of the treatment of the Indians or slaughter of the buffalo are avoided.)

It began in 1938 when Robert E. Nails, a resident of Albany who had been at Princeton and written for the Triangle Club, was asked to write a play about the history of the region for the local high school. From the modest beginning "The Fandangle" grew under Mr. Nails's supervision to a panoramic pageant with 150 to 200 performers and 50 people backstage.

Over the years, the participants constructed vast sets (pulled into the playing area by tractors), built an authentic stagecoach, a replica of a train and a real steam calliope, and sewed hundreds of costumes. The production is staged on a large field surrounded by low hills about a mile outside town.

Preparations begin each year in January. The singers rehearse one night, the men who ride horses and drive wagons another and the small children who square-dance a third night. "The teen-agers are the hard ones," says Marge Bray, who directs the show. "During school they have studies and their clubs and once that's over they're into softball season." During May they held try-outs for the show, called "samplers," and in June the six performances draw more than 10,000 spectators.

"The spectators are fine," Ms. Bray says, "but we do this for ourselves, to celebrate the community spirit and to teach our young people the history of the area."

People from all walks of life and of all ages take part. A good example is the family of Earl Garren. A former oil field worker, Mr. Garren and his wife Marie have appeared in the show for many years. Their daughter Sandra Fox is one of the lead singers. Their granddaughter Becky Pruett dances the can-can in the saloon number and their two great-granddaughters, ages two and five, play settlers' children.

With a population of barely more than 2,000 everyone must pitch in, and they do. Watt Matthews, scion of a family that settled the area, runs the Lambshead Ranch and is also head of the Fandangle Association. He furnishes two buffalo and most of the 40 horses in the show.

The centerpiece of the production is the story of the wild town that grew up next to Fort Griffin, an Army post maintained near here between 1867 and 1881 to protect the ranchers from the Indians. A replica of an entire frontier street is brought onto the playing area, including the barber shop and the Bee Hive Saloon.

The action is one of "Fandangle's" several exhilarating features. The play opens with two rows of cowboys on horseback, riding hell-for-leather toward each other and criss-crossing, each horse ridden with precision between two others at full speed. Women ride side-saddle and young boys and girls ride across the plain at break-neck speed; stagecoaches, prairie schooners and buckboards race through the play. At one point 20 handsome longhorn cattle are herded on and for several numbers the stage is filled with all 150 performers. The spectacle is tremendously impressive.

Equally impressive, though, is the fact that these are local citizens. People play the roles of their forebears and in many cases the roles they play in life. Having people play the lives of those close to them brings the tradition of the area alive in a unique way. At the close of the show the narrators remind the audience of that tradition and ask them to turn toward town and gaze on the courthouse clock tower that has watched over this rugged land and people since it was built in 1883.

Sam Shepard: Bleeding in Red, White and Blue

BY EDWIN WILSON

3/7/80

In his setting for Sam Shepard's "The Curse of the Starving Class," now playing at the Yale Repertory Theater, designer Randy Drake has provided an evocative milieu for the play: a curved backdrop with a blue sky above desert hills: in front—like an object in a surrealistic painting—a drab kitchen not connected to a house; back of the kitchen, silhouetted against the sky, a windmill, its blades broken and rusted from misuse.

These elements—the American setting, the bleak atmosphere, the surreal quality—are hallmarks of Mr. Shepard's recent work, and his use of them has made him one of our most controversial, and most popular, playwrights. Theater Profiles, which keeps tabs on professional productions in the U.S., reports that in the last few years Mr. Shepard has been second only to Tennessee Williams as America's most widely produced playwright. Many people regard Mr. Shepard as the finest U.S. dramatist of his generation, and last year his "Buried Child," a play similar to "The Starving Class," was awarded the Pulitzer Prize.

In disagreement with this view are such people as Otis Guernsey, editor of the annual "Best Plays" volume. He was so incensed by "Buried Child"—and by its having won the 1979 Pulitzer—that he refused to include it in the 1978-79 10 best plays. Describing "Buried Child" Mr. Guernsey used terms like "dismal," "unstructured," "masochistic," and "unbearably tedious."

What kind of playwright provokes such contradictory reactions? For one thing, Mr. Shepard's plays invariably contain striking dramatic images. A major figure in "Operation Sidewinder" is a computer in the form of a six-foot rattlesnake with blinking red eyes. In

249

"The Tooth of Crime" a showdown between a pop music star and a challenger is staged like a Western gunfight, except the weapons are words, not six-shooters.

Mr. Shepard's inventive theatrical images and poetic language led British critic Ronald Hayman to observe that he "has the best claim of any writer since Beckett and Genet . . . to being a poet of the theater."

Since he began writing at age 20 (he is now 36) Mr. Shepard has been intoxicated with words. Listen to Crow in "The Tooth of Crime": "Can't get it sideways walkin' the dog. Tries trainin' his voice to sound like a frog. Sound like a Dylan, sound like a Jagger, sound like an earthquake all over the Fender. Wearin' a shag now, looks like a fag now. . . ."

As is evident from this speech, Mr. Shepard has been strongly influenced by contemporary music, both rock and jazz. Another important influence is cinema. The plays jump from one scene or character to another like quick cuts in a film.

The improvisational quality of Mr. Shepard's plays is one of their strengths, but it is also a source of criticism. The plays are sometimes too disorganized, and Mr. Shepard has admitted that when he was younger he had an aversion to revisions. "I used to be dead set against re-writing," he has said. "My attitude was that if the play had faults . . . any attempt to correct them was cheating."

In recent work, however, there is evidence that Mr. Shepard is attempting to be more coherent. "The Starving Class" and "Buried Child" are models of unity and economy. Both occur in one place at one time: each deals with the affairs of a single family. Themes, rather than thrown out at random, are developed and enlarged.

For example food plays a significant role in "The Starving Class." The daughter has raised a chicken for a 4-H club demonstration, but the mother cooks it for herself. The father fills the empty refrigerator with avocados which the mother tosses out to put in food purchased by a man with whom she is having an affair. The son stuffs himself with whatever food is available; he later slaughters a lamb whose carcass is thrown on the kitchen floor.

In each case the use of food reveals something particular about the characters. But Mr. Shepard goes beyond that to a larger point. These people are also starved for spiritual food: for love, family relationships, a sense of tradition. This brings up possibly the most controversial aspect of Mr. Shepard's work: his vision of America.

As many commentators have pointed out, Mr. Shepard is fascinated by America. He was born in the Midwest, worked in New York for a time and now lives in California. He has filled his 30-some plays with the myths and icons of our country: cowboys, Indians, gangsters, Mae West, Jesse James, people who love the land, people separated from it. His plays written in the 1960s—when he was in his early 20s—reflected the anti-establishment attitude held by many young people then.

Mr. Shepard has focused lately on the disintegration of the American family. His ideas are made clear in the current Yale production of "The Curse of the Starving Class," intelligently and sensitively directed by Tony Giordano. The father (William Andrews) is a drunkard who is deeply in debt and spends most of his time in saloons. The mother (Anne Gerety) wants to find a man who will take her away from husband and home. A son (Warren Manzi) does nothing to make the house and land more livable or productive, but becomes angry when anyone threatens to take them away.

The one bright spot is the daughter (Caris Corfman); she is ambitious and decent. At the end, after several previous attempts, she makes a dash for freedom. But the escape car has been wired with a bomb planted by two thugs and intended for the father. Ironically it is the daughter who dies. There is a great deal of humor in this play—as always in a Shepard play—but the outlook is bleak.

Is Mr. Shepard's view impossibly pessimistic? Some would draw that conclusion. But there have always been two kinds of writers who dwell on the negative aspects of life. One is nihilistic. The other cares passionately about a way of life he considers worthwhile. When it is threatened or destroyed, he laments the loss in the strongest possible terms. Many writers with a tragic vision—from Sophocles to Eugene O'Neill and Tennessee Williams—have been of this type.

Mr. Shepard appears to fall into this category. In "Operation Sidewinder" the character of the young man declares: "I am truly American. I was made in America. I have American scars on my brain. Red, white and blue. I bleed American blood. I dream American dreams . . . I came to infect the continent. To spread my disease. To make my mark, to make myself known."

These could easily be the words of Sam Shepard. Though he does not state it directly, Mr. Shepard's recent plays offer a stern, almost desperate warning: Unless we restore the integrity of the family, unless we renew our spirit, unless we respect the land, the American dream will fail.

Walt's Wonderful World Turns Out to Be Flat

BY MANUELA HOELTERHOFF

DISNEY WORLD, FLA.   7/2/82

Another happy, sunny day. I am having breakfast on Main Street, USA, the long, shoplined street that leads to Cinderella's Castle—the heart of Walt Disney World's Magic Kingdom. Music fills the air. Friendly birds pick crumbs off the restaurant's balustrade. And here's a gaily decked out pony pulling smiling visitors in a festooned wagon.

By day's end, about 35,000 adults and children (adults outnumber kids four to one) will have strolled up Main Street. By year's end, the admirers of Donald, Dumbo, Mickey and Pluto are expected to reach 13.2 million, making Disney World even more popular than the older Disneyland in Anaheim, Calif. Since Disney World opened ten-and-a-half years ago, it has clocked over 131 million visitors. In fact, my travel guide says this is the most popular vacation spot on this planet. That is why I came here and why I am wearing this attractive hat (see inset). As the large 36-year-old child who accompanied me said: "Opera isn't everything, kid. You got to learn about America and talk to the people."

Over there at an adjacent table is a middle-aged couple forking in pancakes. His shortsleeved shirt reveals a tatoo; her print slack ensemble is as happily colored as a flower bed. We chat about their trip and she tells me that he is a construction worker and she a bookkeeper. They are celebrating their 25th anniversary here in Disney. Good choice? I ask. "Oh, God, yes," she says. "We're so amazed. It's better, its more than we imagined. Everything is so clean." They were hoping to spend their next vacation here.

Their satisfaction was echoed in varying decible levels by virtually everyone I spoke to during my four-day stay. "We wouldn't change anything," said a retired couple from Mississippi. "I've been here 11 times; it's an uplifting place," said a young lawyer from Ohio. And a Vermont-based doctor and his wife sang a duet of praise of which one stanza focused on the place's cheerfulness and another on its efficiency.

This joyous ensemble of voices is offered for reasons of balance. I did not have a great time. I ate food no self-respecting mouse would eat, stayed in a hotel that could have been designed by the Moscow corps of engineers and suffered through entertainment by smiling, uniformed young people who looked like they had their hair arranged at a lobotomy clinic. Somehow the plastic heart of Disney didn't beat for me.

Still, I have to give Walt credit for standing in the swamplands surrounding Orlando and envisioning a drained, jillion-dollar amusement/vacation spot presided over by a castle and courtly mouse. Walt's world is simply immense. You need to be Peter Pan to cover its 27,400 acres. As our guide kept telling us: Disney World is much, much more than just the Magic Kingdom with its rides, attractions and restaurants. It's hotels, golf courses, a heap of shops and such other components of the perfect vacation as horsebackriding, boating and swimming. The entire fiefdom is laced together by a battalion of buses and a monorail that zooms above your head and right through the Contemporary Resort Hotel (my happy home).

Anyway, you're thinking, this all sounds neat enough, nobody promised you Paris, poisonous food is at every streetcorner, so what if people smile a lot and what really is your problem, you Fair Isle-sweater-wearing snob? Well, let me offer some highlights of Disney and its parameters, and if it seems really good and you act quickly, you can probably still book a room in the Contemporary sometime next year. The waiting list here is longer than at the George V in Paris.

The Magic Kingdom is divided into various areas bearing such names as Tomorrowland, Adventureland and Frontierland. In Adventureland we stop at an attraction called the Enchanted Tiki Birds, which has a long line of mostly adults waiting to get into "the sunshine pavilion." While we wait, two robot (or, in Disney jargon, AudioAnimatronic) parrots entertain us with a story that starts "many birdbaths ago." One of the many sunny young folks who keep things running smoothly in the kingdom pops out dressed in a disgusting orange outfit. "Aloha!" he shouts. The people stare at him. "I said, 'Aloha,'" he yells smiling madly. "Aloha!" the audience shouts back, making up in volume what it had lacked in spontaneity. "Everyone raise his arm and wave goodbye!" he commands. And everyone raises his arm and waves goodbye.

Any minute, we figured, he's going to have them saluting and clicking their sandals.

We decided to break ranks and headed for Tomorrowland, where we bobbed about in the air sitting in something called sky jets and had some lunch at the Space Port shop. So many choices. We picked Splashdown Peach Punch over a Cosmic Cooler and settled for a Satellite sandwich. In Disney, language lovers will quickly note, Mickey Mouse and Donald Duck worked wonders with alliteration and little rhymes, though it must be said that Walt was no Whitman.

Fortified, we took in a short movie introducing EPCOT (the acronym for Experimental Prototype Community of Tomorrow), a new 600-acre attraction scheduled to open this fall. "Relax and enjoy," says the smooth-voiced narrator as a tenorino begins to croon: "Dreams of the future, lalala, the world belongs to the dreamer, the dreamer inside you." The future apparently includes homes that look like aquariums and people cavorting with dolphins dressed up in pretty outfits. The level of the narration is such that it could be understood by an AudioAnimatronic audience.

In contrast, there is nothing futuristic or fantastical about the next stop, our hotel, except for that monorail speeding through its innards. That was a terrific design idea. And when the hotel opened, the decor had other 21st century touches. But visitors apparently felt uncomfortable with the unfamiliar and the rooms were redecorated. As I dial to a religious program on the TV, I sit on a purple-green bedspread surrounded by swimming-pool-blue plastic furniture, enormous lamps with tumor-like bases and textured green and beige walls. I look out over a parking lot and carefully planted vegetation that is pure Middle America—boring trees and dinky little flowers. I may be in tropical Florida, but there isn't a palm tree in sight. The beach behind the parking lot is as dully laid out as the golf course.

Once outside the fun and games of the Magic Kingdom, the rest of Disney World looks like a condo village. Which is a large part, I would argue, of its attraction. Many Americans spend most of their life preparing for a retirement community and Disney provides a good prelude with its own security force and hassle-free, clean living. Unlike in Europe, you don't have to deal with funny languages, funny-colored money or funny food. And there's no garbage. Never. The smallest scrap of litter is instantly sucked underground, and rushed via pipes to the most fabulous compactor in the universe. The place is obsessively antiseptic. When the Disney characters dance and ride up Main Street in the parade scheduled for every afternoon, a special squad equipped with scoopers follows the ponies.

There's nothing left to chance here, nothing at all. The instant you arrive, you are watched over and taken care of. This place has crowd control down to a science. Mazes set up in front of the popular attractions like "20,000 Leagues Under the Sea," which features plastic-looking, half-submerged submarines paddling past plastic monsters, keep the people-flow smooth and constant. Even though it took us 30 minutes to meet the mermaid, we had the impression our sub was just around the corner. The only time I saw the system break down was in front of the Haunted Mansion. "Disney World is your land" as the song frequently heard hereabouts goes. But not if you're fat. One unhappy girl got stuck in the turnstyle and had to be pushed back out. Like Cinderella's step-sisters, no matter how hard she tried, she just wouldn't fit.

Evenings, too, were crammed with events. One night we dined at the Papeete Bay Verandah restaurant in the Polynesian Village hotel, *the* place if you aren't at the Contemporary. An overamplified and oversimplified combo entertained us as we sipped a Chi-Chi, particularly popular, the menu points out, in Pago Pago, and stared at prawns blown up with breading to look like chicken legs.

But the unquestioned highlight was the Hoop-Dee-Doo Revue at Pioneer Hall in the camping area. "Enthusiastic performers sing, dance and joke up a storm until your mouth is as sore from laughing as your stomach is from ingesting all the food," promises my guide book. I couldn't have said it better. As we sat down, the hearty sextet appeared singing "Hoop-dee-doo, hoop-dee-doo." Then they beat pans and washboards and established friendly rapport with the eating audience. With Robert, for instance, of Virile Beach (could have been Floral Beach, those washboards get noisy). And Chris. Let's hear it for Chris from Daytona Beach! He's 29 today! Let's hear it for Chris! People waved their napkins in Chris's direction. "Hoop-dee-doo" sang the ensemble, jumping up and down.

Our meal—greasy ribs and chicken—arrived in little buckets. When we were done staring again, the hearty sextet reappeared and rubbed their bellies as they sang: "Mom's in the kitchen fixing up a special dessert just for *you*." Out came globs of possibly strawberry shortcake and then more jokes like "You got a wooden head; that's better than a cedar chest. Think about that for a while." Everybody did and whooped and hollered.

Was nothing nice in Disney? Oh, all right. We had a scary time on the roller coaster ride through darkness on Space Mountain; I always enjoy carousels and Disney has one with handsome horses. And I had a fine meal at the Empress Room aboard a riverboat anchored by the shopping complex, probably the only restaurant on the premises that doesn't microwave toast.

The next day, we left Disney World for Cypress Gardens, one of the many attractions beckoning in the Orlando area and bearing names like Sea World, Wet 'n Wild, Gatorland, Circus World, Monkey Jungle. And so on. The landscape is flat and straggled-out. The big thing seems to be gas stations with restaurants attached, chicken salad bars and shacks selling hot boiled peanuts. "Yahoo," says my pal. "Wouldn't mind trying a bag of them hot boiled peanuts." We buy a bag. They are soggy and awful. Our proximity to Cypress Gardens is periodically announced by signs for 12 million flowers and the chief attraction, dramatic ducks. (You're in Luck; A Banjo-Playing Duck).

The gardens are much, much more than just a botanical garden. A water ski show is going on in the stadium. "He hit a wet spot!" exclaims the announcer as a performer disappears into the water. The audience jeers. A child in a carriage leans over and dribbles on my foot. "I wish you'd stop calling America a land of morons," says my friend. "It's not fitting for a foreigner." We pass 12 million flowers and don't miss a one, thanks to helpful signs like: "Look up! Don't miss the orchid." Look has little eyes painted into the o's. "Don't miss the scenic waterfall coming up on your right," warns another sign. "Have you forgotten to load your camera?" wonders a third. "Is America turning into a land of morons?" wonders my companion.

We are too early for the gator show (watch them make pocketbooks right in front of your eyes?). But Bill the Wackie-Quackie man is setting up the duck follies and we sit down just in time to see a duck waddle out onto a tiny stage, and peck at a tiny piano with its beak. "Waddaya call a rich duck?" asks Bill the Wackie-Quackie man of the audience. "A Ritzy Quacker!" he shouts. "Argh, argh" laughs the man in front of us, tugging at his visor cap. Liberace Duck leaves, followed by Kentucky Ducky playing "The Ballad of the Mallard." The Valeducktorian is introduced to a pleased audience as we fly to our car.

We press on to Circus World, which seems to have suffered an unexplained evacuation prior to our arrival. It doesn't seem to affect the place, which looks designed and run by a computer. A sound system keeps churning out electronic organ grinder music, the rides dip and turn even though there is no one waiting to get on. Holding prewrapped cotton candy we stand for a few horrible minutes on the deserted Avenue of Spins and Grins before peering into the concrete Big Top. An announcer is introducing what he calls "our ponderous pachyderms." The beasts do headstands in a ring without sawdust in front of a listless little crowd. The memories of my childhood circuses are stronger than any scent in the wind.

What's it all add up to? The only message I can offer after a few days down here in Central Florida is that America is getting cutified at a far more rapid rate than many of us may be aware of. In gritty New York this mania for babble, alliteration, dumb rhymes—and understandably, sanitation—had largely escaped me. Very few of the places I visited in Disney or its environs seemed to be expecting any functioning adults or intelligent children. They were expecting cartoon characters. And the visitors behaved accordingly. At Cypress Gardens, a number of able oldsters very happily tucked themselves into wheelbarrow-shaped wheelchairs. At Sea World, a theme park offering large fish in large tanks, adults obligingly stuffed kids into dolphin-shaped carriages.

In fact, it was at Sea World that I had a brief encounter with insanity. There I was holding a snack bought at Snacks 'n Suds, wandering past Fountain Fantasy on my way to Hawaiian Punch Village. Shamu, I thought. Got to find Shamu, the much-praised killer whale. So I fluttered about, finally coming to this big pool with a dark half-submerged hulk at one end. It was very still, not showing an inch of killer tail. Then it moved and I thought, this can't be real, it's a plastic submarine. Shamu? Submarine? I just couldn't tell anymore, It was time to go.

And quicker than you could say Mickey Mouse, we were in the friendly skies having another indescribable meal. Hoop-dee-doo, we sang. Hoop-dee-doo.

The High-Flying Price of a Deadly Artform

BY DOUGLAS MARTIN

1/11/80

It's a grand day for waterfowling. As we approach James Michener's Choptank River on Maryland's Eastern Shore, wisps of fog fill the ditches and proud portraits of Chesapeake Bay retrievers adorn mailboxes. In the distance, gunshots crack. Overhead, some 40 canvasbacks coalesce in a purposeful V against the steely sky.

Even to a non-hunter, the prospect of hiking picked-over corn and soybean fields to some reed-covered duck blind or sequestered goose pit seems disturbingly seductive. But we've left shotguns, shells and slaughterous intentions miles behind today. Our interest is the winged inspiration for objet d'art, for we are enroute to the recent Waterfowl Festival in Easton, Md. Here thousands of affluent-looking folks, nattily turned out in a jumble of mink, khaki and camouflage, gather each year to pay soulful tribute to a uniquely American artform: duck and goose decoys.

It is some show. We are greeted by hall upon hall of meticulously crafted waterfowl lookalikes—some sporting $5,000 pricetags—and by a cacophonous gaggle of high-spirited goose callers and seemingly endless paintings of dogs in headlong pursuit of dead bird. "It's a religious festival, where people meet to worship the wooden duck," observes a sociologically oriented observer.

The appeal of these wooden ducks is a tug backward to a richer, wilder past, a remembrance of an unrecoverable era when autumn skies were sometimes blackened by migrating geese. At a time when art theorists are solemnly debating the subtle difference between modern and post-modern art, decoys bespeak simpler stuff. Moreover, they hearken to an old-fashioned Yankee pride that often seems passe now.

"People are kind of fed up with the plastic society," allows a middle-aged decoy carver from Delaware. He buys planks from a nearby sawmill to fashion decoys that sell for up to $3,500.

Indeed, prices of decoys are soaring faster than a startled mallard. One exhibitor points to a goose that has octupled in value to $1,200 in the last decade. An oldtimer says he's been offered $10,000 for a shorebird he bought 40 years ago for 50 cents. Even "Mason" ducks, mass-produced from 1896 to 1924 by a Detroit factory for $13 a dozen now bring down $250 each.

It is thus no surprise that the rolls of serious decoy collectors are said to have rocketed to 10,000 from several hundred 10 years ago. Scores of exhibitions are now held across the U.S. Some feature favored regional carvings, Maine's ocean-going Monhegan Island white-wing scoters, for example, or California's redwood decoys.

Alas, it can all get mighty confusing. "Until recently, very little information has been available, and what has been available has never been accessible," notes Paul W. Casson in his decoy-collecting primer.

First things first, then. Decoys have the diabolical distinction of being the only folk art associated with pioneer America whose success or failure turned on its effectiveness in helping to kill something. As such, the artist's essential goal was to create a believable symbol for his intended and hopefully, doomed audience. Some scholars go so far as to call decoys a form of impressionistic sculpture, suggesting that the most accurate representations may not be those most appreciated by duck or discriminating man.

Whatever, the essence of the things seems dizzyingly Kafkaesque: "You're looking at what a man thinks a bird thinks another bird like him thinks he looks like," says Eleanor Mosca, a dealer from La Jolla, Calif.

Decoys seem to have gotten their name from "coy ducks," those treasonous fowl the British trained to lure others of their species into cages. But there is no evidence that Europeans used inanimate decoys, nor is it thought that settlers here learned much from Indians, who had been using forms of decoys for over 500 years.

Instead, frontier decoys gradually evolved as a tool to harvest the tremendous quantities of protein that waterfowl represented. By the mid-19th century, a confluence of factors boosted their use. First, a burgeoning population was developing a taste for duck; second, firearms improved markedly with the invention of a new ignition mechanism; third, transportation advances made large-scale distribution possible.

Enter the so-called "market gunner" and his swarms of decoys. By the time this savage form of hunting—which involved using virtual cannons surrounded by as many as a thousand decoys—was abolished in 1918, an entire species of duck had been extinguished, and others were threatened.

Market-gunning is nonetheless credited with developing the general criteria for decoy aesthetics. Those aesthetics persist, as a visit to an auction of antique birds reveals. "Where's the Charlie Joiner goose?" demands a nervous man before the bidding begins. Another castigates someone's sanding of the original paint from a Lem Ward duck: "Like to have ruined it," the auctioneer replies in a whisper. Others scribble in thick notebooks and seem to be making furtive deals.

The auction demonstrates the sharpening competition by growing numbers of people for the shrinking supply of antique decoys. Yet interest in the creations of contemporary masters is also soaring. Their creations, with individually crafted feathers and thousand-dollar prices, are done for sitting rooms not swamps. "We're moving into the realm of fine art," one carver proclaims.

The Louvre is not likely to be persuaded soon. Too much of the stuff is frankly imitative; some is plain tacky. Consider: a duck in red and white socks; a goose in a Snoopy flying helmet, or ducks, with their heads emerging Mount Rushmore-like from a tree trunk. A few artisans even offer a grim irony: carved likenesses of dead waterfowl hanging from handsome plaques; thus, an artform created to signify enough life to lure birds to their death has itself been transmogrified into death.

But hunters haven't been eliminated altogether. For a handful of hardy souls, the combination of a wintry wind, the distant honking of geese, a ready shotgun and perhaps a snort of whiskey continues to cry out for a flock of bobbing wooden decoys. "I got tired of hunting over plastic," explains a Moravia, N.Y., schoolteacher, who thereupon became a top-notch carver.

SPORTS

It's 10 Below Zero in Walker, Minn., But at Least the Eelpout Are Biting

BY WILLIAM H. LOVING

1/13/82

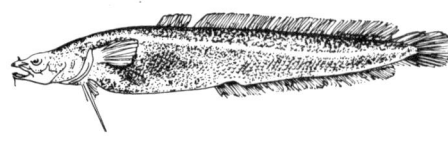

Most people have sense enough to stay away from northern Minnesota in the winter. Particularly in towns like Walker (population 1,037) that make a livelihood from summer tourists, getting through the cold months can be a chore.

In Walker, the solution for the past couple of years has been the International Eelpout Festival, a three-day weekend of mostly drinking, eating and ice fishing. This year's festival starts Friday.

For those who haven't tried it, ice fishing is a sedentary and potentially boring experience that involves sitting on a folding chair in the middle of a frozen lake, dangling a fishing line into a little hole in the ice and wondering how long frostbite takes to set in. (Some ice fishermen install warming huts over the holes.)

At the festival, the ice fishing is competitive. Local merchants furnish about $15,000 of prizes. The purpose of the competition is to catch what many people consider the ugliest, least desirable fish in Leech Lake, the eelpout (alias burbot).

Last year, festival participants reeled in 306 eelpout; the biggest weighed eight pounds, nine ounces. This time, Walker expects about 8,000 visitors. All the town's hotel and motel rooms have been reserved since early December.

Donald Canney, the mayor of Cedar Rapids, Iowa, will be attending for the third consecutive year. "I go up with a group of six or eight guys and we have a blast," he says. Mr. Canney concedes that the eelpout is "a rough fish," but when prepared properly, he says, "it tastes a little bit like lobster."

Other festival events include snowmobiling, ice-bowling and ice-drilling (to determine who can drill a hole fastest through the lake's four-foot-thick surface). The finale is a formal dinner on the ice with eelpout entrees. The chamber of commerce estimates that local businesses took in $300,000 during the festival last year, making it the town's biggest tourist weekend of the year except for the Fourth of July.

Yesterday, the temperature in Walker was 10 degrees below zero Fahrenheit. Kenneth Bresley, the festival's master of ceremonies and owner of a local sporting goods store, says the temperature won't make any difference to ice fishermen: "They're coming up here for fun."

For Football Scouts And College Seniors, Today Is the Future

Pro Draft Can Make or Break Both Teams and Players; How Atlanta Makes Picks

BY JOHN HUEY

Tom Braatz

COLUMBIA, S.C.   4/27/82

In a locker room beneath the University of South Carolina stadium, a dozen beefy football players stretched and groaned in contortionist poses, tuning the winter tightness out of their bodies for the day's trials.

To one side of the room stood a monument to all their dreams: the glass-encased locker of alumnus George Rogers—Heisman Trophy winner, last year's first choice in the National Football League draft, millionaire.

To the other side of the room stood the obstacles between the dream and reality: Tom Braatz, the 48-year-old player-personnel director and general manager of the Atlanta Falcons, and his scouting counterparts from six other NFL teams, all sizing up talent for this year's draft, which begins today at New York's Sheraton Centre Hotel.

Crucial Day

It was a fine spring day a month ago, and the fancies of most young men already had turned to thoughts of love, beer and maybe baseball. But for these seniors eligible for the draft, football was of more urgency than if it had been New Year's Day.

Mr. Braatz, a hefty former Dallas Cowboys linebacker, began his scrutiny with Dewayne Chivers, a big Carolina tight end. The two men talked knowledgeably of lawyers and doctors, discussing various agents and the effects of orthoscopic knee surgery versus medial-collateral-ligament surgery. Then Mr. Braatz measures the player's hand: "10½ inches," he said into a small tape recorder, adding his height, "six feet, four and five-eighths," and his weight, "234." Then the two men headed to the field for a series of stopwatch drills, culminating in the 40-yard dash.

Mr. Braatz, his four assistants, and their opposite numbers around the league have repeated this process on hundreds of campuses over the past year. What they learned will become evident today when each of the league's 28 teams will select one player in each of 12 rounds of draft selection.

For the players, trial days like the one at Carolina can spell the difference between wealth and poverty, fame and oblivion, or simply employment and unemployment. If they don't make the draft, they may become one of 25 to 50 "free agents" signed by each team to try out at summer camp.

If they make the team by either route, they will earn at least $30,000, the union minimum. The average NFL salary is $90,102, but a star can earn much more. George Rogers's contract with the New Orleans Saints reportedly included a $1 million signing bonus plus $125,000 last year, $175,000 this year and $225,000 next year. This year's predicted first pick, defensive lineman Kenneth Sims of Texas, is expected to be equally expensive.

Because the selections are crucial to a team's success, millions of dollars are spent on the preparations. Mr. Braatz says the Falcons spent as much as $750,000 preparing for this year's draft, so he is understandably picky about what he is buying.

"Finding out about these college guys is a lot like matrimony," he says. "Before you take your vows, you dig and you dig and you dig."

He ignores the traditional criteria that sportscasters and fans use. "We don't pay any attention to statistics or awards or all-American teams," Mr. Braatz says. And as for sports publications, he says, he doesn't read them. "I like the New Yorker," he says.

Like everything else in the multibillion-dollar business that the NFL has become, scouting bears little resemblance to the barnstorming days when scouts were part-time hangers-on as likely to choose from Street & Smith's football magazine as from personal knowledge.

"Our business has changed considerably," says Gil Brandt, the vice president for personnel of the ultra-successful Dallas Cowboys. "When I first came into it, scouting was sort of an afterthought. Now

Mr. Brandt, who has used a computer for 20 years, talks about laser-reflex measuring machines and psychological profiles. "We'd like to go and find all the characteristics that make a Medal of Honor winner," he says. "Then maybe we could apply them to football players."

Although the Falcons have been much less successful on the field than such teams as the Cowboys (the Falcons won seven and lost nine last year), Mr. Braatz is regarded as one of the best scouts in the league. Mr. Brandt, without prompting, rates him as one of his top three opponents. And by drafting the likes of Falcon fullback William Andrews as late as in the third round and having him run over 1,000 yards in three consecutive seasons, Mr. Braatz has cemented his reputation in recent years.

Asked about his choosing of the fullback, Mr. Braatz gives a typical scout response: "If I'd known how good he was, I wouldn't have waited until the third round." But in truth, successful drafting, like poker, depends largely on when you throw your chips into the pot.

"Most people can come up with a decent first-round pick," says Mr. Braatz. "The payoff comes with the twos and threes. The trick in this business is to know when to draft them. Not to take them too early and not to let them ride too long."

So when the NFL draft begins today, Mr. Braatz will have a year's worth of strategy mapped out on a wall-sized board in his "War Room" at the Falcons' Suwannee, Ga., complex, ready to relay each move by telephone to his representatives in New York. The board lists the names and ratings of the 336 athletes he thinks will be drafted, as well as his best guesses as to who will draft them. (The Falcons pick ninth this year under the system whereby the teams with the best records pick last).

To compile the information, Mr. Braatz and his four full-time scouts visit some 60 colleges each for full-blown sessions like the one here at South Carolina, where the candidates are put on display in the flesh and on game films from past seasons. Individual scouts also pay scores of visits to other colleges to interview and test one or two potential pros.

Stress on Size and Speed

Before all of this even begins, a good deal of winnowing takes place. "The majority of the players are eliminated outright by their size and speed," Mr. Braatz says.

Every NFL team except the lone-wolf Oakland Raiders belongs to one of three scouting syndicates that do much of the preliminary work, combing through the seniors at some 620 schools to compile a list of the top 600 prospects. A syndicate computer printout lists vital data: jersey number, IQ test score, height, weight, 40-yard speed.

Printout in hand, Mr. Braatz arrived at the South Carolina campus and secluded himself to watch hours of game film. He doesn't see films in the same perspective as a fan. Ignoring the main action in a spectacular passing play, Mr. Braatz replays the film to examine a defensive lineman. "Look at this guy!" he says. "He's dumb. He puts his head down and butts the guy. How's he gonna get to the ball that way?" Commenting on a linebacker, he says, "His shoulders aren't parallel to the line when he moves. That's bad. And his eye's off the ball." When competing scouts are in the room, however, Mr. Braatz says nothing.

Later in the day, the athletes are put through their paces in the stadium. Some are expressionless. Others are obviously nervous about all that is riding on their performance. One is so keyed up he falls down during the most basic drill.

Crucial 40-Yard Dash

The first test is the vertical jump, in which the player must stand by a wall with both feet flat, then leap into the air marking a spot on a chalk board with spit-wet fingers. Next comes a series of three hops in 10 yards for distance. Then the "yo-yo" in which the player is timed while he runs back and forth between yard lines, touching them with his hands. Receivers and running backs catch balls with one hand, and run pass routes. Finally comes the most institutionalized—and telling—of the drills—the 40-yard dash. If the players don't make it here, they don't make it.

"Every one of them says he's a four-four," says Mr. Braatz, meaning 4.4 seconds, an excellent time. "Really most of them are four-nines." And here a tenth of a second can translate into thousands—even hundreds of thousands—of dollars. For draft choices, Mr. Braatz has cutoff points for each position: running back, 4.75; fullback, 4.9; linebacker, 5; cornerback, 4.6; safety, 4.75.

One after another the players shake their heads after running the 40 and say the same things: "I can't believe it. I've never run that slow before."

At one college, a young man Mr. Braatz is interested in is reputed to have been timed at about 4.6, but since then he has had knee surgery, and the scout wants to see how much speed he has lost. He runs it three times and can't do better than 4.8. "Did you see the scar on his knee?" Mr. Braatz asks later. "It looked like a blind veterinarian operated on it."

Second Time Around

When a player runs a poor time, the others can sense it. The scouts all look at their feet or in the other direction. And the saddest cases are those who failed to make the draft last year but show up unannounced at the stadium for the scouts to take another look. "I really want to play, man," says one muscle-bound youth. "I grew three-quarters of an inch this year." When most of these run, Mr. Braatz mumbles into his tape recorder: "He's a double-R," meaning a double reject. There isn't any margin for compassion here.

At such a point in an athlete's career, "he returns to the community he came from as a broken young man," says Cary Goodman, the executive director of the Center for Athletes Rights and Education. "The delusion he's had during college that he's 'making it' is over." According to Mr. Goodman, only one in 10,000 high-school football players ever makes it to the NFL, and then the average career lasts less than five years.

Many of these young men are prepared to do nothing else with their lives. Athletes who seem intelligent in conversation make hopelessly low or wildly erratic scores on IQ tests, even indicating an inability to read. Two-thirds of the players in the NFL haven't graduated from college. But the social implications aren't Mr. Braatz's problem. He considers the tests as one increment in an overall grade, to see if a player can learn and think on his feet.

Once the scouting is complete, Mr. Braatz and his four aides convene at Suwannee, Ga., where they compare notes, conduct mock drafts and give each athlete a grade. The range runs from 99-90, which is "starter-star," to 29-20, which is "training-camp type," to "reject."

The discussions go something like this:

SCOUT: James R. Receiver. Tendinitis in both knees—'80. He's moody type but a good athlete. Workable. He has good adjustment to all balls. He'll go inside traffic and take shots, but he feels he's only semi-tough. Runs average routes with an above-average feel for the game. Above-average runner after the catch. He will block, but he misses and is on the ground a lot. Hands above average to good. He does return punts and kickoffs.

MR. BRAATZ: Is this guy a draft choice or a free agent?

The scouts then try to reach a consensus.

These days, Mr. Braatz has a free hand from the Falcons' president, Rankin Smith Jr., to make such decisions. This wasn't true when Mr. Smith's father, Rankin, Sr., was more directly involved with the team. He likes Southern college football, and his taste was often reflected in the Falcons' draft.

Bobby Beathard, now the general manager of the Washington Redskins, recalls working for Mr. Braatz in those days. "I remember we thought Kenny Anderson (who played in this year's Super Bowl for Cincinnati) was going to be a great quarterback," he says. "But instead, we took Leo Hart because he was from Duke. We also took Pat Sullivan (an Auburn Heisman Trophy winner) when nobody else wanted him, because Rankin did. It was pretty frustrating," as both Mr. Hart and Mr. Sullivan had short pro careers.

Now that it's entirely up to Mr. Braatz, he lives or dies by the draft. After almost 20 years of scouting, he admits to only one hard and fast rule that he never breaks:

"Kickers are an absolute crapshoot," he says. "Anybody who would draft a kicker high is nuts."

Some Old Masters Vault Nine-Foot Bar— And 70 Years

More and More Athletes Vie In Age-Group Competition With Surprising Stamina

BY DORON P. LEVIN

RALEIGH, N.C.   5/28/81

From a standing start, Sherman Burho sprints 55 feet, digs his glass-fiber pole into the ground and gracefully sails over a crossbar nine feet, one quarter inch high.

His jump might not win at all junior-high-school track meets, but it makes Mr. Burho a winner in his pole-vaulting age group—the 70- to 74-year-olds—at the Southeast Regional Masters Track and Field Meet here.

And before the day ends, the 70-year old retired internal investigator for the Treasury Department also throws both the one-kilogram discus and the eight-pound hammer (both less than the usual weights) about 90 feet without any sign of strain other than a healthy sweat. He and about 600 other participants are another indication of the nation's growing obsession with physical fitness: organized competition among people past—often way past—their athletic prime.

Begun over a decade ago by the Amateur Athletic Union, what today is called the Masters program attracts more than 50,000 registered athletes and many more unregistered competitors. Under the auspices of 12 amateur sports groups, these men and women compete in everything from judo to weight lifting to long-distance running.

Swimmers Start Early

Some of the older athletes aren't very old. Swimmers, for instance, can enter the program at only 25—because top-notch competitive swimmers often pass their prime by age 20.

But even people in their 70s and 80s are joining Masters sports clubs, trimming flabby flesh and toning up long-neglected muscles.

In doing so, they are surprising medical experts and destroying old ideas about what older people can do physically.

"The idea that people ought to slow down as they get older is one of the many cultural myths," says Russell Meyers, 77, a retired professor of neurosurgery and avid runner.

An ex-Olympian and captain of the 1927 Brown University track team, Dr. Meyers hadn't run competitively again until two years ago. Since then, he has increased his training to a six-day-a-week regimen: three days of jogging three to four miles and three days of practicing hurdles and sprints.

"A person my age really can't take the wear and tear of sprinting every day," he says, because tendons, ligaments and other connective tissues tend to dry out with age and become more likely to tear. Dr. Meyers learned this lesson the hard way last year, when he tore a quadricep in his left thigh. But he still won the 100-meter dash at Raleigh for the 75-79 age group in 15.7 seconds.

Hip Surgery No Barrier

Other aging athletes seem even more surprising. Marian McKechnie, 76, had to have both hips replaced after a bout with degenerative arthritis, and so she needs help to climb onto the starting block for swimming races. But when the starter's gun fires, she dives in and shows no sign of infirmity.

Since taking up Masters swimming four years ago, the St. Petersburg, Fla., free-style and backstroke specialist has splashed to 16 national records and four world marks in her age group. "I used to go in the water just to swim for therapy, but I have to admit I've gotten competitive," the trim widow says.

The reawakened desire for competition and the camaraderie of Masters athletics—as well as the physical benefits—explain why older people are taking up sports. In addition, Masters athletes generally have the money to buy athletic equipment—a fact that hasn't escaped the notice of Tom Sturak, director of running promotion for Nike running shoes. Mr. Sturak says his company gives Nike shoes and running gear to about 200 Masters athletes. He adds that he believes that the promotional activity "has borne fruit for us."

Surprisingly, many Masters athletes find that modern training and equipment help them match or exceed what they could do years ago.

In 1958, Manuel Sanguily held the world record for the 100-meter breast stroke with a time of one minute, 13.8 seconds. Competing in a Masters meet 23 years later, Dr. Sanguily, a 48-year-old

Tarrytown, N.Y., physician, still swam the event in the only slightly slower time of 1:15.

"What this proves to me is that men and women of our age can achieve limits of stress that weren't thought possible 20 years ago," he says—though he adds that any would-be Masters athlete should have a medical checkup and should exercise in a sensible way.

JOURNALISM

THE ODD COUPLE
Evans, Novak Still Rile Readers After 18 Years of Right-Wing Purity

Column Goes Past Reporting To Press Strident Views, Promote Jobs for Friends

Hot Feet and Genteel Parties

BY JAMES M. PERRY

WASHINGTON 3/12/81

Evans is the slender, debonair one with the sleek, bullet-shaped head. After he spent a year at Yale sleeping all day and playing bridge all night, his father shipped him off to Chicago to work for the railroad. Novak is the short, rumpled one, sometimes called "the prince of darkness." He once managed to set his own shoelaces on fire.

Rowland Evans and Robert Novak

Together they are (Rowland) Evans and (Robert) Novak, journalism's oddest couple, who have somehow shared a byline for 18 years and who have now become the most controversial and talked-about columnists in town.

"I'm fed up with them!" says a prominent politician who has known them both socially and professionally for years. "They've come to believe they're the keepers of the world."

"They do seem to have gotten a little apoplectic," says their old friend and fellow columnist Jack Germond.

What they have been doing—in their column that appears in 223 newspapers, in their newsletter that goes to almost 2,000 subscribers, in their nightly commentary on Ted Turner's cable-TV network and in the more than 50 lectures they deliver each year—is try to hold the Reagan administration's feet to the pure flame of their own increasingly strident brand of conservatism.

They seem to believe that the nation may not survive unless an undiluted supply-side economic program is developed at home and a tougher defense and foreign-policy position to contain the Russians is put in place around the world.

"We don't have much time left," says Mr. Evans, reflecting the doom and despair that permeate the team's reporting.

It's the old journalistic conundrum: Should reporters—and Evans and Novak pride themselves on being shirt-sleeve reporters writing an "inside" column—actually come down out of the press box and take part in the game?

"Dark Foreboding"

"That's what has happened to these two guys," says the editor of a big-city daily who has dropped their column. "They're out there on the field, blocking and tackling and telling the coach what plays to call. I don't need that kind of stuff in my newspaper."

The most recent complaints generally go to their reporting during the transition and the early weeks of the new administration, when they were openly plugging their friends and opposing their enemies for top jobs in the government.

Typical was their report that the administration's failure to name political scientist Donald Devine as the civil-service chief "transformed what should have been a weekend of celebration (for hardline Reagan supporters) into dark foreboding." (Three weeks later Mr. Devine got the job.) In the same vein, they said "a test of the Reagan revolution's tenacity and future prospects" hinged on dumping Alice Rivlin as director of the congressional budget office. (She is still there.)

During the entire period, they tub-thumped for New York businessman Lewis Lehrman, a leading supply-side theoretician. After their first choice for Treasury Secretary, former Treasury chief William Simon, was "stabbed," they plugged Mr. Lehrman for the job. Then, when that hope faded, they plugged him for the No. 2 Treasury job. When that went glimmering, they recommended him for chairman of the President's Council of Economic Advisers. And when that didn't pan out, they pushed him for council membership.

Panic in the Defense Community

Martin Anderson, Mr. Reagan's domestic-affairs adviser, told a colleague that the administration was under "tremendous pressure" to put Mr. Lehrman on the CEA. "Pressure from where?" the colleague asked. "Evans and Novak," Mr. Anderson replied.

So far, though, Mr. Lehrman is still in New York.

Mr. Evans, who is 59, and Mr. Novak, 50, were just as eager to see hard-liners—they don't object to the description—placed in the top foreign-policy and national-security positions.

They were disappointed there, too, never more so than in their Jan. 7 column, in which they said "unease" within what they call the "defense community" had "blossomed into panic" over the way Defense Secretary-designate Caspar Weinberger "has booted out 'Reaganaut' military advisers, trashed their recommendations and at least opened the door for soft-liners."

This is the kind of strident reporting some editors deplore. Others see nothing wrong with it. "They're coming from a certain direction and projecting certain values," says Edwin Roberts, editorial-page editor of the Detroit News. "Readers aren't stupid. They know where Evans and Novak stand."

Evans and Novak themselves make no apologies.

Part of the problem, Mr. Novak believes, is the lingering idea that the columnists once were liberals or, at least, moderates. He thinks that goes back to 1964, when they opposed Barry Goldwater's nomination by the Republicans (they didn't think he could win the election). Some people suggest it may go back to the 1964 convention, when Mr. Novak floored a conservative Young Republican with a single punch. The young man hadn't agreed with Mr. Novak's reporting.

The fact is, Mr. Novak says, that he and Mr. Evans have been out on the field, blocking and tackling, for years. "We caught a lot of flak when we were writing about left-wing subversion of the civil-rights movement back in 1964 and 1965," Mr. Novak notes.

"We got the same treatment over our coverage of the war in Vietnam," adds Mr. Evans. "I don't suppose we ever said, 'Let's unleash the generals,' but there was no way readers couldn't conclude we supported the military effort there."

"And we were never bashful in advising how the war ought to be fought," says Mr. Novak.

Mr. Novak, who is more outspoken and aggressive than Mr. Evans, has another explanation. He says criticism of the column has been sharper in recent weeks because "we are running against the grain of the conventional wisdom within the journalistic community." This, he thinks, is especially true in their economic reporting. "Most journalists find it hard to abandon the viewpoints they have held for years. If supply-side economics works, it will be the death knell for much of the system this establishment has built up over the last 50 years."

Evans and Novak have been together for 18 years, the longest running double byline in journalistic history, they contend. The first column appeared in the old New York Herald Tribune and 44 other papers served by that newspaper's syndicate on May 15, 1963. In it, they said Mr. Goldwater had a chance to win the GOP nomination.

The column was Mr. Evans's idea. He had been badgering his editor at the Tribune for years for a column, finally getting a real taste for it by writing some columns for Joseph Alsop, something of a mentor for Mr. Evans. He was finally told to strike out on his own—six times a week. "No one man could do that," says Mr. Evans. So he went out and recruited a partner.

"The single most brilliant thing Rowly Evans ever did in his entire life was take on Bob Novak," says an old colleague of both reporters.

At the time, Mr. Novak was a 32-year-old congressional correspondent for The Wall Street Journal. He was already something of a legend, not so much for his reporting skill (which was considerable) but for some of his personal habits (which were deplorable).

Smoldering Shoelaces

There is the story, for example, of the time he set his own shoelaces on fire. In those days, Mr. Novak smoked four packs of cigarets a day, never extinguishing them when he was finished but simply dropping them or flipping them over his shoulder. He never tied his shoelaces, either, and one day he managed to drop a cigaret on one of his shoes. The laces began to smolder, then burst into flames.

Another time, he put a lighted cigaret in his pocket before entering the Senate press gallery, where smoking isn't permitted. He became engrossed in the action on the floor and forgot about the cigaret—until his jacket burst into flames.

There are stories, too, about the suits and the food packages his would send him from their home in Joliet, Ill. He would ... all of them under his desk, and they would remain there until ... ge things began crawling around the floor.

"He is still the worst-dressed journalist in Washington," says Art Buchwald, the humorist, whose office is across the hall from the incredibly cluttered quarters of Mr. Evans and Mr. Novak. "I worried about Novak when I heard President Reagan was going to impose a dress code," says Mr. Buchwald. "He could put Novak out of business." (Mr. Buchwald also contends that Mr. Novak's salary is paid out of CETA funds. He thinks either Mr. Evans or Mr. Novak should quit so the other could make really big money.)

Mr. Novak also has a sense of humor, of sorts.

Typical of his wit is the story told by columnist Jules Witcover, another old friend and colleague. Mr. Witcover had just completed his most successful diet—a stern regimen of orange juice, black coffee and tennis—when he encountered Mr. Novak on a downtown street corner. "You've lost a lot of weight," Mr. Novak commented. Mr. Witcover agreed, simpering with pleasure that someone had noticed, and went on to describe how he had lost so many pounds. "I think you got cancer," said the prince of darkness.

He's No Pangloss

John Lindsay, a Newsweek reporter christened Mr. Novak with that nickname and it has stuck. Mr. Lindsay thinks it goes back to the time Mr. Novak buried himself in the works of Spinoza, arriving at the conclusion—which hasn't changed much since—that things were never going to get better.

Outside of his column, Mr. Novak's main passion is sports. He is a fan of the Washington Redskins football team and the Washington Bullets professional basketball team. His 15-year-old daughter, Zelda, is the Bullets' official ball girl.

But mostly he is a University of Maryland sports fanatic. The terrapin is Maryland's mascot, and Mr. Novak is a "Diamondback Terrapin," which means he contributes at least $1,200 a year to the school's athletic-scholarship fund.

Maryland basketball comes first. Mr. Novak travels with the coach, Lefty Driesell, on recruiting trips. He takes players into his office as interns (a recent intern was the Maryland star Albert King). He rarely misses a game, home or away.

He usually travels with John Heise, a local lawyer and another Terrapin fanatic. Mr. Heise remembers the time they flew to Charlotte,

N.C., to make a connection to Clemson, S.C., for a basketball game. But the weather was so bad the connecting flight was canceled.

"Robert prevailed on some contacts and chartered a small plane," Mr. Heise recalls. "We landed at Clemson at night, with no lights on the runway, and Robert had a cab waiting there to take us to the arena. We arrived just as they were playing the national anthem."

A More Exalted Level

For all of Mr. Novak's grumbling about the liberalism and elitism of his colleagues, he is a popular figure with most of them. Mr. Evans, on the other hand, seems to move on a slightly more exalted level. Mr. Evans and his wife, Kay, live in fashionable Georgetown. Mr. Novak and his wife, Geraldine, live in Rockville, an unfashionable Maryland suburb. Socially, the twain rarely meet.

Mr. Evans is a Main Line Philadelphian who breakfasts almost every morning with a source at the Metropolitan Club. He went to a boarding school and briefly to Yale (Mr. Novak holds the pair's only degree, from the University of Illinois). Mr. Evans and his wife entertain with Main Line dignity at their Georgetown home. Greg Schneiders, a former Carter aide, recalls that when he was working in the White House, he was invited to the Evanses for dinner. But Mr. Evans had a preliminary question: Was Mrs. Schneiders "presentable"?

Mr. Schneiders says it was a lovely party. "Henry Kissinger was there, along with the required member of the Senate and the required member of the Supreme Court."

Mr. Evans's friends take exception to the idea that he is something of a dilettante. After all, they say, he was a sergeant in the Marines, while Mr. Novak was a lieutenant in the Army.

Philip Geyelin, the former editor of the Washington Post's editorial page and one of Mr. Evans's oldest friends, recalls the time the two of them hopped a helicopter to go up to War Zone C in Vietnam and observe some of the action. "Rowly took the seat next to the open door—with no strap to hold him in. Suddenly, we were in the middle of an air strike, with Phantom jets all around us. The helicopter was swerving all over the place. I don't know how Rowly held on. I had such a case of vertigo I didn't dare look."

The conventional wisdom is that Mr. Novak does most of the work and Mr. Evans takes most of the credit. Although it is true that Mr. Novak is more passionate and excitable than Mr. Evans, it is also true that they pretty much divide the work evenly.

e been writing the column together for so long that no one which one wrote what. When they look at old columns, they tell themselves. And, whatever people may think of the merits , the column and its spinoffs pay off. Each man earns something excess of $200,000 annually.

During the fading days of the presidential election campaign last year, a young reporter from a local newspaper sidled up to Mr. Novak, who was listening to Mr. Reagan's standard speech, and asked him whether he ever got bored.

"Never," he said. "God help me, I love it."

In Farm Wife News, Rural Readers Write Of Mice and Women

Magazine Provides Fertile Soil For Tales of Bucolic Bliss; Farm Woes Plowed Under

BY LAUREL SORENSON

Behind every successful man who ever hitched his wagon to a star, there stands an exhausted woman who has just spent 45 minutes trying to get the hitch pin in place.

Joyce Carney, Hydro, Okla.

6/15/82

Such bucolic humor isn't the stuff of great literature. Nor is it what you would expect from a woman in these liberated times. But it is standard fare at Farm Wife News, a rural magazine written largely by its readers—women who have cast their lot with the men who till the soil.

Throughout the 48 glossy pages of each monthly issue, farm women speak their piece, seemingly oblivious to the hard times that have recently befallen their barnyards. They exchange recipes. They grumble good-naturedly. They dispense advice. And they relate the trying moments of their lives on the farm ("harvest turns hubby berserk" or "I'm Florence Nightingale of our calf barn"). There is little room here for raging controversy or tales of farming's economic woes; in Farm Wife News, almost everything is sunshine and lollipops.

"I want my farmers to recognize what they have, not what they haven't," explains publisher Roy Reiman, an ex-farmboy from Iowa. "You don't just farm to make money; you do it for the life style, too." Accordingly, the magazine serves up heavy doses of features about robins who herald spring and cookstoves that stir memories of grandmother baking bread. It even draws an occasional spiritual analogy from mundane tasks, asking in a headline, "Have you started your spiritual canning?"

chummy approach fosters intense loyalty among readers, who from rabbit raisers in South Carolina to hickory-nut growers in Wisconsin to corn and soybean farmers in Iowa and Illinois. For example, what other magazine's staffers get letters addressed to "Dear Friends"?

"There's a closeness somehow," says Virginia Morris, an avid reader in Green Lake, Wis. "Farm Wife News is the last thing I'd give up, next to my husband."

This media-age version of the back fence is the oldest and most profitable of several farm magazines published by privately held Reiman Associates of Greendale, Wis. Farm Wife News, which contributes roughly $4 million, or 30%, of the company's revenues, is supported solely by subscriptions, now $11.95 a year.

Readership increased steadily through most of the publication's first 10 years, peaking at 350,660 subscribers in late 1980. But agriculture's recent troubles have taken a toll. More than 6% of the subscribers have canceled since that peak, albeit reluctantly. "My husband and I have had to cut out all but the necessities," said an apologetic former subscriber in Montana. "I appreciate your words and articles of good cheer. . . . We need to know some of us will make it."

Don't bother searching the pages of the magazine for any heartrending tales about those who don't. Farm Wife News treats hard-luck stories like dirty linen that any proper family wouldn't air in public. The magazine does occasionally sandwich a serious story or two—about things like farm stress and futures prices—between recipes and handcrafts, but doesn't dwell on such weighty matters.

Tempest in a Milk Pail

What controversy seeps through is mostly unintentional. Like the astrology column, "Farm Wives Under the Stars," the magazine ran some years ago until besieged by angry letters from fundamentalist readers. "We were told that astrology was the work of the devil," recalls editor Ann Kaiser, who received religious tracts from readers concerned about her spiritual welfare. "And we sure didn't want any devil's work in Farm Wife News."

Recently the magazine's name also stirred up a tempest in a milk pail among more liberal readers. "I don't feel marital status should have anything to do with anything," wrote Liane Hickman, an orchardist's wife from East Wenatchee, Wash., who preferred the name "Farm Women."

Mrs. Hickman's published proposal set off a heated exchange of letters that hasn't ended eight months and 110 letters later. "To get all riled up over taking a title God gave us who chose to be wives seems pretty petty to me," Dottie Estabrook of Monticello, Maine, responded huffily.

A name change isn't expected. Farm folks are a traditional lot, publisher Reiman explains, and don't take kindly to change.

Despite such efforts to please, however, a handful of readers don't much care for the sugar-and-spice stories. Nadine Compton of Fredonia, Kan., stopped reading the magazine after nine months, protesting to the editors. "I don't feel much in common with all those farm women 'paragons' you write about." She wrote: "I am a farm wife, but I do not run our farm single-handedly, raise umpteen children all alone, carry on a full-time outside business and engage in 15 volunteer projects at the same time I'm keeping a perfect house."

While Mr. Reiman seasons each issue with work from professional free-lance writers and the magazine's three-woman editorial staff, more than half of the copy comes from readers. That tradition began early in the magazine's existence, when Mr. Reiman published a plea for contributions, and is encouraged by contests for the best writing and recipes, and "quote'm polls" of readers on issues ranging from estate taxes to land use.

Quality varies wildly, from the woman who described her farm as "irrespressible" to well-considered manuscripts and poems that make it clear that most modern farm women aren't the uneducated workhorses of bygone eras. "Some aren't terrific writers, but it's all there," Mr. Reiman says. "We just sand off the corners and smooth it out."

Some fledgling authors write for therapy. Karen Rowell, the wife of a Berne, Ind., dairy farmer tells about seemingly innocent calves that mischievously kick and bite. "If I write it down, I can look at it and laugh," she says. Others gain self-esteem. "I waved my $35 check (from Farm Wife News) at my husband and told him I made more than his milk did that day," crows Rowena McCarty of Cohocton, N.Y. Mrs. McCarty's recent paean to farm wives received a prominent back-page showcase. "Remember when carrying your own weight didn't include 100 pounds of cow feed?" the article asked.

What else do farm wives write about?

write about love, for instance. "You know you're married to a when he swats you on the rump like one of his favorite cows, gives you that special wink and says: 'Hi, old girl,' " wrote Carol Ann VanderZanden of Banks, Ore.

They write of their mistakes. City-bred Leta Fulmer, of Amazonia, Mo., told of how she mixed cement in the hog feed for two weeks before her father-in-law said that yeast would be more nutritional.

They wax poetic about daily chores. "Full of grain, the new mown grasses lie/Silent and slain, still shining in the sun/Still at the solstice of their song," wrote June Owens, of Richmond, Va.

"There's a great compulsion to express personal feelings to an audience that says, 'Yeah, I know what you mean,' " managing editor Ruth Benedict says.

And that, apparently, keeps Farm Wife News readers coming back for more. "You always find somebody who's gone through the same experience you have," says Marjory Scheufler, 50 years old, who has read the magazine for three years at her Belpre, Kan., livestock ranch. "We all make the very same mistakes, and it's a comfort to know you're not alone."

A Last Remembrance of a Newspaper's Days Past

BY JAMES M. PERRY

1/28/82

Tomorrow's edition of the Bulletin will be the last. But the newspaper that died of red ink in Philadelphia yesterday was nothing like the Bulletin I remember. My Bulletin was big and fat and prosperous—the largest evening paper in the country—and it was an interesting place to work.

It was a Philadelphia paper, staffed with people who knew and loved the city. The editors were tough and the pay was lousy. It was never a great paper (it was always too parochial for that), but for years it was a good newspaper.

In the Bulletin's heyday in the 1950s, you didn't need an advanced degree to get a job. You didn't need much of anything.

One of the regulars was a fellow named Ephraim Gorenstein, who came to the Bulletin from a job as a uniformed usher at a movie theater. He sold watches in the newsroom when things were slow. He also was a master of Malapropisms: his best were called "Ephorisms."

One day, he called his rewrite man from the scene of a ship collision in the Delaware River. "My God," he said, "you ought to see it. People are philandering around in the water." The rewrite man said he'd be there right away. Another time, covering a shooting, he told the rewrite man the wound was in the man's "thig." "Thig?" asked the rewrite man, a college graduate. "Thig, damn it," said Eph, "just above the knee."

As a practical joke, a deskman called Eph once when he was working in Camden, across the river in New Jersey, to alert him that a papal bull was running amok down the Black Horse Pike. Eph leaped in his car and set off in hot pursuit.

Police stations along the way had been alerted to expect him. As soon as he'd rush in, out of breath, they'd tell him the bull already

⌐ through town. Eph had the last laugh, though. The arch- and the rest of the hierarchy were so amused by the joke they ⌐ed for years after that Eph get all their biggest stories exclu- ⌐ely.

The reporter who covered the Phillies baseball team was a big Dutchman with a large handle-bar mustache (the Phillies wrestled him to the locker-room floor when they won the pennant in 1950 and shaved it off. He never forgave them). This reporter—call him Frank—would, as they say, take a drink. I remember the time when the Phillies were coming north after spring training and playing exhibition games along the way. This night, they were in the Shenandoah Valley of Virginia, scene in the Civil War of some of Stonewall Jackson's greatest triumphs.

Frank, as it turned out, was a Civil War buff. Under the influence of strong liquor, he convinced himself he *was* Stonewall Jackson, and he tried to dictate a story to me by telephone that began with these words, "Somewhere in the Shenandoah Valley with Stonewall Jackson." His counterpart from the Inquirer called in later—covering for him—to give us the details of the ball game.

The Bulletin's chief city hall reporter was an impeccably dressed Scotsman (he never removed his jacket or loosened his tie). He never left room 219, the press room, in pursuit of a story, except on Wednesday, when, with great dignity, he would stroll slowly down the corridor to cover the weekly city council session.

He presided, again with great dignity, over the annual shakedown in which all the judges and city officials were asked to cough up cases of booze for the city hall reporters' annual bash at the Barclay Hotel. Enough usually was left over to keep the senior reporters in spirits for the entire new year. Younger reporters put an end to the shakedown, and the Bulletin's senior city hall reporter went into retirement, in high—but dignified—dudgeon.

Jean Barrett was the paper's top court-room reporter, in the days when it was hardly unusual for the Bulletin to run eight or nine columns of testimony from a celebrated case. She had been a Ziegfeld girl when she was younger, and she never lost her show-biz flair. In the big jury trials, she'd come to work the first day in a modest but colorful hat. Each succeeding day, the hats would get bigger and brighter. She could keep it up for two or three weeks, looking at the end of the trial like Carmen Miranda. The jurors were always mesmerized by her performance and so, when the trial was over, they would rush over to her and tell her all about their deliberations. She'd whisper to them they shouldn't talk to the competition. They never did.

The Bulletin had a Washington bureau—a good one too—and sometimes a reporter would travel abroad, but basically it was a local paper. At one time, it had eight reporters in eight radio-equipped patrol cars covering the city. One of them would get up in the morning, stumble to his car, and call the desk to say he was on the job at the police station at 12th and Pine. One day, the deskman asked if he didn't notice anything unusual. "Same as always," he replied. "Funny," said the desk man, "the station's on fire and they just turned in the sixth alarm."

I don't know what happened to the Bulletin. The city changed, the world changed—but the Bulletin didn't. Worse luck, the competition, the Inquirer, the paper we all loathed, was sold to Knight-Ridder, and began to improve, rapidly. It left the gray old Bulletin behind.

The last few years, reporters drifted in and out of the Bulletin news room, tough young kids with dreams of fame and glory. They didn't know much about Philadelphia, didn't think the Bulletin was a home. They'll drift away now too. I guess only four of the old timers remain—Peter Binzen, Sandy Gray, Adrian Lee and Harry Toland. They're all that's left of the real Bulletin.